Elizabeth E. Flagg

Between Two Opinions

Or: The Question Of The Hour

Elizabeth E. Flagg

Between Two Opinions
Or: The Question Of The Hour

ISBN/EAN: 9783744652292

Printed in Europe, USA, Canada, Australia, Japan

Cover: Foto ©ninafisch / pixelio.de

More available books at **www.hansebooks.com**

BETWEEN TWO OPINIONS

OR,

THE QUESTION OF THE HOUR.

BY

E. E. FLAGG,

AUTHOR OF "HOLDEN WITH CORDS," "LITTLE PEOPLE,"
"A SUNNY LIFE."

Hast thou chosen, O my people, on whose party
    thou shalt stand,
Ere the doom from its worn sandals shakes the
    dust against our land?
Though the cause of evil prosper, yet 'tis truth
    alone is strong.
                      LOWELL.

CHICAGO:
NATIONAL CHRISTIAN ASSOCIATION,
1885.

TO DEA. INCREASE LEADBETTER

AND HIS FAITHFUL COMPANION

IN HIS LIFE-LONG WARFARE AGAINST THE SECRET LODGE,

THIS VOLUME

IS GRATEFULLY DEDICATED.

PREFACE.

The writer is aware that the present volume boldly contradicts a certain popular and most mischievous fallacy which seems to date its origin from the time when the anti-slavery struggle for a quarter of a century kept every other great question in abeyance; namely, that there is room in American politics for only one reform at a time

It is true that both the Anti-masonic uprising of 1829, and the temperance movement a few years later went down like driftwood in the tide of excited feeling which followed the labors of the first Abolitionists; but they who would make out of this fact a precedent for all future time forget that we have entered on a new era with totally changed conditions, and every branch of reform work has taken a corresponding impetus

With a nation composed partly of slaves and partly of freemen, or even an unreconstructed South as it existed just after the war, there could be no adequate settlement of these great questions now pressing to the front. But, given a nation emancipated forever from the curse of human bondage, sectional lines obliterated, and a North and South as united in fraternal bonds as the East and the West, and every plank in the platforms of our various reform parties becomes a sublime possibility. The logic of events is fast teaching us this truth. Side by side with the prohibition of the drink traffic comes the labor problem, the Sabbath question, the rights of the Indians and the Chinese. Is it the part of enlightened philanthropy or honest patriotism, or true Christianity to bid these evils all stand to one side while we grapple with the more gigantic and deadly wrong of intemperance? Is it not time to widen our scope both of vision and action? We cannot safely ignore the least important of the many evils now threatening society, for as a certain French writer very truly observes, "Errors are always friends and ready for a mutual embrace." It is in the closeness of that embrace that the secret of their strength lies, and only when Christians unite in one combined onset against *all* evil, shall we see national reform inaugurated on a permanent basis. The Woman's Christian Temperance Union, with its various departments of labor, many of which lie outside of pure temperance work, while all converge to one common end—the extirpation of the liquor traffic—is already acting upon this truth with results that cause saints and angels to rejoice, and time-serving politicians to tremble.

But if the Drink question has a very intimate connection, morally and economically considered, with most of the social problems that now trouble philanthropists, shall we shut our eyes to the fact that there is still another issue as closely related to the rum traffic as the rum traffic itself is to that fountain of crime which feeds our police courts and penitentiaries?

The American party alone has recognized the subtle power of Masonry, and those secret societies of which it is the mother, to uphold with unseen hand the saloon and its kindred evils. But many honest Prohibitionists, even among those who hate the lodge from the bottom of their hearts, are yet inclined to compromise; to say, "Let us kill intemperance, and then we will attack the lodge."

The writer has attempted in the following pages to show the fallacy of such a position; nor has she drawn on imagination for her incidents. They are without exception matters of fact, and scarcely any observing mind who has carefully noted the workings of Secretism in its relations to Temperance could fail to gather a store of similar material

The Temperance warfare has now lasted for half a century. Is it not time for all true Prohibitionists to unite against the secret foe which has so many times betrayed them? Is it not time to drop forever the narrow and one-sided notion that evils must be attacked singly, and, by one grand, Napoleonic onslaught on the enemy's whole line of battle, usher in the longed-for day of social purity and national righteousness?

This can be rendered practicable only by a party with a platform made up entirely of moral issues; which recognizes God as the true Governor of the nations, and his laws as the one enduring basis on which to found the structure of our republican liberty. United to such a party, American freemen need no longer "halt between two opinions," but can cast their ballots equally against the lodge and the saloon, thus striking a deadly blow to both monsters which shall soon consign them to the same unwept grave, among the dead issues of the past.

CONTENTS.

CONTENTS.

BETWEEN TWO OPINIONS:

OR

THE QUESTION OF THE HOUR.

CHAPTER I.

A SON OF THE PURITANS.

His birthplace was an old-fashioned farmhouse among the New Hampshire hills; his parents an equally old-fashioned couple who believed in keeping the Sabbath, doing right by their neighbors and opposing evil wherever they found it. This uncompromising type of Christianity, in the case of the Howlands, seemed to be hereditary, descending from father to son in true apostolic succession. The Howland from whom the family dated its beginning was a Puritan clergyman, who, falling under the ban of the Star Chamber a few years before King Charles lost his head, sought for liberty of conscience in the colonies; but for all practical purposes of this history we need not go farther back than Josiah Howland, the sixth in lineal descent; a plain, hard-working son of the soil, a good farmer and a good citizen, but with nothing about him that distinguished him to common eyes from the great mass of his fellow-men.

Though the family line boasted one or two judges, to say nothing of a score of ministers and deacons, Josiah Howland had never seemed to feel any earthly ambition beyond the desire to raise good crops and stand well with the world. He read much, especially his Bible; prayed much and talked little. He never sought office, nor did office come to him; his voice was never heard in town meetings or caucuses, yet it was a common expression with his neighbors that "though Josiah Howland never seems to say or do much, there isn't another man in the township that would be missed more",—which is, after all, the highest tribute that can be paid to any of us when we leave our earthly places vacant forever.

He had married early in life his second cousin, Phœbe Howland, a woman who combined with sound common sense and great practical energy of character, a deep, almost mystical type of piety. Had her lot been cast among the Quakers she might have developed into a female preacher, but rather being born among those whose traditions and practice were all against a woman's voice being heard in any public assembly, the gift was stifled without anybody's suspecting its existence. Still, she was considered an uncommon girl; and when, instead of marrying a minister or foreign missionary, she quietly united her lot for better or worse with a plain farmer, many people laid her choice to oddity; but Phœbe had no more of this than is common to human nature. The fact was she had a very keen spiritual insight and saw what other people did not see—that Josiah Howland, slow of speech and with none of the varnish of the universities upon him, had the soul of one of God's princes who walk the earth encompassed with an invisible royalty.

Such a couple would not fail to give their children religious training, and the best education their means could afford. One of their sons, at the time our story begins, was pastor of a small country church, while the second was teaching, with prospects of a professorship. But the youngest boy, Stephen, was a secret disappointment to both their hearts, especially his mother's. She had rejoiced with trembling over his queer, wise sayings when a little child, his strange questionings into the infinite mysteries of the life beyond, seeing in every new sign of spiritual precocity, that made old gossips shake their heads with lugubrious prophecies of an early grave, only another gracious indication that the Lord had heard her prayer as he did Hannah's, and her youngest and favorite son might yet prove a second Samuel called of God from his birth. He had passed an exemplary boyhood and youth without the sowing of a single crop of wild oats, but when it came to the choice of a profession, instead of treading in the steps of his elder brother, he shattered all her motherly dreamings and sorely confounded his father by declaring his intention to be a lawyer.

Now this good Puritan farmer had about as poor an opinion of lawyers as is anyway consistent with

Christian charity. He believed that, like the Cretans of old, they were "always liars", busybodies, meddling with other men's matters, keeping up quarrels between friends and neighbors just to fill their own pockets, and browbeating bewildered witnesses till they were ready to say black was white and white was black. Did not even the Bible say, " Woe unto you lawyers "?

But Stephen had fortified himself beforehand against all probable and improbable objections to his chosen career. He reminded his father that the Scriptures made honorable mention of "Zenas the lawyer"; that even if these things were all true of the profession generally, the more need that good men should enter its ranks; that, for himself, he would not stoop to any mean pettifoggery to win the most important case; that he meant to be always on the side of justice, the champion of the weak and oppressed against the powerful and strong; he quoted the resounding and classical words of Hooper: "Law hath her seat in the bosom of God"; and, in short, he argued the matter with a skill and fluency that promised great things for his future clients, and even staggered Mr. Josiah Howland not a little.

He put some more wood into the kitchen stove, over which he was sitting, and by that time he recovered the ideas which had been nearly swept away in the rush of his son's eloquence; very old-fashioned ideas they were, and obtained from a very old-fashioned book, but not yet obsolete in the quiet hill districts of New England.

"Now, Stephen, I want you to be an honest man, and then I don't care what else you are. I don't care how rich, or how smart, or how famous anybody is that ain't honest, and it's next to impossible to be an honest lawyer. It may be there are some that are, but it is like the camel going through the needle's eye, or the rich man entering heaven—a hard rub. To be sure, the Bible tells us that what is impossible with men is possible with God. But we ain't to be presumptuous. Because a thing is possible with God is no reason why we should always reckon on his doing it for us."

There was an unpolished logic in the words of the elder Howland which the younger found it hard to gainsay, but he had as yet advanced only a little way in that knowledge which an old heathen has somewhere declared to be the highest a man can acquire —"know thyself." So he accepted his father's last remark with some slight amendments—that because a thing was impossible with the majority of men, it by no means followed that it was not very possible and easy with Stephen Howland.

"Well, father, I must say as I have said before, I don't see why a really honest man should find it difficult to keep his honesty under any circumstances. The world needs lawyers, and the question is, what kind it shall have. Shall we leave it to the base and tricky to expound our national and State laws? to defend the innocent and unmask the guilty? to sit in the places of Story, and Wirt, and Marshall? Shall we have jurists on the bench, or charlatans?"

"I've had my say, Stephen.   You've got my mind about it," was his father's only response to this grandly sounding speech.   "Now it is time we heard your mother's."

Mrs. Phœbe Howland had not joined in the debate, and even at this direct appeal continued her work of paring and coring apples as if she had not heard it at all.   One who did not know her would have thought her indifferent to the subject; but the truth was she was a woman who never spoke hastily when any important matter was under discussion, and the more deeply her personal feelings were engaged, either *pro* or *con,* as in the present instance, the more firmly did she hold by the rule which in her girlhood she had written out with a list of other resolutions by which to guide her daily conduct.   It ran as follows: "Resolved, when my mind is not clear on any point affecting another's duty, never to open my lips until I feel that God has given me something to say."   No wonder that in her family this Puritan woman was queen, sybil, prophetess; that there was a deep, sweet gravity in her lightest speech, as of one who lived in the constant hearing of heavenly oracles.

So father and son waited, the one in reverential, the other in eager silence.   Five, ten minutes passed, and but for the monotonous leaping of the quarters of apple into the bright tin pan in her lap, it would have been still enough for a Quaker meeting.   Then she spoke:

"It may be, father, that God has called Stephen to

be a lawyer, and what are we that we should withstand his voice? I only want him to be fully persuaded in his own mind."

The point was settled. This Puritan couple, with
their simple honesty, their unworldly faith in God
and each other, had solved the vexed question of
household supremacy without quarreling with either
Peter or Paul. Mrs. Phœbe Howland believed implicitly that her husband was the best man in the
world, and though she had all the refinement and
most of the book knowledge, she gloried in the
rough-barked oak. Mr. Josiah Howland, on his part,
looked on "mother" as a superior being who held
constant communion with the unseen and the eternal;
he followed reverently in the path of her lightest
opinion, and would no more have thought of calling
in question anything she said after one of those long,
sacred "silences," than Dante would have thought of
contending with Beatrice about the right road to
Paradise.

It was under these circumstances that Stephen became a student in the law office of Judge Howland,
a distant relative of his father's, where he remained
the customary period; then, a full-fledged young bar-
rister, he opened a tiny office in a new-made Western
city, hung out his sign, and waited for fortune to
chance that way.

CHAPTER II.

Stephen Howland was waiting for clients with what patience he could muster one raw, cloudy, chilly day, when he heard the welcome sound of feet pausing at his door, and a stranger entered who wanted a deed drawn up.

Even so trifling a job as the drawing up of a legal paper the young attorney did not consider despicable at the present low ebb in his affairs and spirits. So he proceeded àt once to write the required instrument. The stranger, whose name was put therein as Felix Basset, had apparently reached five and forty, was good-looking, well dressed, and agreeable; a man evidently on the best possible terms with himself, as could be seen by the air of self-possession with which he took a seat and let his eye roam over the rather meagre appointments of the little office, in a way that seemed to render superfluous any answer to his careless inquiry, "How goes business with you, Mr. Howland?"

"I haven't been troubled with any rush of clients as yet," returned Stephen, rather dryly.

"Well, I suppose not. A lawyer's practice is like Rome. It can't be built up in a day. But some men make a life-job of success, and never get fairly onto their feet. I don't believe in that, because I think there is no need of it. We are fast learning the truth that mankind are brothers, and as a consequence there are organizations in every city and town founded on this idea, and anybody that wants to get on in the world should join one of these. Now, I started in life with scarcely a dollar in my pocket, and I shall always say that I owe more of my success in business to having joined the Odd-fellows than to all other causes combined."

Stephen only said, "Indeed!" but Mr. Felix Basset was too full of his subject to need any other encouragement to go on.

"Yes; I consider Odd-fellowship by all odds the best order that a young man can enter. It is a system of the most rigid morality as well as the most perfect benevolence. It is even better in some respects than the church itself."

Stephen had grown up with that idea of the Christian church which still prevails in some guileless souls, as the pure and spotless Bride, clothed with the sun and crowned with stars; persecuted, yet full of divine vitality that could triumph over all the fury of her dragon foe; before whose mighty tread every idol should fall, every superstition crumble, every wrong flee away, and the renovated, purified earth become once more a fit dwelling-place for Eternal Love. It was no wonder then that he gave a little start, and fixed his eyes inquiringly on Mr Basset. Both movements were observed by that gentleman, who made haste accordingly to define his opinions with more strictness.

"I see you are surprised to hear me say so, but it is the truth, and the truth ought to be spoken even when it cuts the wrong way. The Odd-fellows take care of their sick and poor. What does the church do for hers? Why, in nine cases out of ten she just lets them alone to suffer and die, or be thrown on public charity. It is a fact that I have heard more than one minister say, both of Masonry and Odd-fellowship, precisely what I am saying now, that they accomplish more good than the churches do."

"I suppose these two orders bear considerable resemblance to each other," observed Stephen, both for the purpose of saying something, and because he really had a vague idea that such was the case.

"Oh, no; they are independent organizations, entirely separate in everything. A man can join both if he chooses, and so get a double benefit. Now a member of the lodge where I belong is not only an Odd-fellow, but a Mason, a Knight of Pythias, a Good Templar, and I know not what besides. But I don't believe in joining so many orders. Odd-fellowship contains enough to satisfy me, and it ought to any reasonable man."

Now it must be confessed that Stephen Howland had an undefined suspicion of anything Masonic. He remembered, when a boy, eating his luncheon with his father one hot day under the shade of the big oak in the south pasture, inquiring between the savory bites of doughnuts and cheese, "Father, what is Freemasonry?"

"It is a bad thing, Stephen, bad clear through. I

hope *you'll* never have anything to do with it."

"But what makes it bad, father?" persisted the boy, whose young curiosity was fully aroused.

"Why, the terrible oaths they have to take, for one thing. There used to be a little book with a blue cover up in the attic, when I was a boy, that had them all written out, and the signs, and grips, and everything."

"Do you know where that book is now?" asked Stephen, eagerly.

"Hain't a notion. I suppose it got scattered along with the other things when we broke up after father died."

"But why do they have to take such oaths?" inquired Stephen, going on with his catechising.

"That's a question, now," said the elder Howland, ruminatively. "Folks ain't generally to all that pains to cover up good deeds, and this is one great reason why I have always stood to it that Masonry must be bad. They say that if a man takes these oaths and then lets out the secrets he is liable to lose his life, and if that is so it is an institution only fit for thieves and murderers. I don't suppose there's a doubt but what they murdered William Morgan out in western New York for writing that little book I told you of. They took him out in a boat at night and drowned him in the river. This was something that happened before my day, but father used to tell about it. It's queer now that there ain't anything about it in the school histories. There ought to be, for it made an awful excitement all over the country, so that the lodge went down everywhere and men were ashamed or afraid to own they ever had been Masons. Somehow the thing had a big tap root, and it beats all how it has started up again. But I tell you, Stephen, don't you ever join the Masons. It is no place for an honest man."

So believed this worthy New Englander, this Puritan of many generations, and so according to his best knowledge and belief did he teach his twelve-year-old son, whose mind, accustomed to consider the taking of human life as the most dreadful crime in the catalogue, was filled with horror at these revelations. So far and no farther could Josiah Howland throw his red light of warning. It is true that on general principles he was opposed to the lesser secret orders, but in his eyes Masonry was the Moses' rod that swallowed up all the others, leaving him with a merely negative opinion about them as of something foolish, but not so absolutely bad and mischievous as to need any special combating. Thus it was that Stephen, as soon as Mr. Basset assured him that Odd-fellowship had no connection with Masonry, felt a sudden revulsion of his previous prejudices, and was perfectly willing to hear more about it.

"I am glad to know I was mistaken in supposing them to be alike," he said, after a moment's pause. "The fact is—I may as well say it—I have heard some things about Masonry not at all to my taste."

"O, you will find that Odd-fellowship has nothing in it to trouble the tenderest conscience," returned

Mr. Basset, with easy cheerfulness. "It requires no oath of its members, only a simple obligation. Be tween ourselves," he continued, with an air of mingled confidence and candor, "there are objectionable features about Masonry. I don't mind saying so, and this is why I recommend Odd-fellowship so highly. It has all the advantages of Masonry, and none of its drawbacks. Here you are a stranger in a strange place. You need friends who will stand by you if you are sick or in trouble, and be interested in your obtaining a practice. Now this is just where Odd-fellowship fulfills the divine law better than the churches do: 'I was a stranger and ye took me in, naked and ye clothed me, sick and in prison and ye visited me.' That is the kind of religion that men understand."

Now in Mr. Felix Basset's coat pocket reposed at that very moment a small volume brimful of instructive facts for all good Odd-fellows, one of them being stated as follows: "Chinese, Polynesians, Indians, half-breeds or mixed bloods are not eligible to membership!" And if any earnest seeker after the truth as it is in Odd-fellowship had looked still deeper into its pages they might have learned that not only were these classes excluded, but all men of African descent, all women—none, in short, being admitted but the free, white males; while even of this favored class the deaf, dumb, and blind, the aged and poor, the halt and lame, might as well, for all their hopes of ever sharing in the exhaustless stream of Odd-fellow beneficence, have been Chinese

, coolies, or negroes whose shoulders still bore the marks of the overseer's whip.

But it is the tendency of human nature to like the sound of certain words. Men have thrown up their caps and shouted themselves hoarse at the name of Liberty, while her most devoted sons were gasping in dungeons or expiring on the scaffold. And Charity, with many people, is almost as potent a watchword. They swear by her name and sound trumpets in her honor at the very moment that she wanders outcast, frightened away by the noise and blare. Stephen Howland believed in mutual helpfulness. He had a generous nature, and was, besides, in that situation which is least calculated to nurture any proud independence of one's fellow-beings. He considered Mr. Basset very kind and friendly, and felt grateful accordingly; and though he could not yet see that it was both his duty and privilege to become an Odd-fellow with all convenient speed, he was willing enough to think about it.

"Now there are some people," resumed Mr. Basset, "whose idea of Odd-fellowship is just a mutual benefit society and nothing else. But that is a very wrong impression. The material good it does is the least part of it. The fact is it is a great moral and religious teacher, and above all it is a temperance order. Now that is a subject in which everybody ought to feel interested. The crime and misery caused by the rum traffic is frightful to contemplate —perfectly terrible."

"It is indeed," answered Stephen, feelingly, for

he had been educated in the strictest doctrines of
temperance. He believed that the legalized sale of
intoxicating liquors was the curse and shame of our
Christian civilization; that it was the solemn and
bounden duty of every man, woman and child to organize and fight to the death the monster Alcohol;
that it was the old medieval battle between St.
George and the dragon acted over again in the living
issues of to-day; and he had even dreamed of grand
and heroic deeds that his own right hand might
some day perform in this warfare. Mr. Felix Basset could hardly have touched a more responsive
chord.

"I am a very strong temperance man myself,"
continued that gentleman, "and though I think the
Good Templars and other similar orders are very
useful, I really believe there is no better organization to promote the cause than Odd-fellowship rightly understood. You see it is just this way,"—and
and here Mr. Basset lowered his voice with the air
of one about to impart information on a deep and
profound subject—"everybody don't understand, not
even the majority of the members themselves, that,
as its teachings are based on the broad foundation
of universal truth, and the greater always includes
the less, it follows that they must in the nature of
things cover all truth that humanity needs to know.
Considered in that light it is, as I said, a temperance
order—nothing less, and every one who enters it
stands committed to prohibition principles. But to
come back to the subject we started on; I believe in

the church. I have been a member fifteen years, and I assert that no single church has a sphere wide enough to do all the charitable and benevolent work that the world needs done. An Odd-fellow who lives up to the requirements of the order can't help being a good Christian, though as a matter of actual practice it is with Odd-fellowship just as it is in the church, inconsistency even among the best."

Mr. Basset sighed, though whether for the inconsistencies of church members or lodge members, or both, was not quite apparent; and, after a moment's silence, he paid the young attorney's modest fee, and left him to his own reflections, which amounted substantially to this: that an institution which could thus combine a man's interest for both world's must be a good thing, and if clients did not come in any faster, he, Stephen Howland, would be standing very much in his own light not to heed the advice so freely and disinterestedly given.

CHAPTER III.

A strange scene now rises before us, and though the reader, at first sight, may be disposed to shrink back, we bid him follow, in all good courage: for this is no assembly of Southern Ku-Klux, meditating a descent on some defenseless negro cabin, but a company of peaceful citizens, who lay aside their masks and disguises when the business which calls them together is over, and separate without the deliberate planning of a single deed of darkness.

But *our* business just now is in an ante-room, where two men stand fronting each other, the older of the two with a blank book before him, in which he is writing down to the following questions the answers given him by the younger, who proves to be no other than our friend, Stephen Howland:

"What is your name?"

"Where do you live?"

"What is your occupation?"

"How old are you?

"Do you hold membership in, or are you suspended or expelled from any lodge of this order?"

"Are you, so far as you know, in sound health?"

Stephen Howland had a good deal of what we may call the "pride of life." He had never wronged his pure and temperate ancestry by a single youthful excess, and his happy New England heritage of mingled plenty and toil had developed in him a vigor and hardihood which hardly knew a day's sickness. So he may be pardoned for answering in the affirmative, with a pleasant consciousness, meanwhile, that his well-knit, manly figure and fine proportions made him goodly to look at, both in the eyes of men and women.

"Do you believe in the existence of a Supreme, Intelligent Being, the creator and preserver of the Universe?"

And again Stephen answered in the affirmative, forgetting that he called himself a Christian, and was now giving his assent to a creed that left out the most essential part of his faith; and which, thus emasculated, neither Jew, Mohammedan or deist could possibly quarrel with.

The recording angel of the lodge, who, by the way, bore the uncelestial title of Past Grand, here put down his pen and shut his book; but he had one more inquiry to make of the young neophyte:

"Are you willing to enter into an obligation to keep secret all that may transpire during your initiation?"

Stephen Howland felt, for an instant, a trifle uncomfortable; but had he not been assured, time and again, of the highly moral and religious nature of the society which he was now joining? So he swallowed his scruples in their first beginning, gave once more the expected affirmative, and repeated, in a clear, firm voice, after his examiner, "I hereby pledge my sacred honor that I will keep secret whatever may transpire during my initiation."

His catechiser then blindfolded his eyes, which gave Stephen another uncomfortable feeling, for he was naturally one of the wide-awake kind, who like to know what is going on about them; and, leading him to the door of the hall, gave three resounding raps. "Who comes there?" was responded from within. "The Outside Conductor, with a stranger who desires to be initiated into the Independent Order of Odd-fellows", answered his guide. And thus introduced, Stephen was led into the hall to where stood three figures, the one on the right and left being in long white robes, like grave shrouds, and each holding an unlighted torch. The middle figure was similarly attired, only in a black robe instead of a white one. The rest of the company wore semi-masks, the upper part reaching to about the middle of the forehead, and the lower part covering the mouth; the funereal aspect of the whole scene being much enhanced by an open coffin, containing a very death-like representation of a skeleton, which was placed in the center of the room.

"You are now within a lodge of Odd-fellows", spoke the black-robed figure, in a kind of recitative singsong; "here the world is shut out; you are separated from its cares and distinctions, its dissensions and its vices. Here Friendship and Love assert their mild dominion, while Faith and Charity combine to bless the mind with peace and soften the heart with sympathy. Those around you have all assumed the obligations and endeavor to cherish the sentiments peculiar to Odd-fellowship; but before you can unite with them you must pass through an initiatory ceremony, which will ultimately lead you to primary truth."

Stephen Howland, standing with his hoodwink over his eyes, doubtful, bewildered, curious, was in a receptive rather than critical posture of mind. It did not even occur to him to ask with Pilate, "What is Truth?" But how shall we excuse his pastor, the Rev. Theophilus Brassfield, who is one of that masked company, and only the previous Sabbath preached from the text, "*I* am the Way and the TRUTH and the Life!"

"The stranger now awaits our mystic rites," sol-emnly pronounced the figure in the black robe.

"Then at once the chains prepare," said the one on the right hand in a disguised and sepulchral voice. And a chain was accordingly thrown over his shoulders, brought around under his arms and tied behind. "Now, bind him to the stake!" chimed in the one on the left; but the black-robed figure inter-rupted this cheerful proposition with, "Hold! Bro-thers! shall we proceed in these, our mystic rites, or shall we mercy show?" And from the masked as-sembly, in a low, hesitating murmur, came the ans-wer, "Mercy—mercy show."

All this did not appear to Stephen nearly as fool-ish as it probably appears to the reader. Whether it be a case of magnetism, or snake charming, or the

mere influence of one set of minds on another, it
generally makes all the difference in the world whether
we are inside or outside the circle. And Stephen was
inside, caught in the whirlpool of all this spiritual
jugglery. He had not the smallest fear of any personal harm, yet his flesh crept with a cold shiver as
the faint tolling of a bell struck on the silence.
When he was a boy he well remembered that sound;
how he used to count the strokes; one, two for the
infant; eighteen, twenty for the youth and maiden;
five and forty for the life gone down in its meridian;
fourscore for the aged and full of days; how solemnly they floated out from the little country church
and reverberated amidst the quiet of those green
hills; and how each one seemed like a separate voice
out of the dim, shadowy shores of eternity, as awful
and mysterious as the voices of the Apocalypse!
And by a curious, but not extraordinary, trick of
memory, as he was led slowly around the room the
clank of his fetters brought to recollection an old
hymn often sung by his mother about her work:

"How sad our state by nature is!
Our sin, how deep its stains!
And Satan binds our captive minds
Fast in his slavish chains."

Meanwhile, he in the black robes delivered a melancholy harangue, intended to deepen still further the
solemnizing effect: "Man in darkness and chains!
How mournful the spectacle! Yet it is but the condition of millions of our race who are void of wisdom, though they know it not. We have a lesson to
impart to him—one of great moment and deep

solemnity; a faithful exhibition of the vanity of worldly things; of the instability of wealth and power; of the certain decay of all earthly greatness." But Stephen hardly heard it in the sense of receiving any definite impression therefrom. It all mingled together — a bewildering, bewitching, stupefying draught of enchantment, till he felt the hoodwink slowly taken off, and was told to "contemplate the scene" before him.

Stephen Howland looked. He saw the coffin, the skeleton, and the two sepulchrally attired figures, one at each end holding up lighted candles which threw into broad relief every repugnant feature of the sight on which he gazed—from the eyeless sockets to the fleshless mouth, on which seemed to be set Death's horrible grin of triumph. In common with most healthy physical natures, he shrank from all sight and contact with such emblems of human mortality. Coffins and graves, skulls and crossed bones he had no morbid fancy for contemplating, but his nerves were strong and he did not even change countenance, but looked steadily as bidden while the dreary harangues went on with their lessons on the instability of life and the certainty of death, which, divested of all their superfluous and high-sounding phrases, might have been found in any child's primer.

Then he was again blindfolded and lead a short distance to where, the hoodwink being once more removed, he found himself confronted by an apparition hardly less startling. It was that of an old, a *very* old man, whose years, to all appearance, rivalled Methusaleh's. He was clad in a long black robe, tied closely at the neck and waist and reaching to the feet; his long grey hairs swept his shoulders, a beard of silvery whiteness descended to his waist, and he leaned on his staff for very age. To this personage Stephen was now introduced with due formality as the Venerable Warden of the lodge, and commanded to listen to his words of wisdom, which unfortunately lost not a little of their impressiveness from the fact that he discerned, or thought he discerned, the voice of Mr. Felix Basset under the trembling accents of this lodge Methusaleh. From thence he was led to the chair of another dignitary, the Worthy Vice Grand. At the mandate of this officer, who was clad all in celestial blue, the chain and hoodwink were taken off and the obligation administered with the assurance that it would not conflict with any of the exalted duties he owed to God, his country or himself. And with his right hand on his left breast Stephen Howland promised: never to communicate to any one unless directed to do so by a legal lodge, the signs, tokens or grips, the term, traveling or other passwords, belonging to the Independent Order of Odd-fellows; never to expose or lend any of the books or papers relating to the records or secret work of the order to any person or persons, except to one specially authorized to receive them; never to reveal any private business which might be transacted in his presence in this or any other lodge; to abide by the laws, rules and regulations of the lodge, the

Grand Lodge of the State or any other Grand or working lodge to which he might be attached; never to wrong a subordinate or Grand lodge to the value of anything; never to take part or share directly or indirectly in any illegal distribution of the funds or other property of the lodge; never to wrong a brother, or see him wronged without apprising him of approaching danger, and should he be expelled or voluntarily leave the order, to consider this promise as binding out of it as in it.

All this while the presiding officer of the lodge, the Noble Grand, had been hidden behind a red curtain, and pretended at first to be exceedingly busy, but finally condescended to appear, dressed in a robe of Babylonish scarlet, and instruct still further the young novitiate; this instruction being supplemented by a long closing lecture from another officer, the Worthy Past Grand, in which he was told that the general design of the order was to teach the principles of universal fraternity, and improve and elevate mankind; in short, to do for him what Christianity has always claimed to do, and actually *done*, in the judgment of many honest souls, who will even point you, in their simple credulity, to numerous facts, both of private experience and written history, that would really seem to prove them right in their belief.

And then the farce was over. Stephen Howland was a duly initiated member of the Independent Order of Odd-fellows, entitled to the fraternal greetings and congratulations of his new-made brothers, as a sharer with them in all its privileges, temporal and spiritual. Of these, Mr. Felix Basset was naturally foremost.

"Now, what is there in Odd-fellowship that a Christian man can possibly object to?" he inquired, with a beaming smile of triumph. "You've found it just as I told you—a teacher of morals and religion all through."

"I must confess that, many times as I have heard its beautiful and instructive ritual," observed the Rev. Theophilus Brassfield, as he too extended a fraternal hand, "they strike me at every repetition with new force and beauty. In this changing age it is good to have a form of sound words which, like the old Episcopal liturgy, time and fashion cannot alter."

The fact that the Odd-fellows' ritual has been altered twice since 1844, was one of which the reverend gentleman was either ignorant, or else it had slipped his memory: and Stephen Howland, who knew as little of the history of the institution he had joined as he did of Voudooism, could only smile assent.

"That is what I always tell people," put in Mr. Green, a prosperous grocer and an enthusiastic member of the order. "I tell them that only we insiders know the first letter of Odd-fellowship; and as to there being anything ridiculous in the ceremonies, I never felt so solemn in my life as I did the night I was initiated."

But Mr. Van Gilder, the keeper of a livery stable near by, who was looked upon by the brethren of the stricter sort, as rather a scandal to the lodge, through his convivial habits, to say nothing of other and worse ones of which he was suspected, seemed to look on the matter in a slightly different light.

"Hang it all, Green," he interrupted, "what is the use of long faces? *You* like a jolly good time as well as any of us."

Some of the brethren chuckled at this hit, and one remarked, "He has you there, Green." While still another member, conscious, perhaps, that the minister, who as chaplain of the lodge was generally present, was not yet out of earshot, took up the cudgels.

"Come, Van Gilder; that is no way to talk. If you don't want religion now you will some time. If Odd-fellowship didn't teach what I call pure religion I shouldn't care anything for it. But I say it does. I always feel, after seeing a candidate initiated, just as solemn as though I had been to a prayer-meeting."

Stephen, on whom the "solemn" effect was fast wearing off, leaving him in a state of general doubt as to whether the whole thing was a religious ceremony or a harlequin play, was glad to get out into the night air and feel its reviving breath on his face. But as the worthy members separated, or rather broke up into little knots which took different streets according to the direction of their several homes, his ears were greeted by another scrap of talk of a slightly different tenor. It was near enough to election for those political straws to be flying about which show office-seekers whether the wind is to blow fair or foul on the all-important day that is to decide their destiny at that throne of King People, the ballot-box.

"Hicks stands a chance to get a good many votes," said one lodge brother, "unless the Democrats put up a stronger man than either he or Putney."

"Hicks is popular with a few crooked sticks," responded the other, with a knowing air, as he stopped to light his cigar; "but of course the third party can't carry the day. It's Putney that has got the inside track, you may depend on that."

"There'll be lots of bolting done."

"Let 'em bolt, then. It won't make much difference. We might get a worse man for Governor than General Putney. He's backed up by all the Grand Army Posts, beside. That's the way he come to be nominated. The thing was worked up neat by Putney's friends. You see I was there and I saw it all. They kept mum till nearly all the candidates were named, and then Judge Dorsey got up and proposed General Putney's name. There was some hissing then and a great deal of confusion, for if the General has got his friends he's got his enemies, too. But the Judge kept cool He had two strings to his bow, and he laid it on so thick about Putney's record in the war, and what a good friend he had always been to the soldiers—how he had worn himself out in their interests trying to get Congress to pass increased pension bills—I tell you when he finished his speech the boys in blue could have been heard a mile."

Only the last part of the talk reached Stephen Howland's ears in any connected shape, but his mind had a natural bent in the direction of politics. He was interested in the movements of parties and the prospects of candidates, while hating political trickery and wire-pulling with all his heart. He had a sincere wish that the people should understand better who and what they were voting for instead of being made mere figure-heads, having a show of sovereignty, while the actual power was vested in a few unscrupulous party leaders, who manipulated the conventions and nominated or rubbed out at their sweet will, without the least regard for what their constituents desired. Though so young when the war ended that the roar of cannon and ringing of bells which announced the fall of Richmond had left only a faint echo in his memory, he had a genuine patriotic feeling of friendliness and respect for old soldiers who had ventured their lives for the Stars and Stripes, and he believed their claims should be ever held in remembrance by the government they had fought to save; and it was natural that he should feel a proportionate indignation when he saw them made the mere puppets of politicians who sought, by playing on their selfish interests, to make them stepping-stones on which to mount higher in the scramble for preferment. He had heard of General Putney, and knew him to be a low, vulgar demagogue. So this was the way he was hoisted into office; by a trick of clap-trap oratory appealing to the selfishness or the gratitude—it was hard to say which—of the country's veteran defenders, for whom he cared not a straw except as they could be made subservient to his own political advancement.

Stephen was thinking it over when a hand was laid familiarly on his shoulder—the hand of one of his new-made lodge brothers.

"Warmest evening I ever saw so late in the season. Step in here and have a glass of lemonade. I'll stand treat."

Stephen was not thirsty, but he accepted the invitation, thinking it would appear churlish to refuse, and followed his guide, nothing witting, into the fashionable restaurant, which was likewise one of the genteel drinking places that, with others not so genteel, flourished under the very noses of the Sons of Temperance, Rechabites and Good Templars to the mystification of many of the worthy citizens of Jacksonville, who could by no means understand why the mice should play when the cat was *not* away.

An hour or two later Stephen Howland was kicking off his boots in his office, which was also his only sleeping-room, with the feeling of one just awakening from an opium dream.

CHAPTER IV.

STEPHEN HOWLAND'S FIRST CASE.

A stone's throw from Stephen Howland's office stood one of the few surviving landmarks that told of a time when the city of Jacksonville was a mere nucleus of log huts surrounded by unbroken prairie. Stephen had often wondered why it was allowed to stand there; and finally reached the conclusion that the owner must be a miserly, grasping kind of man, who was holding on to this bit of primeval property in hopes of a fabulous rise in real estate. Most of our conclusions regarding any eccentric or unusual action on the part of our fellow-beings are about as charitable and as near the truth as Stephen's surmising, who little thought that through this man he would secure his first client.

As he sits in his rude domicile, like a bear in his den, we will sketch his portrait. He is large and powerfully built, with eyes as blue and keen as an Alpine sky. His hair falls in thick, shaggy locks from an ample head, where a phrenologist would find plenty of those unamiable bumps which characterize the born fighter; especially if he be of the combative, destructive, aggressive Anglo-Saxon race; yet when his mouth, shaded by its bristling, grizzly

beard, parts in a smile, it has the winning sweetness
of a child. Taken altogether there is something in
the general cast of head and face strongly suggest-
ive of the portrait of John Brown. Martin Treworthy had often been told that he looked like the
hero of Osawatomie, and no compliment could possibly please him better. In the old stirring days of
border warfare he had been one of John Brown's
men, and when the curtain fell on the tragedy of
Harper's Ferry, the man who had marched under his
orders, bivouacked with him, and listened to his
strong, burning, fateful words, felt the burden of
prophecy in his own soul, as if a portion of his beloved leader's spirit had descended upon him.

"It don't matter to me what folks call him, 'crack-
brained,' or 'visionary,' or 'fanatic,' or anything else
—that's one good thing; and it don't matter any to
the captain, that's another. He was the only one
that dared to *do* instead of writing and speechify-
ing. He struck slavery right at its heart, and it will
never get over the blow. He don't need *me* to stand
up for him, but every time I read in Revelation I
can shut my eyes and see him as plain as day, sitting on a white horse and following the One in the
vesture dipped in blood, with the sharp sword going
out of his mouth. Now I've pondered a good deal
on that passage and similar ones. I tell you the
American people have got a cup of trembling to
drink before the Lord gets through reckoning with
'em. The time is coming when he shall tread the
winepress of the fierceness of his wrath against this

nation, and blood shall come out of the winepress, even unto the horses' bridles."

It was not long before the first gun fired on Fort Sumter startled the North from its dream of peace and safety, and Martin Treworthy, as he buckled on his knapsack and shouldered his musket, knew that the hour of which he prophesied was casting its shadow on the dial.   And when around hundreds of campfires rose the stirring strains of the John Brown song, he only saw, plainer than ever, the soul of the old martyr-hero "marching on" after his Celestial Chief, who had waited in divine patience, while the cries of his enslaved children mingled with the prayers of his saints on the golden altar, till now "the day of vengeance was in his heart and the year of his redeemed had come."

He had been through all the hardest-fought battles of the war, Gettysburg, Antietam, James River and the Wilderness.   He came out of the army as he entered it, a private, his only badge of distinction some honorable wounds that disabled him from active labor.   But he had his pension and a small sum laid up besides, and on this he lived very comfortably.   He was one of the first settlers of Jacksonville, and though the price of the land on which stood his primitive dwelling would have added not a little to his worldly wealth, he had steadily refused all offers to sell, though not everybody knew the reason why.

He had come to Jacksonville when its future greatness existed only in the speculator's brain, a middle-aged man, with life's summer just beginning —a summer like that of northern latitudes, without any spring; for he had been left an orphan in early boyhood, and remembered nothing since but a succession of rough experiences in borderers' cabins, fighting wild Indians; prairie fires and Missouri ruffians; varied, however, we must remark, by one great episode, that reversed the whole current of the reckless backwoodsman's life—his conversion at a Methodist campmeeting, when, among other "fruits meet for repentance," he had given up his favorite indulgence of tobacco; an act which had more of the genuine spirit of self-renunciation in it than many a comfortable, easy-going Christian ever dreams of. The pretty "school-ma'am" who had engaged his affections, an orphan likewise, was a woman as fair and good and true as any of the heroines of Scott or Burns. But alas for human hopes! Scarlet fever broke out in the school in which she was teaching; she caught the infection, and in one short week from the day set for their marriage he laid her to rest under the prairie roses, and tried to keep his heart from breaking by reading the fourteenth chapter of John, and thinking of those many mansions of which the Lamb is the light forever.

"Somehow all this happiness I've been looking forward to don't seem to be for me," he said, when he came out of that first trance of misery which succeeds every stunning sorrow, and realized with a kind of wonder that he could still live on when the desire of his eyes had been taken from him at a stroke. "But I won't murmur at God's dealings. They are all right and for the best. 'The Lord gave and the Lord hath taken away. Blessed be the name of the Lord.'"

But while he bowed himself thus meekly to that mysterious decree which condemned him to loneliness and solitude for the rest of his mortal pilgrimage, he clung to the home that was to have been hers with a tenacity perfectly unintelligible to any one who did not know the story of his frustrated hopes. He had driven every nail with his own hands, exulting in the fact that it was the only frame house in the settlement. He had wrought into its fabric all the dreams and hopes which, in a nature like his, can have but one earthly blooming time; and now that she had gone for whose pleasure and delight he had planned and labored, it still seemed too much a part of her for him to feel contented anywhere else. For, while he had not a particle of superstition in his nature, and denounced unsparingly the rappings, table-tippings, and coarse materializings of so-called "spiritualism" as a fraud and humbug, directly inspired by the father-of-lies himself, he implicitly believed in a world of spiritual intelligences above and around him; nor would he have been startled at any time if soundless footsteps had crossed his threshold, and, looking up, he had beheld once more the blue eyes and brown hair, all transfigured with that tender, immortal light which only rests on the foreheads of the redeemed.

So much for Martin Treworthy, a real old Iron-

side, "born out of due season;" a prophet without
honor save among a few who liked his rugged utterances, or as they would have expressed it, "his way
of putting things." He now sits in his leathern
arm-chair, engaged in earnest talk with a young man
whose shop-apron and sleeves rolled up to the arm-
pits, proclaim him a genuine son of labor; his
shrewd, kindly face indignant and thoughtful by
turns.

"So you mean to appeal to the law. All right.
If you come short, call on me. I've got a little
cash laid by—what I used to spend for tobacco.
See here," and Martin Treworthy took down a tin
box from a shelf over his head, and opening it displayed a goodly store of shining silver coin, "so
much for the Lord that used to go to the devil, and
I say, take it to fight the devil. There's twenty dollars if there is a cent in good solid specie. Come,
now."

But the young man shook his head in decided,
though grateful refusal.

"No, Mr. Treworthy; your sympathy and advice
is all the help I need. The evidence against Snyder
is so strong that prosecuting the case cannot be very
expensive. But poor Tom is pretty bad to-day. It
seems they kept him drinking till he had taken
enough whisky to kill an ox; and then in that condition he was arrested and put into a cold cell with
only a little straw, and not a blanket to cover him—
and it was one of the frostiest nights of the season.
To-day he seems a little out of his head. It is an

outrageous affair, and I'm bound to see what can be done about it. The first thing, of course, is to get a good lawyer to conduct the case—if I only knew what one."

"How many 'good lawyers' do you reckon on here in Jacksonville?" asked his counselor, somewhat dryly. "Count 'em up on your fingers and see."

"There's Greggson. Folks call him smart."

"So is the devil, but I wouldn't want either of 'em to plead a case for me."

"Then what do you say to Simonds?"

But Mr. Treworthy looked no better satisfied.

"I say he is a high Mason, and a poor working-man like you had better keep clear of Sublime Princes and Knights Elect and all such fellows. What are big fish for except to swallow little ones?"

"O, if you come to that," said the other, as he uneasily shifted his left foot over his right, "every lawyer in Jacksonville, unless maybe this young Howland that has just come into the place, is a Mason; and all our business men, to say nothing of the ministers, belong to that or some other secret order. If it is an evil I don't see but we shall have to put up with it or else go out of the world. I know you think all secret societies are bad things, and I am willing to admit that there are evils connected with Freemasonry, but whether they are a part of the system or mere abuses that have crept into it, is a question that I must confess I am undecided about. I believe the trades unions and temperance lodges are doing a good work."

"Why are not labor troubles stopped and the saloons put down then?" queried Martin Treworthy, with blunt and most inconvenient appositeness.

"Oh, well," replied the other, "intemperance is such a giant evil that no single man or association of men seem powerful enough to grapple with it. And as for labor unions, where capitalists are growing more reckless of the laboring-man's rights every year, combination is the only weapon left. To tell the truth, I joined the Knights of Labor a short time ago, and as yet I have seen only good in the organization. The president and many of the members are Masons or Odd-fellows, and appear to be worthy and honorable men as far as I can judge— at least, most of them. Now, I really can't see where the practical difference comes in between a lawyer who is a Mason and one that isn't. Neither want to lose their cases."

Mr. Treworthy's eyes flashed, and he brought his hand down on the table with considerable vehemence as he said:

"Nelson Newhall! I am older than you, and I have seen the workings of this vile leaven as I hope you will never have a chance to. Difference? It can make all the difference between sin and righteousness, truth and falsehood, justice and oppression, heaven and hell. I have seen rogues get clear that ought to have been hung, and far honester men sent to jail in their places; and right here in this very county I know of two murderers at large for no other reason than because Masonic sheriffs would not

arrest and Masonic juries would not convict. Wasn't
I in the war, from the time the first gun was fired
till Lee's surrender? and don't I know a thing or
two you young civilians who never smelled powder
no more dream of than the babe unborn? I could
tell some queer stories if I set out to. As for your
Good Templars and Grand Army posts and farmers'
granges and Knights of Labor, they are just so
many wires to be pulled by Masonic politicians that
want office, and Masonic sharpers that want to line
their own pockets with the earnings of honest farmers and laborers. And if a Masonic murderer, or
thief, or saloon-keeper wants to go clear of punishment, hasn't he got just as much right to pull 'em as
the politicians? Then some innocent man has to
bear the blame, for, as a general thing, if the law
can't get hold of the right one it must have a scape-
goat. These secret lodges, if they are let alone, will
bring the country into such a pass as the prophet
Joel tells of—we're dreadful nigh it now—'That
which the palmer-worm hath left hath the locust eat-
en; and that which the locust hath left hath the
canker-worm eaten; and that which the canker-worm
hath left hath the caterpillar eaten.' That's my
mind."

Martin Treworthy was a man who did his own
thinking. He did not even, as is the case with the
average American citizen, let the newspapers do it
for him. Thus it followed that to be favored with
"a piece of his mind" after it was once made up was
a rather formidable thing, there being none of that

malleable quality about it characteristic of minds
that are formed of the odds and ends of what other
people think and say, and then duly pressed and
stamped into shape by that roller which we call
"public opinion." So it was no wonder that Nelson
Newhall winced under this speech, for he was really
as honest in his way as Martin Treworthy, and had
only joined a secret labor union for the same good
and substantial reason that makes one sheep follow
another down a precipice.

So he sat for a moment in uneasy silence, and
wondered, for he was a simple, honest fellow, with
large capacities for righteous wrath, but without a
particle of guile or duplicity, how so many ministers
and good men could uphold the system if it was
really anything so very bad. For the large majority of mankind, who are neither seers nor philoso-
phers, are apt to assume the existence of any popular evil as the ground of its right to exist. Nelson
Newhall was only like thousands of others. He saw
the lodge in power. It was no abstraction, but a
tangible, unquestionable, undeniable fact. It was
palpable and material as the Scarlet Woman seated
on her seven-headed beast. How came it there?
popular, powerful, entrenched behind such a bulwark
of custom, prejudice and fear. Had not wise men,
good men and great men, lent it their silent influence, bowed before it in slavish homage, seen no
evil in it, and furthermore, refused to see any? and
could such men be wrong, and a handful of fanatics
like Martin Treworthy, right? This is a style of

reasoning which may not be strictly logical, but all
reformers, from Paul to Luther, and from Luther to
Garrison, will testify that it is very common.

Martin Treworthy, having had his say, was content to let the subject pass, and return to the immediate theme in hand. So he remarked after a
moment's silence:

"Why not try this young Howland? You've got
a good case, as plain and straight ahead as the Ten
Commandments, and I wouldn't be afraid to trust
him with it. Melroy—you know Moses Melroy that
lives over in Fairfield—used to be acquainted with
the Howlands before he came away from New Hampshire. Real nice folks, he says they were—folks
that wouldn't lie nor cheat for their right hand.
Such families will throw out crooked shoots sometimes, just as a tree will, but it ain't the rule for 'em
to as long as the main stock holds good."

Nelson Newhall fingered his hat for a moment with
his eye on the modest sign, "S. Howland," just visible down the street. "I'll try him," he said, decidedly, and took his departure. But, like many of our
human decisions, the factor which really determined
him was one of which he was himself hardly conscious. The fact was, he was born in the old Gran-
ite State within sight of those snow-capped hills
which he remembered dimly as in a dream of some
former life, and the flat, rolling Western prairies,
with all their material abundance, had never been
able to blot out the vision, or make him forget his
early home with its stern, rocky soil, its piney odors

borne on every passing wind, its streams of crystal clearness fit to be a type of the river of the waters of life.

But just here we will avail ourselves of an author's privilege to stop and comment on this curious fact: that Stephen Howland's first case in court, one that was entirely to his mind, that stirred up all the chivalry of his nature, and fired his heart with that generous indignation which has been, ever since the world began, the God-ordained force that has set those morning stars of humanity, the souls of heroes, prophets and martyrs swaying in their orbits, did not come through any interest curried for him by the lodge, but in that direct *human* method which lies at the foundation of all true social economy. It is astonishing, when one comes to inquire closely into the matter, how little real aid to success in their worldly business has ever been afforded to honest and self-reliant members by Masonry, Odd-fellowship or any other secret clique whose huge pretensions pass current to-day for no other reason than because it is less trouble to believe a lie than to combat it, and more easy to accept an assertion without questioning than to bring that assertion to mathematical proof. Honest, self-respecting Americans, true to the old Pilgrim and republican traditions bequeathed to them by Puritan and Revolutionary sires, will prefer to gain the favors of their fellow-men in the legitimate method, by probity and strict attention to business, though at the same time they may be paying a large part of their earnings to keep in running

order a machine which they have not the least idea
how to work. That those who *do* know how to work
it, who understand the use of every wire, and just
how it connects with the lobby or the caucus, the
court or the market, must have a larger reserve stock
to draw upon, the larger the number of these ignorant and simple-minded members, is certainly as easy
of demonstration as that two and two make four.

But, as we intend that all this, with other facts
equally curious and instructive shall be duly illustrated in the further unfolding of our story, we will
drop moralizing and go back fifteen or twenty years
to the rocky hill-country farm, now one of the many
deserted homesteads for which that region is famed,
which its owner, Silas Newhall, in an evil hour left
behind him to seek, with his wife and children, a
new home toward the sun-setting. Silas was not a
very active or intelligent farmer. He planted and
sowed and reaped with little regard to any of the
"new lights" in agriculture, and when the soil in
consequence paid him but scanty returns, he grew
discontented and was in just the mood of mind to
listen to an enterprising land speculator who tried to
make him believe, and with very fair success, that
Western farms brought forth spontaneously all that
was "good for food and pleasant to the eyes," and
no more needed to be tilled by the sweat of the brow
than did the original Eden.

To his meek little wife it was a sore trial to leave
old friends and neighbors, but after the first protest
she had no more to say either in the way of remon-

strance or complaint; and so one bright morning saw
their few effects packed, and they themselves on
the way to the land of abundance, to find at their
journey's end only a tumble-down shanty waiting to
receive them, instead of the snug, green-blinded cot-
tage their New England ideas led them to expect.
But this was only the beginning of disappointments,
for the new railroad which the enterprising speculator had enlarged upon as sure to open up a ready
market for their produce, was not yet built, nor
likely to be for an indefinite period; and Silas Newhall found, too late, that big crops, with no prospect
of converting them into enough ready money to buy
a pair of shoes, only made their owner poorer instead of richer. He finally sold his farm and settled
on government lands in a region farther west, only
to repeat the old story of discouragement and failure. He grew despondent and took to drinking,
while the true-hearted wife, who had followed his
fortunes with never a murmur, with the weakness of
a mortal disease upon her, bore a weight of suffering
to which the martyr's brief, fiery trial is as nothing.

Nelson Newhall was fourteen, Tommy ten, and
Dora, the youngest, a pretty child of six, when the
inevitable breaking up came. The father, while intoxicated, fell from a scaffolding in the barn and
broke his neck in the fall. The mother lived through
the following summer, nursed by kind neighborly
hands, and then entered that invisible world where
alone the hidden purpose of love in her dark, tangled
life-web could be made plain. Nelson, stout and

strong for his years, could work his own way; a good, motherly farmer's wife volunteered to take little Dora; but Tommy had been feeble in body and mind from infancy, perhaps a result of that mysterious law which visits the sins of the father upon the children, a law which seems to skip one and take another as capriciously as the cholera or the plague, and what place for him but the county poor house? Thither he went to receive no better and no worse treatment than such unfortunates usually receive in similar institutions. Nelson, to whom he seemed the only living thing left to love and care for, used to visit him weekly, and as soon as he could claim his own earnings took upon himself the burden of his support.

But poor Tom, as a part of the dark legacy so strangely bequeathed, liked the taste of liquor; that is, he was always ready to sip the sweet poison if placed in his way, but he had not as yet developed such a craving for it as would lead him to tax his weak brains with the effort to get it clandestinely; and ordinarily his lack of money was a sufficient safeguard. But being unfortunately enticed one evening into a low drinking saloon kept by a certain Peter Snyder, it was considered a very rare piece of amusement by the bar-room loungers to ply the half-witted boy with bad whisky till the point was reached at which he was incapable of affording them further entertainment, when he was coolly ejected with a kick of his cowhide boots by the proprietor, a pecul-iar and forcible style of argument which Mr. Snyder found handy in certain cases. In this condition he was pounced upon by a watchful guardian of the public peace, and thrust into the lockup after the manner described by Nelson in his talk with Mr. Treworthy. The result was a cold and high fever, which carried him to death's door.

Peter Snyder was arrested and bound over to answer to two indictments: one for illegal liquor selling, the other for allowing Thomas Newhall to be made drunk with whisky sold on his premises, said Newhall being feeble-minded and a minor. He pleaded guilty to both charges and was duly convicted and sentenced; for, as it happened, Mr. Snyder had never been able to obtain admittance into the ancient and honorable fraternity where so many of his particular guild find a safe retreat from the sheriff and other "terrors of the law." We append his own statement of the reason, as given by him in communicative words to his various chums and cronies, only leaving out certain expressions, questionable both on the score of morals and taste.

"I tell ye, now, my opinion of the Masons don't take many words to say it in. They are a set of big, sneaking, rascally hypocrites. How did they treat me once when I tried to get in? I made my application ship-shape and stood all ready to pay my fees and dues fair and square; but I wasn't quite genteel enough for 'em, so I got blackballed. I don't sell liquor because it is respectable or genteel; I do it to make money. Look at Parker and Longman, and lots of others, all Masons and all engaged in the same business, only maybe they carry it on in more style, and durned if I ain't as good as they are!"

It will be seen from the above that many traits of our common humanity were quite highly developed in this poor rumseller; noticeably his tendency to justify himself as being at least no worse than many others. This, with the fact that there had been moments in his life when he thought of his good old praying Methodist mother, and half resolved to quit the vile business altogether and make a man of himself, coupled with the further fact that he had always put it off till "a more convenient season," was certainly clear proof enough that he was, after all, of the same flesh and blood with the general run of humanity. But the liquor business, like the slave-trade, must always have its Pariahs—men from the lower stratum of society who bear on their own shoulders much of the public odium of a traffic that they did not create, and which would fall like a millstone as soon as it ceased to be patronized or supported by any other class. Just as in *ante bellum* days it was very easy to find good people who looked with horror and loathing on the slave-dealer, while regarding with complacency or indifference the system of which that occupation was only the legitimate exponent, so the publican of foreign birth who stands behind the bar and deals out the fiery poison to poor Pat, who goes straightway home, possessed with all the devils of the still, to beat and abuse his wife and children, is an outcast and a wretch to be spurned by all decent people; but what of the voter or legislator who, in blind devotion to party or for the loaves and fishes of political power, is willing to ignore, and thus perpetuate the system which creates the rumseller?

Stephen Howland took hold of the case like a war-horse eager for his first fray. There was in Jacksonville quite a strong under-current of prohibition sentiment, which had been for some time slowly gathering force, and as the case was one which, in its peculiar nature, awakened sympathy, his vigorous and successful prosecution of it gave to the young and almost discouraged lawyer precisely that start in his profession that he needed.

But we cannot do better than to give the reader an extract from one of his letters home:

"Public sentiment is at last roused up, and on the principle of the one toppling brick overthrowing its fellows, there is some hope that Snyder's arrest and conviction will close up other drinking places whose owners are equally defiant of law. For my part I am only too delighted at such a rare opportunity to fight the dragon, for I expect to have more liquor cases on my hands; two came in to-day.

"That Nelson Newhall is a splendid fellow; a grand specimen of the genus labor; and Martin Treworthy is an old soldier who lives all alone like a hermit or a saint. He came and shook hands with me after I had my speech, and told me I had spoken like a young Daniel, and he only wished my folks could have been here to have heard me. I know, dear mother, that from my babyhood it has been your wish and prayer that I might be a Samuel. It hurt me more than anything else to disappoint those wishes and prayers, but if I 'dare to be a Daniel', will not that do as well?"

"It will suit *me* well enough," said Josiah Howland, emphatically, interrupting Phœbe in her reading of the letter. "Be sure, mother, when you write, to tell him that. And tell him, too, that I feel a sight more reconciled to his being a lawyer now that he's given them pesky rumsellers a lesson."

As for Phœbe, she was too full of joy and thankfulness to say a great deal; and there mingled with it, too, a kind of awe. Why is it that the Lord often seems nearer to us when he answers our prayers in a way we are not expecting? In the quiet of the bedroom which had been her "closet" for so many years, she read over again the precious letter; then, falling on her knees, tried to give utterance to her thanksgivings, feeling much as did Eve of old when she exultingly exclaimed, "I have gotten a *man* from the Lord."

But why did Stephen, in all his letters home, never once mention the fact that he was an Odd-fellow? one of a fraternity so moral, so religious, so benevolent! · The reader is welcome to put his own solution to a question that Stephen Howland had never as yet consciously answered, even to himself.

CHAPTER V.

Nelson Newhall, in his vigils by his brother's bedside, had found plenty of time to think, and the result of his thinking was to deepen an already settled conviction that the temperance question was destined to take precedence of all others as a vital, living issue; one which would not much longer allow itself to be thrust out of sight by party politicians; certainly not after every intelligent voter could be made to realize that it was costing the taxpayers of the nation several hundred million every year.

It did not occur to him that behind this question stood another which affected it like an unknown quantity, a disturbing factor in every attempt at solution, though he was aware of certain puzzling anomalies connected with the subject. Why, in the face of a largely increased prohibition sentiment among the people, should prohibition as a political principle make such slow advances? Why were prohibition candidates nominated and prohibition tickets put in the field only for sure defeat every election day?

Tom was slowly coming back to life and consciousness. The pale, wasted face, as it lay on the pillow, seemed to open afresh the fountain of fraternal love

in Nelson's heart, and he felt once more something
as he remembered feeling in the old days when Tommy was his all to guard and love and cherish and
defend, if need be, against the world.

The door opened, and Martin Treworthy, who had
been an indefatigable nurse and watcher, entered
with a bunch of hot-house grapes, which he laid on
the table while he himself took a chair, remarking as
he did so—

"I can read my Bible or the newspaper in one
place as well as I can in another, and I thought maybe there was somebody not far off that would· be
glad to see you for an hour or so."

Nelson colored slightly, but did not wait for any
broader hint. Only stopping to tell Mr. Treworthy
about some new medicine the doctor had ordered, he
put on his overcoat and was gone.

For Martin Treworthy had watched with almost
paternal interest the transacting of a little of the old
Edenic idyl, which has never been quite lost out of
the world, and never will be while that Gospel lives
which has glorified all true human affection by making it the type and shadow of the heavenly union
between the believing soul and its risen Redeemer.
Any young couple starting out in life with only their
bare hands and their faith in God and each other,
might be very sure of his blessing, for as previously
stated he had once been a lover himself, and believed
thoroughly in the New Testament ideal of marriage,
while he had correspondingly small patience with
the low and mischievous notions on that subject

which prevail so extensively in our modern days. Thus it happened that, thanks to Martin Treworthy, the bright-faced little dressmaker to whom Nelson was engaged received that evening a visit from her betrothed that she was not expecting. Martha Benson was a good specimen of the best class of young American women, steady and sensible, not handsome according to any of the generally accepted rules of beauty, yet of so bright and wholesome a countenance that no one could deny her the meed of comeliness. Well educated, she had taught school several terms; well read in solid literature and deeply religious, she was a prize for any man's winning, rich or poor; and Nelson Newhall, unlike many of the masters of creation under like circumstances, was sufficiently aware of the fact to wonder humbly at his own good fortune. Obliged to earn her own bread, she had tried a number of ways to do it, and was now working for an aunt who had a small shop in the suburbs where she carried on dressmaking.

Martha herself answered her lover's knock, and read in his face the good tidings even before he spoke.

"Tom is better! I am so glad. I have been wanting to hear all day. And you really think the danger is over?"

"All present danger," answered Nelson, as he pressed her hand and gazed into her pleased, earnest face. "But it has been a hard pull, and after all, Martha—I don't know—perhaps death would be better than life for him, poor fellow!"

"No, Nelson; don't say that," said Martha, earnestly. "Perhaps this experience will have the effect of checking his appetite for drink. I have heard of such things. Tom is not quite like others, but we must remember that it is a trial permitted by Providence that should only make us more patient with his weakness."

"That is true, Martha, and I love you all the more for thinking and feeling so. Not every woman would. But I honestly believe this cursed rum is at the bottom of all poor Tom's misfortunes, for I remember one day after father began to drink, his giving him a push—it was a push, not a blow—so that he fell and struck his head so hard against the edge of the stove as to stun him for awhile. Mother was very sick and knew nothing of the accident, and father was too intoxicated to realize it, so I did the best I could. I held Tommy and bathed his head, and after awhile he seemed to come to all right, and I thought no more about it till he began to be strange and have fits. Even then it was a long while before I put the two things together as a cause and consequence."

"Oh, this terrible rum business! Can it never be stopped?" said Martha, sighing.

"Sometimes I feel discouraged and think it never will be. Still the local option law works well in many places and is a long step towards it. What do you say, Martha, to going onto a farm and making butter and cheese?"

"I say that it shall be the best butter and cheese

made in the township," replied Martha, who saw the drift of this seemingly irrelevant question better than the reader probably does. "You know I was born and bred on a farm."

Nelson's brow cleared. Evidently her cheerful answer had removed some hidden obstacle in his pathway, but he asked, doubtfully, "Do you really mean it, Martha, that you would be willing to go on to a farm if I could find a good one without going out of the State? In a year, if everything goes right with me, perhaps I could scrape enough money together to buy one. You see how it is, Martha; Tom would be more out of the way of temptation. 'Take care of Tommy,' was mother's last word to me as she lay dying; and if I am ever permitted to meet her in heaven I want to be able to tell her that I have taken as good care of him as I knew how."

"Of course I mean it, Nelson," said Martha, looking up with moistened eyes. "Didn't you suppose I understood the reason the minute you asked the question?"

"Oh, Martha; you are a blessed woman. I ain't half worthy of you. But after all, perhaps if the balance was rightly struck it would be found that I owed more to Tom than he owes to me. Having him to guard and defend has been many a time like the grip of God's own hand on my soul to keep me from going to the devil as I might have done without. To be sure I had a sister, but she must be altogether grown out of my remembrance by this time."

Martha had always regretted this separation, for

she felt a natural desire to be acquainted with her future sister-in-law. She said nothing, however, but sitting down to her sewing machine, stitched away busily.

"You seem in a hurry," remarked Nelson, after watching her for some minutes.

"Only to finish this." And she stopped the whir of her machine and held up to his view the garment she was making. It was an infant's robe, fine and white and dainty enough for any fond mother's darling; but as she smoothed it down and looked it over critically, it struck Nelson that her face was unusually pale.

"You are not well, Martha," he said in alarm. "Or has something happened to trouble you? You look about sick. Do put away your work for to-night."

"I am well, Nelson—only heartsick. Do you know what it is I am making?"

"Nothing more than a baby's dress, is it?" inquired Nelson, wonderingly.

"It is a baby's shroud—another innocent victim to the Moloch of Rum. I am making the last garment it will ever wear, for a child deliberately burned to death by its drunken mother here in this nineteenth century, in civilized and Christianized America! Why, would it have been any worse off—poor thing—if it had been born in Old Testament times when mothers threw their infants into the heated arms of an idol god?"

"Shocking!" exclaimed Nelson. "Do you mean Mrs. McLean's child? I heard it had got dreadfully burned and I knew she was a drinking woman, but still I supposed it was all an accident."

"No; it was the deliberate, fiendish act of a brain crazed with bad liquor. The reason I happen to be making its burial robe is because Aunt used to work in an undertaker's establishment and she had some nice fine remnants laid by that were just the thing. The poor little creature breathed its last in my arms. O Nelson, it seems so awful, so terrible. Will this curse never cease? Must the cry of innocent blood forever go up in vain? O if I had but the power to make every voter in the land hear that murdered babe's dying cries as I heard them! They ring in my ears now."

And Martha clasped her hands over her face in a convulsive shudder.

"It *is* awful, but what can we do? Both our great political parties are controlled by the saloon power. They will dodge and shirk the question, but they won't touch it with a pair of tongs; and as to the Prohibition party, it lacks something—union or zeal, or both—or it would certainly accomplish more. Last year, when there was so much temperance talk done, why were nearly all the votes cast for the old parties? And this year it will be the same. Temperance men will support anti-prohibition candidates for fear of giving away their vote to the other side."

"Well, I am not a politician," said Martha; "I am only a woman, and I suppose I look at such things from a woman's point of view. I believe in men

more than I do in parties, and in principles more
than I do in votes. Most of the political talk in the
newspapers just reverses this, and makes men and
principles the least important things, when they are
actually the only force the saloon power dreads, for
it knows that parties can be controlled and votes
bought, but men and principles, never."

"That's exactly the way it stands, Martha; but I
don't see what is ever going to hammer it into the
heads of the politicians," answered Nelson, with a
doubtful shrug of his shoulders.

"Well, now, Nelson, it seems to me that I have
grown to understand some things lately that I never
understood before. You know I belong to the
Woman's Christian Temperance Union, and I have
belonged to the Good Templars, beside. I have always been interested in temperance work ever since
I can remember, and I have been brought into some
slight association with workers noted in the cause.
Now if there is any want of union in the temperance
ranks there must be a reason for it. Supposing an
army is marching to attack the enemy, and a part
should break up into little squads, each with its own
leaders, its own secret plans and countersigns and
passwords, how long would it be before there would
be an end to all unity of action?"

"Not a great while, certainly; but I don't think I
quite understand your comparison."

"And supposing," said Martha, continuing her
parable, "these same petty squads, after considerable
'big talk' from their leaders of all the feats of valor

they were going to perform, how they only needed
a sight of the enemy to smite him hip and thigh,
should let their arms rust and their amunition spoil
while they sat down on the grass to play games and
tell stories? Now you are wondering why the temperance cause is always meeting with a Bull Run.
But look at it here in Jacksonville; there is no real
unity among our temperance people because they are
broken up into little secret cliques, each trying to
rival the other; and as for good solid work, there is
none done worth the name. It has all degenerated
into play. Now the W. C. T. U. is a grand organization. It is meant for work, and the amount of labor
that some of the women who belong to it perform,
is astonishing; simply heroic. But I have yet to
find, among the Good Templars, a real worker for
temperance, man or woman, who makes a point of
regularly attending the lodge meetings."

"Why, Martha! seems to me you are rather sweep-
ing."

"Not a bit. I have been there and I know. I
don't mean to say that the Good Templars have never
done any good in the line of reform. When a lodge
is first started there are always more or less of the
members who join with a sincere desire to do temperance work, and if some of the W. C. T. U. women
can be persuaded to come in they can't help carrying
a portion of their vim and enthusiasm along with
them. But such ones sink into a hopeless minority
after awhile. They find that the leaders are not
those with the most executive ability. They are the

ones who can sing the best songs and tell the best
stories, and contribute most to the general fund of
amusement; and so the working spirit all dies out,
slowly smothered to death, and the lodge comes to
be a mere social club—what saloonist ever stood in
dread of *that?*—a place where you can go and meet
your acquaintances and have a good time.   The last
Good Templar meeting that I attended was just before the State election.   There was a strong prohibition tide setting in, but instead of planning how to
take advantage of it, I cannot remember that the
subject of temperance was even once alluded to all
the evening; nor was it made a specialty of at any
of the meetings.   Half the time was spent in drill-
ing us in the secret work of the order, and the other
half in talk that had no more to do with the subject
of temperance than it had with political economy.
Now, the more I think about it the more convinced
I am that no good work for God or humanity can be
done if ·we start with a wrong principle. 'Can a
fountain send forth at the same place sweet water
and bitter?' "

"Then it is the secrecy you disapprove of," said
Nelson, who felt uneasy under this talk, without exactly knowing why.   "Now, I can't see· any harm in
it, necessarily.   In the Knights of Labor, for instance, the secrets are so few, merely the grips and
passwords, that they don't really amount to anything."

"Then why have secrets, anyway?   If they don't
amount to anything, what good do they do?"

Nelson felt posed. It was such a perfectly common-sense question, and Martha asked it in such a cool, common-sense way, that it was decidedly surprising, as well as inconvenient, not to find any answer ready. So what could he do but repeat at second-hand the old Masonic argument, with which his connection with the Knights of Labor had made him tolerably familiar:

"Why, society is so constituted that secrecy is necessary sometimes. Why do Grand Juries sit with closed doors, and Congress hold secret sessions? and even the family—what is that but a secret institution?"

Martha's eyes flashed.

"Don't name the lodge and the family in the same breath. It is profanation. Privacy and secrecy are two different things. Senates and juries publish the results of their deliberations to the world, which is all that the nation or the community is interested in knowing. And furthermore, such secrecy is only a temporary arrangement; senators and jurors do not take solemn oaths *never* to reveal anything that is done behind closed doors. And as to the family," and the flash went out of Martha's eyes in a gleam of good-humored laughter, "you had better not try to exact any such vow from me. Just think of a family with its members pledged to keep all they say and do forever secret from the rest of mankind! I am sure that nothing would induce me to pass a single night under their roof for fear that murdering travelers and confiscating their effects might be among those precious 'secrets.' But there are other reasons in my mind why such societies must always be a drag on the temperance cause. As a Christian woman I believe that the gospel and the gospel alone is the true reforming agency for the world, and all organizations for that end will be successful just so far as they work by Christian methods. Good Templarism requires its candidates to believe in a Supreme Being, but all through the ritual the name of Christ is mentioned but a few times, his atoning work not once. Now, I don't believe that drunkards can be saved by pledges and good resolutions. They need something else. They need to be told of a Divine Helper who will stand by them just as they are, in all their vileness and degradation, and battle with them and for them against the demon of the still. They need to be told the old, old story of Jesus crucified for sinners, bleeding his life away that the vilest might look to him and live. Tell the drunkard *that;* guide his trembling, shaking hand till it touches, only touches the hem of Christ's robe, and his feet are on the Rock of Ages, and he is a saved man. But this is exactly what Good Templarism never does."

Martha spoke with quivering lips and eyes that shone through unshed tears, while Nelson gazed at her roused and kindled face with a kind of wonder.

"You talk like Martin Treworthy," he said.

"If I do it is because one Spirit has taught us both," she answered, resuming her work, which she had dropped in her momentary excitement. "Now,

the Good Templars profess to be a religious order,
or why do they have prayers and an altar and a chaplain?   Yet, as I said before, the lodge does not and
cannot convert the drunkard, and without conversion
I do not believe in a permanent reform.   I don't
mean to say that there is no Christianity in its teachings.   There is just enough to make them dangerous, for what more fatal delusion under heaven than
a Christless Christianity?   As a matter of fact the
really religious members of the lodge fare about as
bad as the workers.   It is the worldly, irreligious
element that invariably gets the upper hand.   I have
known a man who could hardly spell his way through
the ritual elected chaplain just for a joke, and not a
single voice raised in rebuke or dissent.   Yet there
were Christian men and women present; I was there
myself, and I remember feeling shamed and indignant at first, and then laughing with the rest at his
manifest exultation at being promoted to the chaplain's desk, and the funny way in which he mispro-
nounced his words.   I blush when I think of it, but
there is a mysterious something about these nightly
gatherings that acts like a draught of enchantment.
I have known professed Christians to say and do in
a Good Templar lodge what they would not have said
or done anywhere else.   I am sure of one thing:
Christ isn't there, and the Holy Spirit isn't there.
Why should they come where their work is persistently ignored and set aside for mere human methods?
The lodge is like the house in the parable, 'empty,
swept, and garnished;' and Satan enters in and dwells

there, and the last state of man or woman who joins
it expecting to be helped thereby, or put in the way
of helping others, is worse than the first. After
attending the meetings for a few times I began to
feel a strange deadness and indifference when I took
up my Bible or tried to pray. I lost my relish for
prayer-meeting; even for the dear old hymns that I
used to sing over my work. I knew that something
was wrong and it made me miserable, but I could
not imagine what. I tried to think that it was only
a common experience, a mere passing cloud, and I
should feel all right again soon. All the while I
knew better. I knew I had backslidden, but what
had made me? Now if I had been enticed into attending some place of amusement, professedly worldly, like the ballroom and the theatre, I should have
known in a moment; but how could I lay my spiritual darkness and trouble to attending the meetings
of an organization that claims, for its sole object,
to save men and do them good? I will tell you
what opened my eyes: an Anti-masonic tract that
fell in my way. I was familiar enough with temperance tracts, but this was something new; so I took it
up, half curious, half indifferent, thinking to myself,
'Women are never Masons; how can the subject possibly concern me?' But I found that it did concern
me, and in more ways than one. I saw that it was a
system square against Christianity on one side, and
every principle of our republican liberty on the
other. And I saw besides, as plain as two and two
make four, that the same line of argument which

condemns Freemasonry condemns Good Templarism."

"Oh, nonsense, Martha. You are so conscientious
that you are like an over-careful housekeeper, who is
always finding dirt and disorder where nobody else
would think of looking for it. Now, I have seen
books that claim to expose Masonry, and granted that
they are true, what possible likeness between their
barbarous, blood-curdling oaths, for instance, and the
simple promise, or 'obligation', which is said to be
all any of these minor orders require?"

"Just the difference that there is between a glass
of champagne and a tumbler of stiff old Bourbon,"
answered Martha, promptly. "What makes the fas-
cination in any kind of spirituous drink? Just the
alcohol, more or less, that it contains. So these
minor orders are fascinating just in proportion to the
amount of secrecy which they cover. Now, the
whole of Good Templarism could be just as well
taught in one degree as in half a dozen; and all the
object of the Charity, Fidelity and Council degrees,
so far as I can see, is to serve the double purpose of
making the principle of secrecy so familiar that the
gradation to Masonry and Odd-fellowship will be
easy and natural, and to shut the mouths of conscientious non-Masons. Now, Nelson, let me ask a
plain question: are *you* just as ready to express your
honest convictions about Masonry as you would be
if you did not belong to a secret order? Don't you
feel, without exactly knowing why, that there would
be an inconsistency in *your* denouncing it? that it

would certainly draw down upon you the dislike of the Masonic members of the lodge if you did so, and on the whole you had better let it alone?"

Nelson Newhall was decidedly an exemplary young man who would not have told a lie for the world. He neither smoked nor chewed; was a regular church-goer, and taught a class of boys in a mission Sunday-school. I am afraid he was only a step removed from a well-meaning young Pharisee, though Martha, looking at him by the light of that glamour with which a true affection always invests the beloved object, saw nothing of the sort.

"I don't know but it is so, Martha," he answered, after a moment's hesitation, "though I never though of it before."

"But there is another side of the question. How can temperance workers admit into their ranks as co-laborers men who are bound by oath to protect every saloonist who can give the Masonic sign of distress? Will not their best efforts be constantly checkmated, and their plans betrayed when Masonic interests come in collision with the temperance cause? For my part I am not surprised that prohibition makes such slow progress considering how many politicians have to be accommodated with office every year—like Gen. Putney, for instance."

"But they say the Grand Army Posts put him in."

"And who originated the Grand Army? Who are its leaders? Poor, simple, private soldiers with no political aspirations, or Masonic ex-generals who want their votes? I desire no clearer proof than

Gen. Putney's nomination that the Grand Army is a mere political machine manipulated by men without a single patriotic impulse in their bosoms; with whom self is first, party next, and country last of all. It is worse than folly to let corrupt secret rings control the elections and then clamor for reform."

"All I can say about it is that the people are to blame," returned Nelson. "If every temperance man would go to the polls resolved to drop all party interests and vote for none but out-and-out prohibitionists, without any regard whatever to party leaders, the tide would soon turn. But why have you never told me before how opposed you were to secret societies?"

"Because I was really not aware of it myself. I joined the Good Templars without the least suspicion of any harm in the organization. The worthiness of the professed object blinded me to all the folly and sin; but now the beam is cast out of my own eye, perhaps I can see clearly to pull the mote out of my brother's eye."

"I know what is coming, Martha," answered Nelson, with a comical look of resignation in which there mingled, to a critical observer, the slightest shade of vexed annoyance. "I am ready for the operation, however, if you will engage not to hurt more than is necessary."

"Well, now, Nelson, as a laboring woman who intends to marry a laboring man, I ought to be interested in all that concerns the working classes—secret trade unions like the Knights of Labor included."

"Oh, come, Martha! what do *you* know about the Knights of Labor? Capitalists can and do combine, and why shouldn't workingmen? I have no high opinion of the Masons or the Odd-fellows either, though I don't know much about them; but a harmless trade union is quite another thing. And besides, I hardly ever attend the meetings. I just pay my dues, and that is about all."

Martha held her peace. She was a prudent woman, and did not always speak the thought that lay uppermost.

"You see all the other workmen were joining," continued Nelson, after a moment's silence; "and they urged me a good deal. It is all very well to talk about independence, but a man must be fair to himself and fair to his fellows. The labor problem presents entirely different conditions from what it did fifty or even twenty years ago. Now I feel perfectly able to stand alone and fight my battles with the capitalist on my own hook, but that isn't the case with one in a hundred. How can an ignorant, unskilled workman with a large family protect himself against the greed and injustice of employers? He will just as surely be driven to the wall as he attempts it. The class increases every day, and if it were not for these protective unions he would be in a condition little better than white slavery. Shall the strong, just because they are strong, stand off selfishly each by himself and let his weaker brother stumble along as he can? That isn't the way I read my Bible, and I am sure, Martha, it isn't the way you read yours. As for the secrecy part of it, as I said before, it don't amount to much—only enough to prevent imposition."

"Insurance companies are imposed upon sometimes. Why don't they need the protection of secrecy just as much?" queried Martha.

"Oh, that is a different thing. Business is guarded by red tape, which is something plain workingmen don't know much about. Some secret signs are necessary to enable those who actually belong to make themselves known when they are traveling from place to place, and at the same time keep out bogus members."

"*I* think it is a great deal more important to keep out unscrupulous leaders," returned Martha, dryly; "for among the other uses of secrecy you forget to mention that it is a most convenient cover under which such men can do pretty much as they like."

"Oh, well," said Nelson, as, with a half laugh and hasty glance at the little French clock on the mantle, he got up to go; "we might talk on this subject from now till next week, and then stand about where we did when we begun. I can't afford to spend time and strength fighting secret societies when there are so many worse evils in the world. I want to see this rum business put down, and I am willing to give up all I have, even life itself, to do it. But still, I agree with you in thinking that these societies have not done as much for the temperance cause as they pretend. And as to the Knights of Labor, if I become a farmer that will sever my con-

nection with them, and leave us nothing to quarrel
about unless I join the Grange.   But now, Martha,"
he added, dropping his half-jesting tone, "try to put
this dreadful thing that has happened out of your
mind.   You couldn't have helped it or prevented it.
It is only a specimen of what is continually going
on, and will keep going on till the people rise in
their might and refuse to bear it any longer.   When
the liquor traffic finally does go down, I believe it
will be in such a whirlwind of popular wrath that
the whole cursed thing will be destroyed root and
branch, and swept as completely from the land as
ever slavery was."

"God hasten the day," ejaculated Martha, solemnly.   "Amen," returned Nelson, as solemnly.   And
so they parted, one in their hatred of the dark, destroying saloon power, yet divided by that subtle
spirit of evil which stands at its right hand—the
spirit of the secret lodge.

CHAPTER VI.

Colonel Gail Hicks, the nominee of the Prohibition party, was a man the intensity of whose moral convictions was only equaled by the unsullied purity of his public and private life. He was pre-eminently a man of the people, and chosen by the people with that divine instinct which generally shows itself when any great question opens the way for independent political action. The Republican nominee was first and last a demagogue, whose military career had been chiefly remarkable for disastrous blunders, unredeemed by any personal bravery, and whose large fortune, it was more than suspected, had been filched from the government in its hour of deepest distress. The choice of the Democratic side was a man who, when the war broke out, openly aided the Confederate cause, and who now sympathized with the rum interest exactly as he had once sympathized with slavery. This being the character of the two leading candidates, they, with the factions that supported them, found the saloon vote a necessity, and thus the liquor power was placed in the embarrassing position of having two suitors, either one too powerful to offend; but it was fully equal to playing a double game in which both parties were made to truckle to it, and vie with each other in their general subserviency.

The prohibition wave in Jacksonville was one of those phenomenal tidal movements which occur as often and with as startling an effect in the social and political as in the natural world. The saloonists, rendered careless by long security, had scarcely made a pretense of keeping within the strict letter of the law, and this sudden turn in popular feeling surprised them too completely for any attempt at organized resistance.

"We must have a grand rally at the polls," said Mr. Basset, who dropped in one morning to talk over the situation with Stephen Howland. "The ballot is the only argument the liquor party can understand. There's nothing like keeping people's minds stirred up on this subject. A little temporary excitement won't do. We mustn't stop rowing till we've fairly touched shore."

"Jacksonville seems to be stirred up pretty well now," returned Stephen. "Such a case as that McLean woman burning her own child to death ought to be enough to wake up any community that calls itself Christian."

"That was an awful thing," responded Mr. Basset feelingly. "Now we've had two saloon murders in Jacksonville in less than a year, to say nothing of the terrible profanity and Sabbath breaking. Iniquity runs down our streets like a river. It is really dreadful to contemplate such a state of things."

"Well, now, Mr. Basset," said Stephen, candidly,

"I have not been altogether satisfied with the method pursued thus far. For my part I'm tired hunting down small vermin. What is the use of arresting such men as Snyder and shutting up their drinking holes while all the restaurants and hotels have their open or secret bar? It is neither justice nor policy. I am glad they have planned a descent on Parker of the Phœnix House, for it is safe to say that two-thirds of his profits come from the liquor he sells, and not from his legitimate business."

"Ah! I hadn't heard they were going to arrest Parker. But of course," added Mr. Basset, quickly recovering the self-possession which this information had seemed for some reason to momentarily disturb, "it is always best to be thorough in the work and give no quarter to respectable offenders."

"I appreciate as much as anybody," resumed Stephen, "the necessity of making a good show at the polls. The Prohibitionists must let all the numerical strength they have got be felt, but I don't think it reasonable to expect to carry the State this year. We are working for principles, and principles triumph slowly. Prohibition is surely coming, but it must come through an increasing aggregate of local successes. Every neighborhood thoroughly stirred up on this question, provided the interest is not allowed to abate, makes a kind of nucleus for reform; and when we get a sufficient number of them they will carry the State. Now I believe if temperance people will only work together we can carry Jacksonville for no license this year."

"Now that's exactly my idea," cheerfully responded Mr. Basset, as he took his departure. "Reform,
like charity, must begin at home."

Stephen sat down once more to his interrupted
study of certain complications which had arisen in
one of the liquor cases he was just then prosecuting; for, without any seeking of such honor, he had
come to be a prominent leader in the movement in
Jacksonville, and was already engaged as one of the
chief speakers at a meeting to be held a few days
before election in the interests of the temperance
party.   He was young, ambitious, and high-princi-
pled.   He felt that he was engaged in a glorious
cause, and metaphorically he girded on his armor
and longed for the trumpet to sound for battle.   Mr.
Basset did not quite suit him.   He thought there
was a great deal of talk in him to very little action.
Still he never distrusted his sincerity.   Had Stephen
been more deeply conversant with the workings of
that system of mingled religion and morality to
which he had so recently joined himself, he would
not have been surprised that the proprietor of the
Phœnix House should step out—nobody knew where,
nor for just how long—a few minutes before the
raid on his establishment: from which, by the way,
every vestige of the bar, which he was known to
keep in cool disregard of the terms of his license,
had vanished like a dream in the night.

Stephen was not only surprised, he was disgusted and wrathful, the more so that another prominent
liquor-seller, whose conviction he had looked upon

as a foregone conclusion, seemed now likely to escape through certain newly-discovered technicalities of the law. But he comforted himself with the old saying that it is an ill wind that blows no good. People would finally learn that prohibition pure and simple was far more easily enforced than the most ingenious license law whose ramifications were only so many loopholes through which the liquor-seller could slip and· thus evade conviction; that behind the saloon power lay a masked enemy whose arrows were shot in secret, an argus-eyed foe that never slumbered, wily, treacherous, that with its deluding *ignis fatui* was leading himself and others a fool's dance over bogs and morasses foul with miasma and death—this was an idea that never came into his head. But though Stephen did not know why so many finely-laid schemes of the Prohibitionists went "agley," there is no reason for keeping the reader in like ignorance.

The proprietor of the Phœnix House was an Odd-fellow as well as a Mason, having joined both orders for several reasons. In the first place he wished to shed all the respectability possible on his traffic, and he knew very well that Odd-fellowship was considered more respectable than Masonry by a large class of moral and Christian people. He knew also that owing to the close and beautiful relationship existing between the two he would get more advantage from Masonry by being an Odd-fellow, and more advantage from Odd-fellowship by being a Mason. That he was right in this opinion the sequel will show. For quite in a neighborly way Mr. Basset accosted a Masonic acquaintance whom he happened to meet a few steps from Stephen Howland's office, and informed him—all as a mere piece of friendly gossip—"that Parker stood as good a chance to be hauled over the coals as any of the common saloonists, and he knew on good authority that his arrest was already planned." Whereupon his Masonic friend did exactly what Mr. Basset supposed and expected he would do—promptly "warned" the hotel keeper "of impending danger." Nor was this the first time that Mr. Basset had played with success the *rôle* of "Mr. Facing-both-ways." He had once turned a lawsuit in favor of a brother Odd-fellow by refusing to agree with the other jurymen on the verdict; he had contrived in a number of cases to have worthy employes turned off and their places supplied by men who could sport the three links on their shirt fronts; besides otherwise seeking the good of the order by a system of vigorous proselyting that would have done credit to any olden Pharisee or Mormon bishop.

"But a Christian man, and a Prohibitionist too—impossible!" exclaims the astonished reader. Know, dear sir, or dear madam, as the case may be, that though Mr. Basset was a temperance man he was an Odd-fellow first, and he held his Christianity on the same secondary principle. He believed in the church as a highly convenient institution, which, as it obligingly took in all that numerous class that the ark of Odd-fellow salvation passes by, could not well be dispensed with; but his relative valuation of the two may be inferred from the fact that while he was seldom or never absent from the brethren on lodge nights and always paid his dues with promptness, he was invariably short of funds when called upon to aid any department of church work, and never found time to attend the prayer meeting—a very common state of things among that portion of the secret fratern'ty who are trying, like Mr. Felix Basset, to play the part of the scriptural Issachar. But lest the reader should look upon him as a sinner above all other men, we will state what we know to be a veritable fact: that the keepers of two restaurants had been "warned" in like fashion only the day before, by a Mason who was also a Good Templar, and as such had been freely trusted by the small but determined body of Prohibitionists who had set out to suppress the illicit saloons, but found themselves betrayed without any clue to the traitor.

Martin Treworthy laughed sardonically when he heard them wonder who divulged their plan, asserting that the liquor power, by means of its sworn Masonic allies scattered up and down through the length and breadth of the temperance camp, could hear what was whispered in their secret chambers. He had said the same thing a good many times before without anybody's heeding or laying it to heart, and with the grand persistence of a true prophetsoul he was willing to keep on saying it to a generation that only mocked and despised his words.

But Jacksonville was, as Stephen expressed it,

very thoroughly waked up, and in a way not to be mistaken by saloonist or Prohibitionist. How to allay the excitement or keep it at fever height was the respective problem discussed by each with very various answers. One important wing of the Prohibition side had a plan of their own concocted, of which we shall hear more anon. Meanwhile the idea was industriously circulated that General Putney was a temperance man, with a record as high in that respect as the average, and consequently temperance men could vote for him without sacrificing either their principles or their standing in the glorious old party that had abolished slavery and saved the Union. Men who had voted with that party from its birth hour, to whom its very name was a storehouse of glorious memories of grand deeds and noble leaders—gray-headed men who still loved it, with all its venality and corruption, almost as a father his erring first-born, wavered, glad to catch at a straw. There was still another class who halted between two opinions—men who believed in prohibition and wanted to see it triumph, yet could not make up their minds to leave the party in power and thus resign all expectation of office or preferment at its hands: while another class, still more numerous, comprised the floating political driftwood; men ready to support either side according to circumstances; men with votes to sell and willing to sell them; and men with principles, but deterred from taking that unpopular article to the polls by the newspapers and stump orators with their black prophecies of woe and ruin sure to follow the defeat of the Republican party. And they also halted between two opinions.

Stephen Howland, on the contrary, had no party fetters to break. He believed the time had come for all true men to separate themselves from factional interests and vote only for candidates that would truly represent their convictions; and we will not pretend that he had not his own private, yet most worthy, ambition to become a leader in this new party of truth and righteousness. So he stood upon the platform primed to the fingers' ends with facts and figures; feeling sure that truth, invincible, eternal, was on his side, and with a great deal more faith in his power to convince the crowd before him of that fact than if he had been a little older or a little wiser. But though composed of all the incongruous elements mentioned above, it was a good-natured crowd, ready to laugh and applaud any specially clever hit; and Stephen Howland had the faculty of making a brilliant off-hand speech on almost any subject.

"What has the Republican party done? I ask," he said, in closing. "You point to the broken shackles of four million slaves. But who thirty years ago in the legislative halls of this very State voted for a law that should rescind every hunted fugitive, man, woman, or child, back to the master from whose brutality they had escaped, and made it a penal act to offer them even a cup of cold water in the name of our common Lord? Who but the very man on whom the Republican party of this State now pro-

poses to bestow gubernatorial honors! You point
me to a Union preserved through seas of blood and
tears. Far be it from me to speak a word which
should be a blot on the glorious record; but who,
while ostensibly serving his country in the field, was
silent partner in a company for cheating the Government and its brave defenders with shoddy contracts?
Again I repeat, who but the very man the Republican party now delights to honor?

"But let these things pass. Time is a great con-
queror of prejudices, and the gallant General is
doubtless on the way to make as good a Prohibitionist as he is now an anti-slavery man. Perhaps the
Republican party can afford to wait for him. It is
good at waiting. [Laughter.] It has done nothing
else since it came into power; but the *people* can't
wait. This red-handed Herod who slaughtered the
innocents must be dethroned [applause]; and what
more fitting than that this same Republican party
which dealt the death-blow to slavery with the sword
should strangle intemperance at the ballot-box. So
we have said, so we have hoped through all its de-
lays, its compromises, its persistent ignoring of the
great question at issue. Like the mother of Sisera
as she looked through the lattice, we have cried,
'Why is his chariot so long in coming? Why tarry
the wheels of his chariot?' And the wise among us
have answered; yea, we have returned answer to ourselves, 'Have they not sped? have they not divided
the prey?' [Laughter and applause.] Yes; that is
the trouble. Sisera won a great victory a score of

years ago, and he has been busy dividing the spoil ever since. Meanwhile shall we sit still while an enemy steals the wealth of our nation, desolates our homes, and slays not its tens but its hundreds of thousands, or quit us like men, like freemen, by casting our votes to-morrow for Col. Hicks and prohibition?

"What we want, what we *demand* of the Republican party, is present action, not a barren record of past achievements, however glorious. This want remains unmet. This demand has been received with open or silent contempt. It has quarreled over office spoils, split hairs over the tariff question, and passed bills to restrict Chinese emigration; but on the monstrous evil of the liquor traffic, an evil which is eating out the very vitals of our nation, it has nothing to say. Parties die, principles live. The Republican party totters to-day on the brink of dissolution, but the sublime doctrines enunciated by her first leaders cannot die. They are everlasting as eternity. When men are dead we bury them; when parties are dead we do or should do the same—whether in hopes of a future immortality must depend in either case on the question whether they have lived worthy of that immortality. I, for one, have a great deal of faith in the Republican party, so much that I can help bury it without a tear in the firm belief that it will rise again [applause] baptized with a new name, its mantle of old corruptions dropped, and animated once more with the spirit of its early founders. As one on whom a double portion of that spirit has fallen, I name the Prohibition nominee for the governorship of this State, Colonel Gail Hicks—a man in all respects worthy the support of every true citizen. I call upon all such without any regard to previous political affiliations to go to the polls resolved to vote, not for a party but a man, not for the saloon but the home, not for the lie of the rumseller but the truth of God, not for license but for prohibition."

There had been slight attempts at disturbance from the license element, which, however, did not amount to much beyond a few groans and hisses that were effectually silenced in loud and long continued applause when the young orator ended his speech.

"Good timber in that fellow now," muttered Martin Treworthy, who stood in the crowd, flashing keen approval from beneath his shaggy eyebrows, while Nelson Newhall close by was contributing his share to the burst of acclamation with an enthusiasm not to be mistaken.

The next to occupy the platform was Col. Morrison, editor of the *Jacksonville Patriot*, a stirring Decoration-day orator, a Mason, and a Grand Army man. He perfectly agreed with the position taken by the first speaker in regard to the rum traffic. He was a Prohibitionist to the backbone, but did not believe that the Republican party was dead or in a dying condition. It was still sound at the core for all the abuses and corruptions of party managers. If brought back to the purity of first principles it could extinguish intemperance as easily as it had slavery; and he put it to their common sense—one could always trust the common sense of an American audience even in the fever of political excitement—whether prohibition would come soonest by working for it in the ranks of an old and established party, or by joining a third, which, as it lacked all the elements of popularity and strength, must be years in achieving even a doubtful success. For his part he preferred the half loaf to no loaf at all. Why give their votes to the Democratic nominee and thus help to secure a triumph for the saloon? General Putney had been caluminated by his political enemies, and these calumnies he was sorry to hear repeated by the eloquent young speaker who had preceded him. He could state from personal knowledge that General Putney was a consistent temperance man, who could be depended on to enforce the law. True, he had once voted a pro-slavery bill in a pro-slavery era. That era had passed forever along with the days of witchcraft in which the good and learned Puritan, Judge Sewell, knew no better than to commit judicial murder. Let him who had no sin of ignorance to answer for cast the first stone."

"The Colonel means to be elected Representative to Congress next year," said Martin Treworthy, in another grim aside. "No half loaf of prohibition for him, but a longer nibble at the whole loaves and fishes of the Republican party."

The next speaker, Dr. Haynesworth, agreed with all the main points of Col. Morrison's speech, and could confirm his statements by remarking that he had been told only the day before by one of the most prominent of the Prohibition leaders that he was in constant correspondence with the General and could vouch for his temperance principles.

"There is treachery, O Ahaziah!" muttered Martin under his breath. "But this ain't the first time I've known the leader of one hostile army to be in correspondence with the other side."

The doctor deprecated discord between brethren. Prohibitionists should wear the same colors or there was continual danger of mistaking each other with fatal results to the cause. He would be willing to work for a third party if temperance men everywhere would join it, but as a matter of fact the large majority were faithful to old political friendships; and he was more and more convinced that no better standing-place for union could be found than that same Republican party in which they had been nurtured, which had once so gloriously lead the vanguard of Reform, and might again. And he drew such a glowing picture of that happy time when all differences, forgotten in the joy of victory, high license and low license men, prohibitionists and moral suasionists, should lie down together like the lion and the lamb of prophecy, that it provoked another side remark from Martin Treworthy:

"This is going to be like the witches' cauldron"— for, unlettered backwoodsman though he was, Martin kept a copy of Shakespeare in his hermitage, which he occasionally studied in the intervals between his

Bible and his newspaper—" 'black spirits and white, white spirits and gray, mingle, mingle, ye that mingle may.' An out-and-out speech for prohibition might ruin his chance to be mayor."

Stephen had been led to suppose that all the speakers would be unanimous for a third party, and he was simply astonished at this unexpected change of base. He felt that he had been treated unfairly, for though he would not have altered his speech one iota, had he known beforehand what was to be the tenor of the other addresses, it would have prevented his speaking at all and thus saved him from the awkwardness of having to defend his position among assumed friends. But to hear this weak apologizing for party corruption and misrule added a feeling of shame and disgust to his sense of injury; and when the climax was reached by claiming General Putney as a temperance man, his old lie-hating, truth-loving Puritan blood stirred within him. When he attempted to answer, however, there was a scene of tumult between the saloon element which sought to prevail by dint of noise, and the cries of "Go on," "Give it to 'em," and sundry similar exclamations from the third party men, who knew their champion when they saw him, complicated still more by a settled disposition on the part of the managers of the meeting to make him reply at a disadvantage by allowing him only five minutes, on the pretence that there were a number of others yet to speak.

But Stephen bethought himself of a certain newspaper paragraph which had attracted his attention

sufficiently to be saved, as just the thing to turn the
tables on these political time-servers. So quietly
remarking that he believed it to be one of the laws
of parliamentary usage that he who makes the opening speech should also make the closing one, he
waited till all had said their say, including one or
two rather discouraged advocates for a third party,
followed by another seeker after loaves and fishes,
who devoted himself to picking up the chips in the
wake of Morrison and Haynesworth. Stephen then
rose to his feet and simply observed that as there
seemed much confusion of opinion as to General
Putney's prohibition principles, he would, to set all
doubts at rest, read his own testimony on that point
at a recent political gathering: "The time has not
come for us to take up the temperance issue with
safety, *and I repeat once more I am not in sympathy
with the fanatics who are trying to force this question
on the Republican party, knowing that it will bring
disruption if not absolute ruin thereto.*"

Stephen read this from the slip of paper which he
held in his hand, and then paused for a moment before adding: "Gentlemen, you have now the witness
of his own mouth that he cares less to protect the
homes of the nation than to protect a party, and
more for the votes of the liquor interest than the
wail of its murdered victims. But their cries have
entered into the ears of the Lord God of Sabaoth,
and

'E'en now from lone Mount Gerizim and Ebal's starry crown,
We call the dews of blessing or the bolts of cursing down.'

The question of the hour confronts us. As free American citizens what answer shall we give? Shall we put our necks under party yokes and cower before the crack of party whips, or shall we assert our blood-bought right to vote as we choose, asking no consent from political demagogues? It stands before us like the Sphinx, and it will not down at the bidding of fear or interest. That question has got to be answered. Every election day it will stand by the ballot-box sterner and more awful till we are compelled—a word for slaves, not for freemen—aye, *compelled* to answer it one way or the other. Oh, for a voice that shall go forth to-morrow from every voting precinct in this State, and sound like the trump of doom in the ears of 'them that build a town with blood and establish a city by iniquity,' but clear as the clarion of victory and tender as the voices of pitying angels in the hearts and homes made desolate by the liquor traffic: 'Down with this giant abomination, down with legalized robbery and murder under the name of license! But up with the snow-white banner of Prohibition! Fling it wide to the breeze with the name of the noblest of her leaders blazoned upon it, the name of Col. Gail Hicks. And may God forever speed the right.'"

Stephen stopped, his whole frame quivering like a racer's at the goal. His ingenious flank movement had succeeded. Those who had hoped to see the meeting end as it had at one time threatened to, in a ridiculous fizzle, were doomed to disappointment.

"If he didn't floor them fellows handsomely, now,"

chuckled Martin Treworthy. "A sight of their faces was worth all the specie in my tin box."

"Well, I must say I'm disappointed in Colonel Morrison," replied Nelson, discontentedly. To stand up for prohibition and Putney in the same breath is 'good Lord and good devil' with a vengeance."

"Oh, it only shows how well the Masonic lodge is educating our politicians," returned Martin, with a grim smile. "The result is, they stay politicians. They can't grow into statesmen under lodge training no more than the dwarf trees that I've read the Chinese raise in thimbles can grow into real oaks and elms."

"But all our public men are not Masons," objected Nelson.

"No; but the lodge influence goes everywhere like malaria, and they can't help breathing it in, and then good, simple souls wonder what ails Congress that we have such crooked goings on—back salary grabs, and Credit Mobilier schemes, and Star Route swindles, and nobody knows what else. They can't imagine why there is so much boss rule and party spirit and so little patriotism; so much cheating of the government and so little common honesty; so much practical infidelity and so little practical Christianity. Now, Nelson, you are a sensible fellow on the whole, and I want you to look at this thing just as it stands. The lodge takes three dollars from each of its members where it pays out one to help them in return. What is that but a lesson in swindling? Then it puts on a great show of piety and religion, and calls it benevolence. That is lesson in hypocrisy number two. It demands obedience to all its laws and requirements, and no questions asked. There is lesson in boss rule number three. It refuses to expel a traitor to his country—Jeff Davis or Benedict Arnold, it makes no difference which—because treason is not a Masonic sin. There is lesson in disloyalty number four. It tears Christ's name from his own New Testament and preaches another gospel. There is lesson in infidelity number five. And so I might go on to the end of the chapter. Will politicians trained in such principles, think you, sacrifice a jot of their self-interest to put down all the saloons in the land? Do men gather grapes of thorns or figs of thistles? Do you think we can have the lodge in every city and village and town and not have to take the fruit of the lodge along with it? Can we sow the wind and not reap the whirlwind? Yes; if history and the Bible can go back on their own records and contradict themselves. But that ain't a thing they are likely to do in a hurry, thank the Lord! not even to please the politicians."

Nelson Newhall turned away in gloomy silence. His sanguine hopes of an overwhelming prohibition vote had fallen to zero. Even the young lawyer's fiery eloquence had failed to make the meeting any thing but a wet blanket on the prohibition cause, and he felt uncomfortably sure that the leaders, for reasons of their own, had so intended it from the beginning. Like King David, he was ready to say

in his haste, "All men are liars." He was besides
conscious of feeling half impatient with his old
friend, which added a slight touch of compunction
to his sense of discomfort, for he loved and reverenced Martin Treworthy, and only wished he was not
such a fanatic on the lodge question. Were there
no paramount issue to be met it might be well
enough to discuss it, but prohibition was *the* question of the hour, and it was nonsense to think that
any other issue could be prior to it in magnitude or
importance.

So reasoned Nelson Newhall. Whether he was
right or wrong the sequel of this story will show.

CHAPTER VII.

A NEW FACTOR IN POLITICS.

The morning of election day rose in a chill mist, a perplexing, uncertain mist which might roll away by nine o'clock A. M. and leave a clear sky, or might with equal probability grow denser and darker and finally settle into a downright storm. In one sense it was very appropriate weather, for it exactly represented the political sky as it appeared to many a voter—Nelson Newhall for one. His first conscious thought on waking was the election, and yet for ordinary politics he did not care the snap of his finger. It is only as we look at them through the small end of our object glass, that is to say, the lens of our own private hopes and fears, that political questions assume large proportions. Nelson Newhall was a common working man to whom the suppression of the liquor business had grown to be a vital subject, for it meant not only release from a constant, wearing anxiety, but the temporal and eternal welfare of one to whom he was bound by ties that in their protecting tenderness were almost maternal.

He sprang out of bed and began hastily dressing himself, making as little noise as possible that he might not waken his still sleeping brother. But the latter stirred and began to cough. In an instant Nelson was bending over him.

"I hoped I shouldn't disturb you, Tom. I will get you a spoonful of your cough medicine and then perhaps you will go to sleep again. It is very early yet."

He measured out a spoonful of the syrup and administered it as deftly as a woman; then he built up the fire which seemed to share in the general depression and needed much coaxing to boil the chocolate or toast the bread, for Nelson always prepared his own breakfast and his invalid brother's before going to work. Tom, though much better, was still feeble. On bright, warm days when his cough did not trouble him much he would drag himself down stairs and sit in the sun, finding amusement in the society of their landlady's children; and she, a buxom, motherly, Scotch-Irish woman, cheerfully agreed "to look after him a little," while Nelson was absent in the shop.

"He ain't a bit more trouble than a chip sparrow, Mr. Newhall, and he keeps the children so still I'm sure it is a real favor to me to have him round. I had a brother once that was something like him— the quietest, gentlest soul that ever God made, if he didn't know quite as much as most folks. Many's the time I've wished I was as near the kingdom as poor brother Sandy."

And good Mrs. McGowan wiped away a tear with the corner of her apron while Nelson responded gratefully: "Tom has but one failing, and you know what that is, Mrs. McGowan. But I don't think he is half as much to blame as the men who make and sell the cursed stuff, or those in power who are willing for the sake of a little more revenue to license it."

"Just what I've always stood to, Mr. Newhall. I say that money got in that way is blood money, and if it is enough to make a man lose his soul, I can't see for my part how government can take it and expect to prosper."

Mrs. McGowan was a woman and unversed in political subtleties. Furthermore, she was a good Presbyterian who made a conscience of reading her Bible straight through in course—not skipping one of its terrible burning words against those "who decree unrighteous decrees," "who build up Zion with blood and Jerusalem with iniquity;" and the reader must excuse her if she had not yet attained to the broader and more enlightened views of some of our modern statesmen.

Martha Benson, when she stitched the burial robe for the murdered innocent whose little life had gone out in such cruel tortures, felt every holy instinct of womanhood rise in revolt against this awful traffic in human anguish. And as womanhood is pretty much the same the world over, the sacred fires of a noble indignation and a brave purpose to do what they could were burning in many other hearts—that fire from the Lord which first kindled the Woman's Crusade, that flashed like a meteor and was gone, yet not before it had kindled in its turn a flame that

has gone on increasing till now it lights the whole
country from the Atlantic to the Pacific.

The Woman's Christian Temperance Union has
come to be a recognized power. Politicians may
coolly ignore its inconvenient requests and snub the
petitioners. None the less do they tremble before
the oncoming tread of the Divine Deliverer who has
sent before his face these silver-tongued messengers,
saying to the haughty Pharaoh of the liquor traffic,
"Let my people go that they may serve me." With
their simple weapons of faith and prayer they have
wrought miracles. We of this present century can
not estimate the full scope and power of the movement. We are too near; but the coming generations
will see it as it really is, in many respects the grand-
est, the most unique of all those moral and spiritual
revolutions that have stirred modern Christendom.

Nelson knew that a band of white-ribbon workers
had been organized in Jacksonville to meet the approaching crisis, for so Martha had informed him,
adding with a smile and an arch shake of her finger,
"You men will find out after awhile that you can't
get along without us women. Politics have got into
the muddle they are in now by a law of nature, just
as a house will get to be dust and cobwebs from top
to bottom when there are no women to wield the
broom and the scrubbing-brush."

"Well, Martha, God knows I would be willing to
have the women vote if they could help us get rid of
this rum curse; but as things are I don't really see
how they are going to accomplish much."

"We can pray."

The words leaped from Martha's lips like an inspiration—so suddenly that Nelson felt for a moment as if a supernatural voice had spoken. Was there not such a thing as a divine lever "which moves the hand that moves the world?" and was there not a bare possibility that the weakest woman laying hold of God's eternal strength was mightier than he, "the sovereign citizen" at the ballot-box? Nelson believed in prayer, but the atmosphere of the workshop had covered his faith with a coating of something a little more like skepticism than he would have been willing to own. If he could have accompanied Martha, as the reader is privileged to do, that gray, foggy November morning into the vestry of the First Presbyterian church in Jacksonville, he might have had his faith strengthened, and even discerned a gleam of light in the political horizon, cloudy as it appeared.

The little throng before us, composed entirely of the non-voting sex, who, perhaps for the very reason that they are excluded from expressing their convictions at the ballot-box speak them all the more eloquently and freely in the ears of Infinite Justice, contains a few faces that are a study—sweet with the pathos of a nameless endurance, beautiful with those fine heroic lines that only start out under the chisel of a life-long sorrow. Yonder, for instance, sits one who for ten wretched years felt the iron of a great legalized wrong enter into her soul; but, womanlike, all her sorrow was swallowed up in joy when her husband, a man of education and brilliant talents, reformed and even began to win some reputation as a popular temperance lecturer. But one night he failed to meet his engagement; was missing forty-eight hours, and then brought home dying. King Alcohol had recaptured and this time slain his victim; but it was in a properly-licensed saloon, and with liquor that had paid its lawful share of the government tax, and what could be said except that it was all legal and constitutional? Only this woman believed like poor Chloe, when her husband was sold South to die under the slave-whip, that "thar was suthin' wrong about it somewhar;" and singularly enough it did not reconcile her in the least to know that the price of his blood had added a few cents less or more to the nation's treasury.

And here sits a noble-looking woman clad in Quaker gray, with shining silver curls framing a dear, motherly face as bright and peaceful as the new moon when it rises over the hill-tops on a summer night. Yet hers had been a trial by fire. This Christian mother had one son whom she taught to say, "Our Father," and "Now I lay me down to sleep," morning and night; whose tottering steps she guided to the house of God, and into whose young mind she labored to instill all right and pure and holy principles. But, alas! the drink taint was in his blood and he fell—fell into a deeper abyss of degradation and ruin for those sun-crowned heights where a mother's love had placed him. He rests to-day in a drunkard's grave. It is all over—the long, midnight vigils, the tears, the agonies of prayer. She has been robbed of her boy, and the liquor traffic under the shield of law has done it.

Near by sits another who has suffered cold and hunger and abuse, yet through it all has clung to her drunken brute of a husband instead of taking the advice of friends who urge a legal separation; for after all there are times when the brute is a man, when the light of the old affection is in his eyes, and he weeps over the past and makes all kinds of vows for the future—and she? well, she half believes him, knowing all the while they are vows written on the shifting sand. Of course she is a fool, but haven't you, dear lady, who "wouldn't for the world live with a drunken husband and don't think it is any woman's duty to," read somewhere of a divine foolishness that confounds all earthly wisdom? In spite of the doctrine zealously advocated by many of the political prophets of our day, that "prohibition don't prohibit," this woman labors under the singular delusion that her husband would not drink if there were no saloons. And so she has come here to-day ready to add her mite of prayer and effort, though not the weight of a finger may she or her sister sufferers lay on that only lever which can move law and law-makers out of the ruts of legalized evil—the ballot-box.

Others there are from comfortable and happy, even luxurious homes, large-hearted, refined, noble Christian women who have heard, over all the demands of pleasure and fashion, the bugle call of duty, and sprung to answer it with no half-hearted zeal—

women that are known in their respective social circles as prudent managers, careful mothers, and faithful wives.   But we need not spend more time in in-
troductions.   This is the Jacksonville branch of the
W. C. T. U., who having, as we hinted in the last
chapter, a plan of their own for election day, are here
met to spend a few brief moments-in prayer before
the opening of the polls will leave them free to put
it in execution.

Meanwhile we are not unconscious of a host of
grumblers and objectors at our elbow.   "I don't
hold to such things," remarks very decidedly a gentleman on our right.   "I don't believe in a woman's
neglecting her husband and children to go gullivant-
ing round the country holding temperance conventions."

We notice that the gentleman wears the three
links of the I. O. O. F. conspicuously displayed on
his watch-chain, and a little bird of the air takes occasion to whisper in our ear that his invalid wife is
left to long evenings of uncheered solitude while her
husband is at the lodge, generally detained to a late
hour on important business.

But let us hear Mrs. Orderly.

"At this hour in the morning these women ought
to find enough to do at home.   A pretty plight their
kitchen must be in!"

Not so fast, my dear madam.   Did you never at
the call of pleasure or duty leave your own domestic
establishment to run itself for a day, secure in the
thought that every necessary preparation had been

made and every needful direction been given the night before? All this a woman may do to go to a picnic; but reform work, especially if it trenches on the forbidden realm of politics—oh, that is another thing.

But these women of the W. C. T. U. are actually preparing to go to the polls and persistently urge every voter, seconding their persuasions by cups of the most excellent tea and coffee, to vote for "no license." And strong in their faith and courage they are willing to even encounter the tide of profanity and tobacco-spitting at the ballot-box, from which the respectable, easy-going male citizen is so apt to shrink back into his comfortable home privacy, feebly crying, "Have me excused." These women are not partisans nor politicians, yet all their labors and prayers and hopes are with the minority that from a feeble beginning have risen to hold the balance of power between the two contending factions that are now bidding for the vote of the saloons; and by interviewing local candidates and pressing the claims of prohibition on young or doubtful voters they have done work in a quiet way which will tell in the election returns. They mean to have Jacksonville a no-license town, and at the same time they are painfully aware—for some of these good women have sons—how inadequate is local option to the real needs of the case.

"For my part I think mothers would do more to stop intemperance by staying at home and training their children," says a voice at our left; and as a general chorus of "amens" follows this view of the subject, which is really the most sensible objection that has thus far been made, we will stop to consider it at length.

Would it satisfy a mother, who knew that a panther was ranging over the country, to procure a work on zoology, and gathering her children about her show them from the pictures how a panther looks? Would she consider it enough to give them a familiar description of its haunts and habits, and warn them to be careful when they went berrying to keep a sharp lookout for its gleaming eyes, its stealthy tread, its cruel spring? Would she not, rather, if she had a true mother's heart in her bosom, shoulder a good trusty gun—if there was no one else to do it —and attempt herself the death of the monster?

"But it seems unwomanly to be mixed up with such dreadful goings on as they so frequently have at the polls," puts in a feminine voice at our right. "Why, it is almost as bad as voting."

For our part we think it considerably worse, and on this slight basis of agreement let us call for a general truce.

The president is now addressing a few words to the little assembly—no other than the matron with the silver curls, Mrs. Judge Haviland. Every woman present loves and reveres her, not because she bears a distinguished name in society, but because she is exactly what she is, so motherly, so Christlike, of so grand a courage, with such far-reaching sympathies that the poorest and most sor-

rowful feel uplifted and strengthened though they
touch but the hem of her garment. The real magnetism which pours life into faint, discouraged, sin-
sick souls must come from actual, personal, daily
contact with Him who is the heavenly Magnet for
all earth's sorrows. There are human hands whose
lightest touch is healing; but they are hands that in
the mountain-top or in the valley, in darkness or in
light, in storm or sunshine, have never let go of the
crucified One.

"My dear sisters, our enemies sometimes accuse
us of seeking notoriety, but every calumny will fall
harmless at our feet if we only go forward trusting
in the Lord alone. And here do we not make a mistake? We, at least many of us, desire the ballot.
We desire it, not for purposes of selfish ambition,
but to protect our homes; and so far we are right.
Our error, it seems to me, has been in looking to
man to give what is really not his to give. Does
not our Father hold the nations in the hollow of his
hand? Is not he the true author of all national and
civil polity? And in his own good time how easily
he can cause the gates of brass to fly open with a
touch. I think he is now teaching the women of the
W. C. T. U. a great lesson—to depend more upon
him and less on man. We have petitioned legislatures, political conventions, men in high official positions, and though certain Michaels—all honor to
them—have stood up and helped us, we all know the
story. We stand to-day without the shadow of hope
from either of the two great political parties. Poli-

ticians have united to ignore us—we have no votes
to give them.   But all our petitioning and memorial-
izing has not been in vain if their failure but drives
us nearer God.   Let us cease from man and pray:
'Give ear, O Shepherd of Israel, thou that leadest
Joseph like a flock; thou that dwellest between the
cherubim, shine forth.   Before Ephriam and Benja-
min and Manasseh,·stir up thy strength and come
and save us.'"

And in the deep ground-swell of the old Hebrew
psalm we seem to catch the voices of all the martyr
generations that have gone before—an innumerable,
palm-crowned multitude who once were faithful unto
death, and now recognize kindred souls in this band
of earnest-eyed women.   It is the cry of finite
weakness to infinite strength, which, though feebler
than the dying sparrow's, can pierce the veil of the
unseen, and above the song of the seraphim, above
even the triumphal chants of this redeemed, sound in
the ears of One who, as grand old Augustine has
said, "is patient because he is eternal."

But we feel moved to turn aside once more for a
brief converse; first, with the politicians.

Men in high places who stand to-day as the representatives of this free Christian Republic, can you
disregard the appeal of such women and be guilt-
less?—not of a great moral wrong simply, but of a
great political blunder.   Does not the prosperity of
a nation centre in its homes? and what of the policy,
what of the statesmanship that would license an evil
which more than any other is at the bottom of our

frequent divorces; which causes most of the cases of brutality and desertion, to say nothing of the domestic unhappiness that never gets into the papers because it never rises to the dignity of tragedy? What sort of political economy can we call it that allows a traffic which takes nine hundred millions from the wealth of the country that it may put a matter of eighty millions or so into the nation's exchequer? or that completely ignores every axiom of political science in proposing to lighten the burdens of State taxation by dividing among them the surplus revenue from that, which, as the chief fountain of crime, misery and pauperism is likewise the chief source of all the taxation that oppresses honest industry?

But we have a word to say to the voters. Honest-hearted, hard-handed farmers and mechanics, how long will you be led by mere party interest—which only means the interest of some party leader who wants your votes—to support men and measures with whom and with which your whole moral sense is at war? Is it wise to do so? Is it patriotic? Is it *safe?* With all our seeming peace and prosperity, thoughtful, far-seeing souls tremble as they catch at intervals gleams of subterraneous lightning playing below our social and political horizon, and hear the low, ominous rumblings that warn of a terrible volcanic-power beneath our feet that may find voice to-morrow in the earthquake shock startling continents. More and more American cities are getting to be the resort of Communists, Nihilists, dynamiters—men who hate law and every institution based on law; and more and more both our towns and cities are gathering a mass of inflammable material precisely fitted under such leadership to enact on American soil the scenes of blood and terror that we have grown to regard as the legitimate fruit of old-world serfdoms only. "And what will ye do in the day of visitation and in the desolation which shall come from far," if you vote to license the liquor traffic? or, what is the same thing, cast your ballots for rulers and legislators committed to its interests? Liquor to the passions of a mob is as the torch to the powder magazine, the match to the fuse. What warrant have you for the safety of life, property or home, if, to maddened crowds goaded by real wrongs and inflamed by the harangues of socialist leaders, liquor can be dealt out freely, thus priming them for murder and violence and rapine? Truly, there is a whole eternity in the word longsuffering, yet let us beware that we weary not that patience beyond which there is nothing but a certain fearful looking for of judgment and fiery indignation on a guilty people.

The neat sign up at every polling place, "Hot tea and coffee served free," over the letters W. C. T. U., was a surprise which caused the saloon party to gnash their teeth; for their plan had been kept as entirely to themselves as if bound by any number of oaths 'ever to conceal and never reveal it"—a fact which we commend, by the way, to the attention of those gentlemen in the Masonic order, who, when questioned as to the reason why the lodge so rigorously excludes all the weaker sex, sauvely reply, "O women can't keep secrets, you know."

Though Nelson Newhall in his inmost heart disliked the idea of any feminine meddling with the mysterious machine of politics, he was perfectly sincere in what he had said to Martha—he was ready to welcome any instrumentality that promised to overthrow the haughty, tyrannous, ever-encroaching saloon power; and when Mrs. Judge Haviland herself handed him a no-license ticket with the request that he would vote it, he could not help feeling that this royal woman, who might have sat for an artist's dream of universal motherhood, did not look so very much out of place after all.

"Shure, an' its a fine cup o' tay; and thank ye kindly, ladies;" spoke up a rough-looking Irishman who had just treated himself to a cup of the steaming beverage, and then he looked a little doubtfully at the ticket placed in his hand.

Though poor Pat had neither money nor learning, at the ballot-box he counted for as much as if he was a millionaire or had a whole string of college degrees attached to his name, and usually the Democratic side had secured his vote by liberal supplies of cheap whisky and equally liberal doses of that peculiar species of political oratory vulgarly denominated "buncombe." Like too many of his countrymen, he fell a victim at periodical intervals to the attractions of the saloon; and, as it happened, the one to which he usually resorted was kept by an old-

time Democrat, who had suddenly turned into an
ardent Republican, under the stimulus of promises
to wink at all future violations of law on his part if
he would but give his vote and influence towards
electing Gen. Putney.   So Pat had lately been in the
way of hearing talk which had quite revolutionized
all his political ideas.   He had learned to his astonishment that it was the Republicans and not the
Democrats who had all along been the defenders of
the poor man's rights.   Gen. Putney, he was told,
was a strong "protectionist," and ought for that reason, if no other, to have the votes of all laboring
men; for the Democratic hobby of "free trade," if
once allowed, would mean starvation wages for the
workman, colossal fortunes to the capitalist, and,
most horrible of all, an influx of Chinese to which
the Egyptian plague of locusts could not compare
for a moment.   That neither he nor his instructors
could for their lives have given the dictionary mean-
ing of the terms they used so glibly was but a
trifling matter.   Pat had come to the polls sure that
he comprehended the whole political situation.

But this poor Irishman, though capable of swallowing whole any lie that political demagogues chose
to tell him, had a heart and a very respectable bit of
a conscience.   He loved his wife and children, and
for their sakes had made more than one manful
struggle against the whisky jug, but what availed it
when the saloon with its tempting free lunch of salt
fish, or some other equally thirst-provoking viand,
stood always open, its attractions seconded by the

cravings of an ill-nourished physical system, and the utter lack of any mental resource as a refuge against bodily weariness? And whicH is the most to be despised, poor Pat or the Congressman who sits down to a luxurious dinner with half a dozen courses of wine, and now and then goes off on a grand spree at the nation's expense? In our humble opinion Pat is decidedly more of a man, inasmuch as he always pays his liquor bills himself.

To this adopted citizen of great and glorious Columbia did Mrs. Judge Haviland now address herself with all that sweet and persuasive tact which is the gift of woman.

"We want to have no saloons in Jacksonville this year, and we ask you as a personal favor to vote for no-license. You, and I, and everybody else would be better off if no liquor was allowed to be sold anywhere. Your vote may go a great ways towards accomplishing what we so much desire."

Pat had been asked for his vote before, but never so winningly; and he thought how glad it would make Katy, *his* Katy, who had the brightest eyes and reddest cheeks for miles around when he wooed her in the "ould counthry," if he should never get drunk again. And if nobody was allowed to sell him liquor how could he get drunk?

Of course if Pat had been a politician he would never have reasoned in this simple fashion. He would have doubted whether laws restricting the liberty of the individual citizen to eat and drink what he chooses are constitutional. He would have point-

ed to the difficulty, if not the utter impossibility, of
enforcing such laws as a proof that they originated
in a narrow and ill-regulated zeal; and he would have
capped the climax of his arguments and objections
by saying that, so long as taxation was the nation's
only source of revenue, the true policy was not to
prohibit liquor but to tax it so heavily as to make it
the servant and ally of government, even letting it
pay the entire school bill of the Union; and thus
lifting the whole business to the dignity of a permanent institution based on national interests.

But, unfortunately, this poor, unenlightened Hi-
bernian had never been instructed in those peculiar
views of political economy which prevail among so
many of our statesmen at Washington; and in his
new hope of getting the upper hand of the whisky-
jug forever, must we say that he forgot, with all the
reprehensible fickleness of his race, every one of his
oft-repeated promises to vote only for the Republican candidate!

"It's all thrue, what ye say. I'd be a sight better
off, and Katy and the childher, if there warn't a drap
o' the vile crathur to be had in the wide worruld, let
alone Jacksonville. And if Col. Hicks will be
afther shutting up the dramshops, Pat Murphy is
the man that'll vote for him, and glad to do ye a
favor, mum." And Pat went up to the ballot-box to
enjoy for the first time since he took out his natural-
ization papers the full exercise of his freeman's
right; while one of Jacksonville's leading saloonists
who did a large business in so-called "temperance

drinks," and considered himself in a modest way as decidedly a benefactor to society, expressed rather loudly his opinion that "it was a shame for respectable women to be bull-dozing poor laboring men into voting away their personal liberty. They had as much right to their beer as they had to their bread."

Martin Treworthy, waiting with the throng of voters, heard this speech, and was moved by the spirit to reply.

"If this is the kind of bull-dozing they practice, all I can say is it's a pity we can't have more of it. They've made the polls for one day a fit place for a decent man. You are dreadful tender of the poor man's right to his beer, but why not turn the tables once in awhile and give us a talk about the rights of his wife and children to their bread? It would be a kind of refreshing variety, now."

The vender of "temperance" drinks found too many in the crowd against him to make much reply, and slunk away discomfited; while, heedless of everything but their one object, this brave detachment of the great white ribbon army, through evil report and good report, kept steadily at their posts; pouring out the steaming cups and handing no-license tickets, till the polls closed with this united testimony from friend and foe that never before had so orderly an election been held in Jacksonville.

Its results we will leave for our next chapter, while we transport our readers once more to that farm-house among the hills where another letter from Stephen has just arrived, to be read and re-read and talked over, and then laid carefully away in a corner of the square mahogany desk, which, according to authentic tradition, formed one of the few earthly possessions of the exiled clergyman previously alluded to as the founder of the Howland line; and which was, therefore, dated less than half a century after the sailing of the Mayflower.

This family ark, the sacred depository for the family valuables, Mrs. Phœbe Howland now proceeded to reverently unlock and open, while her husband, wearied with his farm work, leaned back comfortably in the feather-cushioned arm-chair and contemplated the fire; his thoughts traveling meanwhile over quite a circle of new ideas opened before him by Stephen's letter. Finally he broke out:

"I don't care what folks say about 'woman's sphere;' it is always right where God puts her, and I'm glad for one that the women are rousing up to stop this saloon business. I hope God will give 'em grace to hang on till the whole cursed system falls as flat as the walls of Jericho."

Now Mrs. Phœbe Howland was the most conservative of New England matrons, which is saying a great deal. The only place where she allowed her native gifts to have full scope was the female prayer meeting. There, her wonderfully earnest petitions, her pointed exhortations and eloquent appeals to Christian duty made her a natural leader. But there were times when her heart was thrilled with such a deep longing to give out more freely and fully of what was in her that it was almost pain; yet her soul, naturally tuned to the grand and the heroic, fitted itself to the humblest daily duties without a murmur, and the result was no actual narrowing of her spiritual powers, but rather a condensing, as of some exquisite perfume under the distiller's art, so that whatever she said or did was like a drop from the alabaster box of ointment. Its fragrance filled the house.

"Women followed Jesus to the cross," she said, coming back to her seat and her knitting (four pairs of lamb's wool socks destined for the absent Stephen). "I think I could follow him to the polls if I felt certain that God called me there. But I greatly fear that in this movement there may be many who will not stop to take counsel of the Spirit, but run before they are sent, to the harm and hindrance of the cause. I rejoice at everything that looks like a fulfillment of the prophecy, 'I will pour out my Spirit upon all flesh;' but in this calling of women to public work I can only rejoice with trembling, for they are human as well as men, and if they don't keep close to the Lord I know how it will be. Pride and ambition and self-seeking will come in and spoil all they are doing."

And there fell between the two a long silence, broken again by Mr. Josiah Howland whose thoughts though they seemed to be pursuing another track, had really followed logically in the line of Phœbe's last remarks.

"Mother, there's one thing I've noticed about Stephen's letters lately. He don't say a word about

religion, yet I think he gave good evidence before he
went from home of having met with a change, and I
feel kinder afraid that he's letting his mind get all
taken up with other concerns. Temperance work
can't be carried on to have it amount to much without Christ behind us, and I wish when you write to
him you'd say something that will draw him out a
little to speak of his spiritual state. I'm glad he's
prospering and getting on; tell him that. I don't
grudge a dollar I've spent on his education. 'But
what shall it profit a man if he gain the whole world
and lose his own soul?' "

To this Puritan couple this problem held in
solution every interest of time and eternity; for what
were riches, learning, or fame, but as the small dust
of the balance weighed against immortal life?

CHAPTER VIII.

Martin Treworthy's hermitage looked as inviting as a bright light and a good fire could make it. The furniture had all been bought in reference to that marriage which never was to be; and so it happened that many tasteful bits of ornament scattered here and there through the homely apartment seemed to shed over it the light of a gracious feminine presence, as if the one who was to have been its pride and joy had only left her sewing-chair in the corner for one brief moment.

On a bracket in one corner stood a vase of dried grasses; *her* hands had arranged them. In the window stood a pot of ivy; she had rooted it from a tiny slip. There was not a niche or corner to which Martin Treworthy's eyes could turn without resting on some momento of her he had loved and lost, and he liked to have it so.

He was really one of those crystallized poets whose *feelings* move to rhyme and rhythm while they generally talk the most rugged, matter-of-fact prose. He had a dim idea, which he could by no means have explained, that there are vibrations of soul as well as of sound and light, so that even in the ineffable glories of the New Jerusalem the spirit of his beloved might be conscious that he still remembered her with an affection stronger than death. And who shall say that it is not so? What warrant for believing that earthly love founded in heavenly hope can perish? The blossom may be nipped, but the root is perrennial and native to Paradise.

It was a disagreeable evening. A keen, raw wind was blowing the clouds in great dark masses across the sky—treasuries of snow and hail that only waited Jehovah's bidding to be unlocked by the angel of the elements and scattered broadcast over the shivering earth. Nelson Newhall occupied one corner of the settee that extended its comfortable length before the fire which was blazing brightly under Martin Treworthy's vigorous application of the poker.

"Seems as if the cold weather was setting in uncommon early," the latter remarked. "If signs mean anything we are going to have a cold winter. I met an old comrade of mine 'the other day—perhaps you've heard of him, Dan Carter—he was with me in Kansas, but he's settled down now to the trapping business; been at it ten years; and he tells me he never saw the fur so thick on the musk-rats as it is this season."

But Nelson just now was not interested in weather prognostications, and abruptly changed the subject.

"I want to know how long we've got to submit to having our rights over-ridden in this fashion. With a fair ballot and a fair count Jacksonville could have been carried triumphantly for no-license.

Now we must stand the saloon curse another year. It is perfectly infamous and outrageous to play such a trick on temperance men in the first place, and then deny us the right to a recount."

Martin Treworthy drummed gently with the poker a moment before speaking.

"'The Lord reigneth; let the earth rejoice.' I've known times when it was like pulling eye-teeth to say that; when it seemed as if the devil was reigning, and every good man ought to hide his head and wear sackcloth and ashes; when I saw husbands and fathers shot down like dogs on the plains of Kansas just for defending their right to a free home on a free soil; when I saw the flag of my country, the blessed old Stars and Stripes, turned against me, and waving over ruffians that were hunting me down for no other crime than because I had tried to be a refuge for the Lord's outcast ones. Nelson, you hain't got into the deep waters yet. 'If thou hast run with the footmen and they have wearied thee, then how wilt thou contend with horses? and if in the land of peace, wherein thou trustedst, they wearied thee, then how wilt thou do in the swellings of Jordan?'"

"I can't help it, Mr. Treworthy. Your blood was hot as mine once. Submitting to God's will is one thing, and submitting to injustice and fraud is another. There has been too much of this last kind. Why, if all the men who call themselves Prohibitionists had only voted according to their convictions we should have elected our man by a good majority."

"There ain't no reasonable doubt of that," placidly returned Mr. Treworthy.

"Well, it just makes me mad to hear Christian men talk about the evils of intemperance and pray, 'Thy kingdom come,' and then eat their own words by voting with rumsellers and distillers at the bidding of a party. It's the inconsistency of the thing *I'm* looking at."

"Don't you know," returned Martin Treworthy, leaning forward in his chair and giving the fire an extra poke, "that these good men believe all the while they *are* voting for temperance. They are humbugged and don't know it. 'He that letteth will let till he be taken out of the way.' There's a lying spirit abroad in the world, in the church, everywhere —an organized Satanic power that will either plant itself square in the way of every honest reform, or if it has got too strong to be stopped, checks and hampers it; puts a bridle round its neck and a bit in its mouth, covers it with fine trappings, and then rides on it just where it wants to go. Look at the Good Templars, started in 1851 when the temperance reform was thirty or forty years old, and had got too strong a grip on the hearts and consciences of the people to be shook off—who were its chief engineers? High Masons. And what has it done for temperance? Well, I'll tell you. It has humbugged a great many temperance folks into sitting with folded hands and trusting to the lodge to do their work for them; it has humbugged lots of others into joining, and then kept them busy with childish nonsense; it has humbugged thousands of Christian men and women into supporting secrecy as a principle; and in short it has been nothing else but a first-class humbug clear through."

"But what has all this to do with temperance men voting for Gen. Putney?" asked Nelson, rather impatiently.

"I hain't come to it yet," answered Martin Treworthy, serenely, still keeping his hold on the poker. "It's a long story; it's got as many coils and ramifications as the old Serpent himself. Now take the Grand Army of the Republic. I believe the rank and file of the members are honest men, but *they* are humbugged. They are made to believe that all the reason for loyal soldiers banding together in secret like a company of robbers is to cultivate fraternal feelings and assist one another, when the real object is to get offices for the leaders. Take all the secret orders in the land—and their name is legion—they are nothing but different manifestations of one lying spirit—Freemasonry. Good Templars, or KuKlux, or Nihilists—it is all the same. Men that will be humbugged by a secret order will be very easily humbugged at the polls. Men that will bind themselves by an oath, or an obligation—I don't care which—to obey leaders they never saw or heard of, will be just as easily made slaves to a party, especially if that party is itself nose-led by the lodge. There's the whole thing in a nutshell. Gen. Putney has been elected by the votes of old soldiers, prohibitionists and liquor men; and I can tell you how it

has been done. In the first place he was nominated
over the heads of other and better candidates by
Masonic leaders of the G. A. R. who all had axes to
grind of one sort and another. The G. A. R. is a
grand machine for getting fraudulent pensions, and
there's lots of bounty jumpers who ought to bless
the General for his work in that line when he was
Representative. But does anybody who knows Joe
Putney and has got as much common sense as you
can put on the point of a cambric needle, think for a
minute that he cares for the soldiers any more than
just to catch their votes. Then the next thing was
to dupe the Prohibitionists with lies and fair speeches; and how was that done? Why, by means of
Masonic influence controlling the secret temperance
orders just as it controls the G. A. R.; magnifying
the Republican party, belittling the prohibition
movement, ridiculing the prohibition leaders, and
lauding Gen. Putney for a temperance man, when it
is a fact that brewers and distillers all over the State
have poured out money like water to secure his election. Maybe you don't know it, but every saloonist
in Jacksonville is a Republican, because the party
managers have given him to understand that that's
the side his bread is buttered. 'Support our ticket
and we won't interfere with your business.' That's
the word; and when every bar-keeper is a Mason, or
an Odd-fellow, or a Knight of Pythias, or all three,
they know pretty well they don't run much risks
promising. So the lowest groggery becomes a trap
to catch the votes of the drinking class, and we are

treated to a spectacle that is enough to make the devil
laugh in his sleeve, bar-keepers and temperance men,
church members and drunkards, ministers and rowdies, all voting together for the same man!"

"I must say you are making out the political situation to be in even a worse muddle than I thought,"
observed Nelson, with a shrug of his shoulders.
"But if I have been told once I have fifty times that
the G. A. R. was not in the least a political organization."

"Tell that to the marines. No; to somebody a
great deal greener than the marines, a jack Mason;
but don't you go to riling me up by talking as
though *you* believed any of that stuff, Nelson Newhall, or I vow, I don't know but I shall be tempted
to show you the door."

Nelson laughed quietly, as a threatening flourish
of the poker; which had been buried long enough in
the coals to show a red-hot tip, gave emphasis to the
words.

"Their hand has been plain enough in this election, I'll confess. It's an idea I don't like. I am
not down on secret orders hammer and tongs like
you, but I hold to their keeping their fingers out of
the political pie and not making a worse hocus pocus
of it than it is."

"Might as well say that a cat ought to go against
its nature, and not catch birds and mice," retorted
Martin. "It is the nature of the lodge to want
power, and the way to power is through politics.
The saloon party has played us a trick"—

"Which they won't do another time," growled Nelson, who felt that his indignation was most righteous; for through a purposely ambiguous wording of the ballots it was found that many Prohibitionists had voted Yes, on the question of license, believing all the while that they were voting No—a fraud which doomed Jacksonville to another year of rum-rule, the just demand for a recount having been refused.

"Not the same trick, but maybe another just as bad. When the lodge and the saloon strike hands what can honest men expect? Years ago the Lord opened my eyes to see that lodgery, and slavery, and rum, and every other evil that is opposing the reign of Christ, were so many links in the devil's chain; and, Nelson Newhall, the day is coming when your eyes will be opened, too."

Martin Treworthy spoke with a strange solemnity which impressed Nelson too much to ask him what he meant; and in the silence which followed he began to think—feeling almost angry with himself meanwhile that the recollection should occur to him at just that moment, for what could it possibly have to do with Martin Treworthy's prediction?—how the day before he had been visited at his lodgings by a stranger who represented himself as an agent of the Union, empowered to look into matters connected with the works where Nelson was employed. In his immaculate broadcloth and spotless beaver, with his massive gold watch and chain, and his fat, white hands bedecked with rings, this champion of the laborer's rights seemed so evidently to belong to that class of humanity which like the lilies of the field "toil not, neither do they spin," that Nelson did not feel inspired with any particular confidence; but he answered his inquiries frankly. There had been a recent cut-down in the wages which he considered unjust and unreasonable, and this had caused some dissatisfaction among the workmen. But when asked "if there was any talk of a strike," he had bluntly answered "that with the winter just on them and promising to be a hard one, he shouldn't suppose anybody but a fool would talk of such a thing. The capitalist could barricade himself behind his dollars, and then when the strike was over start up again with perhaps an improved market, while ten to one the men would go back to work at the old prices." This vigorous speech was met by the agent with the smooth reply that it was the settled policy of the Union to avoid strikes if practicable, and indeed it was in accordance with this policy that he had been sent out to make these inquiries. But the assurance for some reason did not allay Nelson's feeling of distrust; and still further was it increased when he picked up and began to read a paper left behind him, either accidentally or purposely by this white-handed and be-ringed representative of labor. It was a Socialistic sheet filled with accounts of many real wrongs and abuses and some fancied ones; but with the same false, dangerous, unrepubli-can remedies for all. He read it awhile, then threw it into the fire with an impatient "pshaw!"—for Nel-

son Newhall, as a typical American workman, desired most devoutly the elevation of his own class,
but with ideas rather than dynamite.

There was reason why Martin Treworthy's words,
though not remarkable in themselves, should impress him like a solemn prophecy of things already
close at hand. Side by side with his rough, practical common sense ran a vein of that spiritual fire
that burns in the souls of prophets and seers; his
rough border experience, filled with episodes of un-
written heroism, had fanned the divine flame. Altogether Martin Treworthy was a unique character who
never could have been developed on other than
Western soil, with a dash of the Yankee, the Puritan
and the backwoodsman, all combined. His newspaper had educated him as it has many an American
citizen with few early advantages, so that he could
talk in a pungent, practical style with no very serious grammatical lapses; while his daily study of the
Bible had given him a kind of Hebraistic turn of
thought and feeling. Nelson had heard of his
strange foretelling of our great civil struggle, and
for an instant he felt vaguely thrilled and startled—
that involuntary shiver that passes over the spirit
when touched by the breath of the supernatural.

"Well," he said, rising with a sigh from his seat
before the fire; "this seems home-like, but I must go.
Tom don't seem to be quite so well to-day. I wish
I could get hold of something that would cure his
cough."

"Oh, you must keep up heart. Cut and try, cut

and try; that's the way. Now there's Balm of Gilead buds, with a little ipecac and balsam of fir; I've known that to cure a man given over in consumption. I've got some of the buds; always calculate to keep them on hand for sprains and bruises." And Martin Treworthy began to rummage among his rather heretogenous stores on the shelf where he kept his "tin box" with a brisk cheerfulness which might have wakened a heart of hope in the very bosom of despair.

But we must not forget Stephen Howland, who still continued to live with a Spartan economy, satisfied with the thought that he was laying the basis for a legal reputation which would not dishonor the Howland ancestry. Stephen felt not a little honest pride in the good old Puritan stock from which he sprang, and in fighting the liquor oligarchy was he not doing just what they did two or three hundred years ago, only in a different shape and fashion?

He was also fast becoming a good Odd-fellow, according to Mr. Bassett's idea of the term—that is to say, he attended the lodge regularly and was slowly beginning to see some of its peculiar advantages. He had passed all the degrees of Friendship, Brotherly Love and Truth. He had acted over the story of David and Jonathan and the parable of the Good Samaritan with a promiscuous company of church members, ministers, deists, and we must add, profane swearers and libertines. And in all this stealing from Holy Scripture never a mention of that Name above every name which is the central pivot

on which all divine truth turns! He had been shown
various instructive symbols, such as the All-Seeing
Eye, a skull and crossed bones, a coffin, a Bible, and
a serpent lifted on a pole, but never a hint of God's
wonderful plan of redemption; for even the latter
symbol was explained to him as bearing merely the
pagan signification of Wisdom, and not as typifying
that atoning sacrifice for human guilt once uplifted
on Calvary.

To be sure, Stephen was familiar enough with
Bible truth. Like young Timothy he had known the
holy Scriptures from a child; but the lessons that he
learned at the lodge were softly, slowly letting down
a veil over his spiritual sight through which the doctrines taught him at his mother's knee, of repentance, of a new birth and faith in a risen Redeemer,
appeared as dim and indistinct as the images and
sounds about him to one half-locked in slumber.
He never thought of Odd-fellowship as a form of
salvation or even a form of religion, and had he been
questioned would have emphatically denied it was
either. He would have scouted the idea that these
nightly meetings with their Christless prayers, their
equally Christless morality, and ceremonies borrowed
from pagan sources, had stolen from him his early
faith. And why? Simply because the lodge knows
that to keep its victims unconscious of the robbery
it must substitute in the place of those truths sham
semblances to counterfeit them, as a wax figure coun-
terfeits the living, breathing human form. He read
in the Odd-fellow's manual, kindly lent him by Mr.

Bassett, that "his initiation into the order was the
same thing as regeneration by the Word;" that "it
was a leading characteristic of all the ancient rites
from which Odd-fellowship was copied that they began in sorrow and gloom and ended in light and
joy," just as in the Christian religion the soul passes
to the joys of salvation through the narrow gate of
conviction and repentance. He read, furthermore,
that "the order was a miniature representation
among a chosen few of that fraternity which God
has instituted among men"—in other words, of the
Christian church, the holy nation, the royal priest
hood, the peculiar people; that Love (not the love of
Christ which constrains us to act justly and mercifully by all men, but that kind which excludes from
its bowels of compassion more than four-fifths of the
human race) "was the hidden name in the white
stone;" and, to crown all, that he had only to be a
good Odd-fellow, practicing all its three cardinal virtues "to have the bow of hope span his last resting
place," and "find the mysteries of heaven unveiled
to his admiring vision."

One who has taken a deadly dose of laudanum may
seem to be only in a sound, natural slumber, while
every moment is locking him faster in the sleep that
knows no waking. This was the trouble with
Stephen. That old-fashioned couple in their hill
country home who held to the old theological landmarks with a pertinacity quite in keeping with the
rocky, stubborn soil from which they drew their live-
lihood; who believed in the inspiration of the Bible

from Genesis to Revelation; who held that the deepest conviction of sin could not fathom the awfulness
of that guilt which cost the Son of God his life; who
looked upon time as the only preparation for eternity, and on all departed souls gone into the invisible
as beyond the power of any prayer or ceremonial
rite whatever to alter their final state, could not understand, what Stephen had never told them, that he
had been spiritually chloroformed by the false worship of the lodge, which fascinated him with its
dreamy, shadowy semblance of the true religion, as
the mirage with its vision of palm-fringed lakes fas-
cinates the desert traveller.

Not that he was wholly satisfied, for it sometimes
crossed his mind that he did not fancy standing in
fraternal relations to men of such free and easy
morals, as Van Gilder, for instance; and he even had
strong suspicions that many of the members secretly
adjourned after lodge meeting was over to some of
those very bar-rooms upon which he, as attorney for
the Law and Order League, had been waging such
vigorous warfare. Indeed, he once hinted as much
to Mr. Basset, who answered him with a reassuring
Scriptural quotation.

"Wheat and tares, wheat and tares. They've got
to grow together in the lodge as well as in the
church. As to Van Gilder, I don't stand up for the
man; you know I don't; but still he's no worse than
a good many others, and if we went to expelling all
the unworthy members I don't know where we
should stop. We all have sins and shortcomings

enough to lead us to deal charitably with weak and erring brethren."

Stephen felt rebuked, as if Mr. Basset had delicately accused him of Pharisaism, not reflecting that such a man as Van Gilder might easily be in possession of too many secrets (which was in fact the case) affecting the reputation of seemingly respectable members of the fraternity to be safely expelled. And as to the vexatious and needless drawbacks which he had met with in prosecuting liquor sellers —it is true that Stephen himself had solemnly promised "to warn a brother of any approaching danger, whether from his own imprudence or the evil designs of others;" but he would have repelled with scorn and indignation the idea that this could ever mean shielding a criminal from the consequences of his crime, and he was far too honest and fair-minded to impute any such understanding of it to others.

From all this the reader will see that Stephen Howland was very thoroughly humbugged, and would have afforded a fine illustration for Mr. Treworthy with which to point his arguments and facts when discoursing to Nelson.

CHAPTER IX.

A NEW KIND OF MACHINE.

Chronologically speaking, this chapter is out of place, for it belongs to an early epoch in our story, when Stephen Howland was patiently waiting for slow-footed Fortune in the shape of his first client, Nelson Newhall.

Fairfield is one of the pleasantest of prairie villages, and the finest farm therein is owned by Israel Deming, himself as fine a specimen of the well-to-do Western farmer as one often meets. At the present moment he sits on his shaded back porch discussing the news and the crops with Uncle Zeb, and at the same time enjoying the cool breeze that has sprung up after a day of unusual sultriness. Uncle Zeb is a lean, dried-up little man who might have sat for a picture of Timon after the goddess turned him into a grasshopper, so much did his long, thin legs, and a certain lively quirk in his. voice, to say nothing of a happy faculty of living without work or worry, remind one of that musical insect.

"They say corn is going to yield more to the acre than it did last year, Mr. Deming," remarked Uncle Zeb, briskly. "Them frosts we had along back didn't do no great damage arter all. I see your wheat is coming out heavier than the average.

Some folks think it is all luck, but I believe what Solomon says, 'The hand of the diligent maketh rich.' And I tell 'em if they'll only pattern after Israel Deming, always up and at it, early or late, rain or shine, they'll have as good luck as he."

"Anyhow I don't get much more than my living," replied the person thus complimented; "and no farmer can with these high freights and middle men taking all the profits. These confounded corporations lobby round, and wheedle and bribe Congress into voting away the people's land and money to make the rich richer and the poor poorer. Farmers ought to combine like other working men to protect their own interests, *I* say."

Now the wrongs of the farmers was a theme on which Mr. Deming always waxed into a fiery indignation, and if some of his strong speeches on this subject could have been uttered in the ears of the Senatorial "dough-heads" (his mildest term of contempt for law-makers who truckle to class interests) it might have made their ears tingle, but would cer· tainly have done them no harm.

"They says there's going to be a farmer's grange started in Fairfield afore long," responded Uncle Zeb.

Mr. Deming broke off a head of orchard grass that peeped through the lattice, and chewed one end of it reflectively.

"To tell the truth I ain't certain about these granges. No offence to you, Uncle Zeb, but I want nothing to do with anything that is patterned after

Masonry, and I have always been suspicious that the grange was a kind of Masonic institution. But then I don't *know* anything about it."

"I ain't one to give offence, Mr. Deming—leastways not when I know it—and I never take what I ain't ready to give," was Uncle Zeb's reassuring reply. "I'm a Mason, but not one of your thin-skinned kind. There's bad and there's good in Masonry, and I see no sense in acting as though the thing was a powder mill, and if anybody said a word it would blow up. But I'll tell ye how I look on this 'ere matter of the grange. It's jest a new kind of machine. Farmers must test it and take their chances. It may break down arter usin' of it awhile and cost more for repairs than its wuth. And it may be hard to get the hang on't. Some machines are awkward things if a green hand tries to run 'em without knowing how; get caught in 'em and they'll pound a man to jelly or cut him up into inch pieces. And then agin, —"

How far Uncle Zeb's lively imagination would have carried him in picturing all the possibilities of "the machine" must forever remain among the things untold, for he was interrupted at this juncture by a pretty, girlish figure suddenly framed in the doorway, while a voice, saucy and sweet as a bobolink's, cried out,—

"Now, Uncle Zeb, what do you mean, saying such awful things? Father will be more prejudiced against the grange than ever, and I was hoping they would start one in Fairfield right away."

"I only called it a machine," said Uncle Zeb, composedly. "I had to make some sort of a comparison, and they use machines for everything under the sun, nowadays, so that seemed to come handiest. I never said whether it was bad or good."

The nymph in the doorway tossed her bright head. She and Uncle Zeb were used to bandying words with each other, and both enjoyed the exercise.

"Well, *I* think it is good. I don't like Masonry, but I like these societies that women and girls can join as well as men and have a nice time. And they do have splendid times in the grange. Mrs. Thompson told me all about it."

"Marthy Washington!" ejaculated Uncle Zeb, who had an odd habit of using the name of that distinguished lady when he felt the need of a mild expletive. "They say women never can keep secrets, and now I shall believe it sure enough."

"Oh, nonsense, Uncle Zeb. You know I didn't mean that Mrs. Thompson told me anything she hadn't a right to. She says the grange is really nothing but a farmer's club, only the secrecy makes more fun. You will join, won't you, father?"

"I don't know, Dora. I shall have to think it over first. Of course its natural for young folks to like a frolic, but a society that's all play ain't going to benefit the farmers much."

"I don't fancy the idea anyhow," put in Mrs. Deming, very decidedly, from her seat by the open window. "I remember how it was with the Good

Templars. When a lodge was started here I let
Dora join because I thought it a good thing for
young people to get interested in temperance work.
But the way they carried on! The last time Dora
went they had a dance, and she didn't get home till
after midnight. I never let her go again, and so
many of the other parents in Fairfield thought as I
did that the lodge died down in less than a year
without reforming a single drunkard, so far as I
could find out."

"I can see into that easy enough," said Uncle Zeb.
"I've known plenty of drinking men that jined the
Good Templars, and thought they'd reformed as
much as could be, but when they had gone through
it all there wa'n't anything more behind to hold 'em;
and so they'd go back to their cups, and their 'latter
end would be wuss than their beginning,' as Scripter
says."

"That just goes to prove what I've said all along.
If you want to reform a drunkard better try and
hitch him on where there *is* a power strong enough
to hold him up. I never knew a reformed man to
join the church and give good evidence of conversion
and then go back on his pledge. It is in reform as
it is in everything else. If we want to accomplish
anything worth speaking of we must buckle down to
real, right-down, honest work; turning work into
play won't answer."

"That's so," assented Uncle Zeb, with an energy
of speech not at all abated by the fact that he cherished a mortal hatred to work of all kinds.

"Well," said Mr. Deming, "I'm a good deal of my wife's way of thinking about the Good Templars. But the grange don't pretend to have any moral aim, I take it; and just as a mutual benefit and improvement society for the farmers, I don't see as there would be any harm in starting one and seeing how the thing worked."

"And just remember, Mr. Deming, that when a man invests his money in a machine that *don't* work he's so much out of pocket."

Which was touching her husband on a weak point —a smooth-tongued agent having once beguiled him into doing that very thing, buying a new kind of patent reaper which proved worthless when it came to the test.

Uncle Zeb gave a mild chuckle of inward amusement. "I guess you're about in the right on't, Mrs. Deming. Well, I must be a going. Looks as though we might have a dry spell. I see the moon turns up considerable."

And Uncle Zeb shambled off to finish his evening round of gossip somewhere else, while Mrs. Deming called to Dora to come in and pick over a pan of beans for the next day's dinner.

Dora obeyed, thinking meanwhile just such thoughts as come naturally into a young and foolish girl's head. She was pretty and she knew it. She was fond of admiration and a good time, and all the reason why she wanted to see a grange started in Fairfield was because its meetings promised to supply her with both those desirable things.

Mrs. Deming's rule over Dora (who, as the reader has probably guessed, is no other than Nelson Newhall's sister) had been vigorous enough; but it was the vigor of real, maternal affection to which we can forgive an occasional hardness supposed to be for the good of the subject. Dora was Mr. Deming's pet; he never crossed her in anything, and she would certainly have been in a fair way to be spoiled if her adopted mother's sound common sense had not come to the front.

Under this combination of influences Dora Deming had grown up a bright, merry, thoughtless creature, loving her foster parents dearly, popular among the young people of her own age, with a general desire to do right; and sometimes, under an especially moving sermon, or when there was a period of religious awakening, feeling a vague longing after something higher and nobler than her life had yet developed. In short, her's was a nature of that very common and mortal type from which most of the happy wives and mothers about us are made. But as she stands in the Paradise of her maiden innocence we have grave fears for Dora—unbalanced, undisciplined, ignorant of her own heart, when the serpent whose trail is over every earthly Eden whispers in her ear his subtle temptation, will she be wiser, stronger to withstand him than was the first Eve? God grant it.

Mrs. Israel Deming has spoken for herself. She was a good woman, active and stirring, who placed laziness in the same category with dirt and flies as

a thing to be held in utter abomination; but at the
same time she tolerated Uncle Zeb with a good-
natured, half-contemptuous tolerance much as she
would a monkey or a parrot. The fact is, everybody
has a tender side for the village gossip or the village
joker, and Uncle Zeb, in a small way, practiced both
vocations.

Mr. Israel Deming was, like his wife, a staunch
church member, a law-abiding, law-upholding American citizen, who wanted to see everything of a rascally nature put down—so effectually that it would
stay put down, whether it was polygamy in Utah or
a whisky ring at Washington. He was also an Anti-
mason, though not very thoroughly instructed. He
had a plain, honest man's dislike to fuss and feath-
ers as savoring of monarchial rather than republican
institutions. But the idea of the grange fell in with
his weak side. He was told that it was a society intended to unite American farmers in one grand combination against the gigantic monopolies that were
driving them to the wall.

Now there were some things Mr. Deming understood as well as the average Congressman. He knew
that our patent laws, which could be so grossly pros-
tituted as to tax, in the interests of great moneyed
corporations, everything used in working his farm
down to the very material with which he built his
fences, needed a thorough overhauling. He knew
that gamblers in grain were allowed to depress or
inflate the markets at their own will to the injury of
consumers and producers alike; and railroad mag-

nates to filch their heavy dividends on watered stock direct from the pockets of the long-suffering farmers; while Congress, which had not passed a single bill of any importance in aid of the agricultural class since the Homestead Act, was squandering millions in land grants to corporations of its own creating, and closing up vast sections of the public domains to the poor and honest settler. Naturally enough, he thought, it was time that government should be made to see that it was killing the goose which laid the golden egg. But what spirit of madness and folly could lead honest, intelligent Israel Deming, and thousands of others like him, to imagine that monopoly could overthrow monopoly, that ring rule could banish ring rule, and the devil of organized selfishness cast out the devil of political bribery and corruption?

Mr. Deming disliked secrecy, and all dark-lantern ways in general, but to such infinitesimal doses as the grange offered him, coupled as it was with a vague promise of unknown good, he felt no great objection. And in spite of Uncle Zeb's oracular warnings and his wife's plainly-expressed antipathy to the whole thing, Mr. Deming concluded to try "the machine," with a result which we will leave for future chapters.

CHAPTER X.

IN WHICH THE QUESTION IS MET FACE TO FACE.

Nelson went to his work day after day with a strange new sense of uneasiness. There was an ominous electricity in the air—the presence of unknown forces which he could not guage or analyze any more than he could that mysterious power that can change the face of the solid land and fling up mountain peaks in mid ocean. A strike in the dead of winter, with all its entailed idleness and pinching want, was a folly that he found nearly as difficult to understand as voluntary suicide. Nor did he believe that the men themselves, if left to the dictates of their own common sense, would adopt a remedy so much worse than the disease; but he strongly suspected what really proved to be the case, that the same Union agent whose advances he had so bluntly repelled was secretly and with no inconsiderable success laboring to foment discontent among the other hands. Some hundreds were employed in the works, foreigners and native born, as miscellaneous in their political and religious creed as in their nationality, but nearly all bound together by the tie of the secret Trades Union.

"The fellow is a disguised socialist," he said to Martha; "and I believe he is doing a great deal of mischief in his smooth, quiet kind of way. The majority of the men are too ignorant or too unthinking to see that any attempt to injure capital is simply cutting their own fingers. They know they are unjustly treated, and the impulse is to strike in a blind, blundering fashion at what they think is hurting them. They don't stop to consider that three or four months of enforced idleness, during which he will receive no wages at all, is an injury far more real to the working man than to be docked of a portion, however unfairly. But I've talked till I begin to think the wisest way is to keep silence. I believe already some of the men—and they are honest fellows whose good opinion I value—are beginning to look upon me as taking sides with their employers, and acting the part of a traitor to my own class."

"And if the order comes to strike?" queried Martha.

"I shall obey it, of course. To do anything else would be like trying to stem the tide of Niagara. If it was merely the local Union one had to withstand, resistance would be possible; but behind every subordinate Union stands the National Union, and simply to attempt resistance would be to be ground between the upper and the nether millstones. You know I don't mean to go back on what I have always said," added Nelson, struck by a sudden sense of incongruity which he felt that the keen-witted Martha would be sure to note. "Some people call this depotism; I don't. I grant that the National Union wields a tremendous power, but it is only what the workingman needs to counterbalance the money power of the capitalist. I grant, too, that like other kinds of power it is liable to abuse and incidental disadvantages. A locomotive is an excellent thing, but it sometimes runs off the track. So is a steamboat, but it sometimes bursts its boilers; and then we have an investigation, and a verdict of criminal carelessness, or ignorance, or incompetence, on the part of somebody or other; but no one suggests that we had better go back to stages and sailboats."

Martha knew better than to hint that all this elaborate and uncalled-for display of argument was a confession of weakness; an attempt to convince himself rather than her; and Nelson continued after a moment's silence:

"Of course I have my private reasons for not desiring a strike just now. My board will be paid by the Union, and something additional for Tom's support, but in his present state he has to have a good many things in the way of food and medicine that would not be taken into the account. If the strike is long continued I shall have to fall back on the money I have laid up. The result will be a longer deferring of our marriage and the spoiling of a good many of my plans. Still I don't want to look at the matter selfishly, as if my own interest was the only thing to be considered. If Jacksonville could have been carried for no-license last fall, I shouldn't mind the strike half so much. The new mayor may talk temperance as much as he pleases; I don't trust him.

He was elected by liquor votes, and when a pinch comes he won't dare offend the party to whom he owes his office. So this is the way the few govern the many. I was foolish enough once to suppose that the majority ruled, but I'm beginning to change my mind." .

It will be observed that in thus declaiming against the liquor oligarchy, while he patiently submitted to the ordering of a few irresponsible lodge leaders, Nelson was straining at a gnat and swallowing a camel in the sweetly unconscious fashion of our inconsistent humanity generally.

"I know I was terribly disappointed with the results of the last election," said Martha, thoughtfully; "and I don't think I felt quite right about it till Mrs. Haviland talked to us so beautifully at our last W. C. T. U. meeting. She gave us a Bible reading from the eighty-first psalm, dwelling especially on the seventh verse: 'I answered thee in the secret place of thunder; I proved thee at the waters of Meribah.' She said some among us could look back to the days of the Crusades when we were small and weak, with no weapon but prayer, and remember how gloriously God answered us 'in his secret place of thunder.' Now we are an army with banners marching in to possess the land. If he allowed the wicked a momentary triumph it was only to prove us as he proved Israel at the waters of Meribah. We must put down every feeling of discouragement and rest patiently in the promises; and when we had thus prepared the way for him in our hearts we should see his salvation. Nelson, I held my breath while she was speaking. I am not a perfectionist. I don't believe the best of us live without sinning, yet I could never see a single human weakness in that woman. I remember reading somewhere that refiners of silver consider the process finished when the metal perfectly reflects the face of the person who bends over the crucible. I always think of that when I see Mrs. Haviland and remember what she has gone through. I never look at her nor hear her speak without gaining a more vivid and personal conception of Christ himself, as a real, living, ever-present Saviour."

Nelson did not answer for a moment, and then he said with a sigh, "I suppose I ought to have a stronger faith, Martha; but I believe women are always more gifted in that line than men."

"Well, you see it gave me a kind of new revelation. I went away from the meeting perfectly satisfied. I hate this dreadful business as much as ever, and my heart is just as sore over the misery it causes; but I know God hates it worse than I can and pities its victims infinitely more. And I feel so sure the day is hastening when he will answer the prayers of the souls crying under the altar that I am willing to see the politicians play their little game a while longer. I am even willing to see the beauties of 'high license' illustrated in Jacksonville the coming year."

"High fiddlesticks," said Nelson. "I believe it is worse in one sense than the free, unlicensed sale, for it is a greater swindle and delusion. A few of the smaller fry among the saloon-keepers will have to go under, but that will only make better standing room for the others. This compromising with evil, I hate. I want the lines sharply drawn. If there are but a handful on the right side and God with us, I don't care. Let it be war with the liquor traffic, and war to the knife; but for heaven's sake none of these disgraceful, halting compromises that only make the evil worse."

"Precisely my sentiments, Mr. Newhall; but how is Tom to-day?"

"I think he is improving. He's certainly stronger and don't cough near so much. I have been careful not to give him liquor in his medicines in even the smallest quantity, and since his sickness he has seemed to show no desire for it. All will be well if his appetite for drink can be kept dormant. But, O Martha, just think for a moment what this dreadful traffic in human misery has done for me and mine! How it has orphaned us, crushed the mind of my only brother, and made me a stranger to my own sister! And yet Government sanctions it, coolly puts the wages of blood into its treasury. What do they care, these Congressmen, only to keep their places and draw their salaries."

Nelson spoke bitterly; but, reader, put yourself in the place of this young workman as he looked back over his shadowed childhood and sorrowful youth, and remembered that the very government under which he was born had made itself a party to his wrongs.

"Nelson," said Martha, taking up her pocket Bible, "let me read you something that has comforted me a great many times when everything looked all wrong and mixed up. 'Fret not thyself because of evil-doers, neither be thou envious against the workers of iniquity. For they soon shall be cut down like the grass and wither as the green herb. Trust in the Lord and do good; so shalt thou dwell in the land and verily thou shalt be fed.'"

Nelson's brow cleared. It seemed so like his mother's own voice that he felt a strange calm enwrap his soul as she read. The eternal rock of God's righteousness stood firm; and what was human wrong and injustice but passing waves that dashed against its immovable base to be swept into the tide of the yesterdays, and leave not a trace behind on his grand to-morrow, when there shall be a new heavens and a new earth; but no more sea, no angry whirlpool of opposing moral issues, but for every great and burning question that agitates the nations to-day a final, irrevocable settlement by the laws of everlasting Right.

"Thank you, Martha," he said when she finished. "It has done me good."

The next day—it was about two weeks before New Year's—the order came to strike. It was a cold, cloudy morning, the call to work had just sounded, and the men were trooping in with their dinner-pails, but in an hour the whole place was deserted and silent. A Napoleon might have envied the power which had only to issue its mandate and be thus

obeyed.   To be sure it is a power fraught with some
danger—more particularly in a republic which as-
serts every fourth of July as its foundation doctrine,
the sacred, inalienable rights of the individual citizen, which would seem to include among other
things the right to sell his own work at his own
price.

During the day the men gathered in little groups
and talked over the situation.   There were rumors
of a compromise.   It was said that the employers
had expressed themselves willing to make certain
concessions if met half way, and were conferring to
this end with a committee from the Union.   The result was awaited hopefully by some.   Others, in
whom was working the socialistic leaven, were less
anxious for a peaceful settlement of the difficulty.
Nelson found himself in the course of the day in the
midst of one of these groups.

"Newhall don't believe in strikes; thinks the manufacturers ought to be allowed to make their pile of
money and grind us working men into the dirt,"
was the greeting that fell on his ears as he came
up.   Nelson happened to know the speaker very
well, and thought this a good chance to prove to
his fellow-workmen that he held opinions of an
exactly opposite tenor to those imputed to him.

"Now be fair," he said good-humoredly, "and let
me tell you what I really do think.   Granted that
every manufacturer in the country is making his
money unjustly, don't that money go to create more
capital?   And how can cutting off the fountain

which supplies us with our wages make us any better off? It is playing a game in which we have hardly one chance in a thousand of coming out ahead. But I don't believe, and I want you to understand that I don't believe, in tamely submitting to wrong. I am only talking against the kind of resistance that bounds back on ourselves and leaves us worse off than we were before. What hinders us working men from putting our money and brains together and running factories and shops and mills on our own account? Now *there* would be a kind of resistance based on justice and common sense."

"What hinders us? Hain't these moneyed rascals got the staff in their own hands? and don't they mean to keep it there?"

"How did they get it in the first place?" asked Nelson, coolly. "Most of our rich men began life with hardly a cent. Now I think it is a pity if three or four hundred working men, if they are sober, industrious and skillful at their trade, can't be equal to at least one capitalist."

"That's all fool's talk," growled the leader in the group, a man of German parentage, but American born and bred. "The power is all on the side of the rich, and there's got to be a revolution, a turning upside down of society before things will be righted."

"But just remember," answered Nelson, good-naturedly, "that when this general overturning comes on if you and I should happen to be under the heap it might be awkward for us. Volcanoes and earthquakes may be necessary things, but it always seemed to me that I had a *little* rather keep out of their range. The fact is, Schumacher, you have read these papers that talk as if American working men were all in a state of serfdom till you have begun to believe it It is no such thing. Not a capitalist under heaven could 'grind us into the dirt' if we all understood as we ought to that labor has got a vantage ground of its own. Our numbers are our defenced city, and, to make it as impregnable as Gibralter, we only need intelligence, sobriety, economy, and I am going to add, though I know you have thrown both these things overboard, faith in God and hope in a hereafter."

"Hang your religious rubbish. What do we know about a hereafter, whether we shall be nothing or start up cabbages."

"For my part," responded Nelson, "I had rather a good honest cabbage should spring from my dust and that be the end of me than to go into the other world weighed down with all the rascalities and meannesses that some men have to carry with them, and if your belief helps to make life more cheerful, why I am glad. It would have just the opposite effect on me. But we are wandering wide of the question. What hinders us working men? What is the foe in the rear that is always hanging on the skirts of the great army of labor? It is these thousands on thousands of legalized dramshops scattered over the country. So long as we are content to keep an army of lazy saloonists living on the fat of the

land there is no sense nor reason in our cursing capitalists. Just look at this thing a minute. The nine
hundred millions that it takes every year to keep
the country's one hundred and seventy-five thousand
dramshops running means so many millions less to
run its shops and stores and mills; and do you suppose because you are neither drunkards nor tipplers
yourselves that you can escape paying your share of
this enormous tax when it is money taken right out
of every honest business by which working men earn
their living? This monstrous traffic sucks industry's very life blood, and which side, think you, feels
the drain the most, the capitalist who, when he sees
a hard time ahead, can haul in his sails with no
great inconvenience to himself and wait till the
storm blows over? or the average working man to
whom a 'shut down' means less food, less fire, less
of everything that makes life comfortable and pleasant? Take off this terrible tariff, this millstone
round the neck of labor, and what would be the result? Why, it would increase its earning power at
least one-third, which is the same as to say that you
let rum take one dollar out of every three you earn,
and bear it patiently, while you grumble and growl
if a manufacturer cuts you down in your wages
twenty cents!"

Two of the men laughed. The third one looked
thoughtful. The fourth member of the party, which
was Schumacher, shrugged his shoulders.

"We are not Grand Moguls. Liquor will be sold
and drank for all us."

"So it will while we allow it. As a class we hold the sovereign power in our own hands, and if, instead of listening to political demagogues every election, each working man would make his ballot a straight shot at the rum power, I warrant that it wouldn't be a great while before our Senators and Representatives at Washington would get some new light on the subject. Better read over again the fable of Hercules and the wagoner. If we working men are ever to improve our condition the help must come from ourselves first. And it won't come by sitting still and railing against the rich. If they oppress us the worst is their own, but at the least they give us work and wages. What does the liquor power do for us? Cripples and paralyzes every single industry by which we earn our bread. Let us roll that burden from our shoulders and then labor will be prepared to resist the tyranny of capital to some purpose."

But talk like this was making Nelson unpopular, for though his fellow-workmen dimly realized that he stood on a higher mental plane than the most of them; had read more, thought more, and observed more—still there were many, as he told Martha, who construed his words into a tacit desertion of their cause, and turned the cold shoulder on him in consequence.

He went back to his boarding-place feeling as if it was a strange new kind of Sunday without the Sabbath peace and spirit of devotion. Tom was sitting in his old place coughing feebly, and watching with dull, vacant gaze a belated fly that was slowly and stiffly buzzing about in a streak of cold, white sunshine.

Outwardly Tom bore a much closer resemblance to his mother than either of the two others. As nature had given him at the start a much weaker physical frame than the stalwart Nelson, so she had cast his features in a proportionately finer mould; and the epileptic fits which had fastened on him in childhood, the result of that injury to the brain received from his father's drunken blow, however they might dim his intellect could not wholly mar the original beauty of the chiseling.

"Well, Tom, old fellow!" was Nelson's cheery greeting; "I'm going to stay with you all day. What do you say to that? It seems good to see the sun coming out. Let me wheel your chair into it."

Nelson had devoted himself heart and soul to his unfortunate brother without the least idea that he was doing anything very noble, or worthy of particular remark. There are natures that seem to be morally "born in the purple," and the most unlimited drafts on their generous self-devotion are honored at first sight with the confidence of one who has in his soul a whole royal exchequer to draw from.

So he had fought Tom's battles with a rude and scornful world, and no wonder that he seemed to the latter a perfect incarnation of wisdom and strength. Tom stood somewhat in fear of him, it is true, but it was that kind of fear which we are told in Scripture is not inconsistent with the highest love; and when

his fit of coughing subsided, he showed Nelson with
much delight a newspaper on which he gravely
marked with his forefinger a length of about two
columns and a half.   To make believe read was one
of Tom's amusements, and Nelson always humored
him by taking the matter very seriously.

"All that this morning! You've done bravely,
Tom, since I've been gone.   I'm thinking you'll be
lots of help to me when I get my farm."

Tom smiled contentedly.   That farm was his
Eldorado.   His feeble mind made his anticipations
of its freedom, plenty and varied delights like a
child's, a pleasure from which all elements of care,
worry, or possible disappointment were entirely
eliminated.   Though Nelson did not now feel in just
the mood for such castle-building, he went over the
story again for Tom's amusement, and when he could
think of no further enlargements or additions that
could be truthfully made to it, he began to sing in a
melodious, baritone voice—

> "On Jordan's stormy banks I stand
> And cast a wishful eye,
> To Canaan's fair and happy land,
> Where my possessions lie."

In singing to Tom he generally chose old-fashioned hymns.   They chimed in best with his strong,
thoughtful, earnest, nature; and they reminded him,
besides, of his mother.   How she used to satisfy the
hunger of her homesick heart with Watt's grand old
lyrics!

When he reached the last line of the hymn Tom
was asleep.   Nelson got up, poked the fire a little,

and then took the newspaper which Tom had dropped. He looked over the usual list of murders, wife-beatings, and brutal assaults in which, strangely enough, high-licensed whisky appears to be just as prolific as the more plebeian sort which lacks that peculiar stamp of respectability; and then he passed to the column headed, "Labor Troubles." Everywhere there seemed to be an epidemic of strikes. In the coal-fields Molly Maguirism was cropping out, and the whole industrial world appeared to be generally in a state of upheaval and disturbance.

Nelson took a pencil and figured up on the white margin something like a rough approximation to the sum lost by labor per week. Startling as were the figures, he knew he had under-rated the factors by which he had obtained this result.

And what of that vast sum lost every year by the liquor traffic? Nelson was enough of a political economist to understand with Adam Smith that the one great law on which all equitable trade is built is the law of corresponding values; in other words, that value taken must always mean value received in something of direct profit or service to the buyer. And when the liquor business ignores utterly this underlying law in political economy, this rule of reciprocal giving and taking, and decrees that all the profit and advantage shall be on one side only, can such mischievous violation of so fundamental a principle help reacting disastrously on trade? Is it not laying a hand on the very main-spring of every lawful industry? and must not the legitimate fruits be dull times, poverty, distress, and that remedy worse than the disease—strikes?

And what of the liquor power as a ruling force in government? Did not every election prove that its immense wealth was simply a bribery fund? To this corrupt and corrupting factor in politics with its hundreds of millions annually stolen from the people, could anything be said to be impossible in the way of chicanery and fraud? One wrong fostered, one injustice upheld made room for others to gather their foul brood under the same broad shield of national law; and legislative integrity thus sapped, on what could the poor man base any reasonable hope of being protected from the greed of unscrupulous money kings and soulless corporations?

Nelson wanted to confront the question fairly. He believed he had done so, when in reality he had seen but one side of this double-faced Janus.

CHAPTER XI.

At this juncture we perceive a growing restlessness among some of our readers. Countless voices
are raised in defence of their own pet insurance
society, and learned college professors hope we shall
not be so unwise and unjust as to include their beloved Greek letter fraternities in the same condem-
nation. And as many of these good people take
pains to assure us that they are opposed to Masonry;
that they have some adequate idea of its ability to
corrupt the courts, paralyze the hand of justice, and
shield every murderer, rumseller, or bank defaulter
who puts his trust in its shadow, we will stop the
thread of our story long enough to relate a certain
episode in the career of Napoleon, which, though un-
familiar to the average student, was one of those
hidden factors of Providence which bring about the
mysterious and unlooked-for results that so often
baffle human calculations.

At the very threshold of his conquests, at the
very moment when his hand was stretched out to
grasp imperial power, he met, like the heroes of
Greek story, a dragon to stay his farther progress.
That dragon was Freemasonry. Masonic lodges

covered alike Protestant Germany and Catholic Spain. Under their mask aristocrat and anarchist, free-thinker and Jesuit, could plot together in a horrible unity—the unity of the pit. Already it had overthrown the Puritan commonwealth in England, and lighted in Paris the lurid flames of the French Revolution.

Two courses lay open before him. He could grapple with the monster—crush, annihilate it if possible; or he could make it his tool, his slave, his faithful ally. The "Man of Destiny," whom neither Alps nor Russian snows could daunt, and at the tread of whose armed hosts all Europe was shaking in terror, quailed before the first alternative and chose the second. At his dictation his own trusted generals and marshals entered the various lodges, became their leaders, and controlled them completely in the interests of imperialism till St. Helena ended the drama.

t was not the first time that Masonry has been paid in her own coin, nor will it be the last that this spiritual sorceress in her trade of duping and fooling men has been made herself the dupe and fool of crowned and mitred heads. This shrewd stroke of Napoleonic policy was only a slight variation of her own favorite game, and one which she is now playing in our own free Columbia with much success.

Odd-fellowship and the hundreds of minor secret orders she officers with her own most tried and trusted generals, and has no desire—indeed would have the greatest objection to see the rank and file turn Masons. She well knows that they make far more tractable subjects as they are. Vowed to obey unquestioningly Masonic superiors, and those superiors sworn in turn to obey all above them in continual gradations till the apex is reached at the top of which sits the commander-in-chief in the shape of a most Sublime and Illustrious Sovereign Grand Inspector General, we can easily see how with only the bridle of a minor temperance order the whole body can be turned about in any given—Masonic—direction.

The strike continued, with no prospect of a speedy end; and many of the workmen found their unoccupied hours dragged less heavily if passed in some place of common resort. Unluckily there were enough saloons left in Jacksonville to supply that want; and they furnished precisely the soil needed for the sprouting of socialistic tares, though the previously mentioned "Union agent," having finished his seed sowing, had some time before left for "pastures new." The saloon-keepers, warned by the popular storm which had so nearly wrecked their business, and with some little fear of the W. C. T. U., practiced more circumspection and more secrecy; but bar-rooms fitted up underground may be as favorable gathering-places as the cave of Adullam for "every one that is discontented" with the prevailing order of society; and it is certain that over the fiery potations there dealt out strange threats were sometimes uttered, and the speeches of noted communistic leaders quoted with a gusto that would have been far from pleasant to peaceful and law-abiding ears.

"I believe there is more drink sold in Jacksonville now than before the strike," said Nelson to Martin Treworthy one morning in the latter part of February. "What is our 'temperance' mayor about?"

"Fulfilling his Masonic obligations," growled Martin. "Liquor men and Good Templars voted together for him last fall, so now he's got to be 'all things to all men' in a sense the Apostle Paul never dreamed of. But then it comes tolerable easy to a man that has taken a dozen or two of Masonic degrees."

"The strike ought to have been at an end long ago," said Nelson, choosing to ignore this explanation of the case. "I know men that were steady and industrious before it happened, and now they spend in drink half the money allowed them by the Union to support their families. It is ruinous, it is suicidal—this long, fruitless strife in which nothing is gained and everything lost on the side least capable of bearing loss. It is the ambition and selfishness of men like Gerrish and Reynolds that is prolonging this state of affairs, and I've about made up my mind to break with the Union entirely if I've got to be under such leaders."

A dry smile curled Martin's lips. He was not at all averse to seeing this young Hercules of labor chafe under his lodge fetters. Perhaps Nelson did not see the smile. He went on.

"They have stood from the first of it right in the

way of any adjustment of the difficulty. The manufacturers were ready for a compromise long ago,
that the majority of the men—I for one—would
have been willing to accept. Here we are losing
money and time, and suffering all the demoralizing
influences that come from idleness. But what do
these men care for that? They don't want to see
the wrongs of labor righted. It is for their interest
to keep up this strife and contention. It is the way
they get their living. They are too lazy to work,
and to beg they are ashamed, but they manage some
way to get all the offices themselves, and wear their
kid gloves and draw their comfortable salaries, and
we working men must submit to their tyranny."

The reader may perhaps remember that Nelson
had once himself innocently informed Martin Treworthy that the leaders of the Union were generally
Masons or Odd-fellows. But the latter made no allusion to this fact as furnishing a possible key to
the mystery of these easy berths. Experience was
beginning to teach Nelson a good many truths before unheeded, and he was quite willing to leave
him for awhile to the tutelage of this stern in-
structor.

"The fact is they represent no interests but their
own, and I don't wonder the manufacturers refuse
to treat with them. I should in their place. I heard
to-day that the works were going to start up next
week with a large force of non-union laborers, and if
the new hands can't be intimidated or bought off
there will be trouble. I see it and feel it."

"And that no man might buy or sell save he that had the mark or the name of the beast or the number of his name," slowly repeated Martin Treworthy.

"But I always thought the beast was popery. Commentators explain .it so," added Nelson, innocently.

"When I see prophecy fulfilled right before my eyes I don't have to go to the D.D.s" returned Martin, dryly. "But I hain't got no -grudge against Masonry for anything it has done to me, though I remember in one of the first battles of the war how, as we were retiring, I turned right back in the very face of the rebs as they were dashing down hill—I don't know what possessed me unless it was the spirit of Gideon—and picked up our colors and carried them safe into camp; but I never got any promotion for it, though I was told if I'd only been a Mason I should have got promoted fast enough."

'That was shameful injustice," said Nelson, indignantly.

"I want you to understand," replied Martin Treworthy, coolly, "that its losing me a pair of shoulder-straps don't make it that there's any debt or credit account between us. Why, I read that thirteenth chapter in Revelations nigh a hundred times on my bended knees before the Lord revealed to me what it meant. It was the Spirit of the Lord that taught me to hate Masonry, not anything it has done to me or mine. It seemed as if I could see the beast, and the long procession of worshipers filing up—lawyers that wanted clients, and ministers that

wanted pulpits, and politicians thåt wanted office;
and all the murderers and adulterers and rumsellers
that wanted to get clear of the gallows and the jail;
small and great, rich and poor, bond and free, wearing his mark on their foreheads or in their hands.
Then the thought came to me that worship always
implies a religion of some kind, and so the beast
must represent some universal religion. And as it
was in the likeness of a lamb, but not the Lamb as
it had been slain, it must be a religion of works
without any atonement. And with that the Holy
Spirit flashed the truth right into my mind. As
Masonry required worship without Christ, and promised salvation without repentance, it was the only
religion that would suit the natural heart everywhere. And I saw that in its pride, lust of power,
blasphemy, and spirit of persecution, it was an
image of the old papal beast; and every secret order,
whether it was in Russia, Africa or America, was an
image of Masonry. A religion that will suit everybody, Jew or Christian or heathen, must be the same
in principle the world over, and yet be able to
change its outward shape. That is what Masonry
does in all the little secret orders; it changes its
shape, but it is the same thing at heart—anti-Christ,
whose coming is with all manner of deceiveableness.
And when the Lord showed me this I was astonished
like Ezekiel by the river of Chebar. But I knew
there was more light to come. So I considered further on the matter, and I saw that until the time of
the end all the great world powers like slavery and

rum and Mormonism would 'agree to give their
kingdom unto the beast.' And from the day that
the Spirit of the Lord revealed this to me—mind, I
hadn't read a tract, book, or paper about it then—
I've fought the evil thing with might and main, and
I mean to keep on fighting it to the last. To see the
victory will be for younger eyes than mine, but I'm
satisfied so long as I know who my Leader is."

And the grizzly-headed hero of more and different
battles than Nelson ever dreamed of took his departure, leaving the latter feeling rather uncomfortable. He was thoroughly disgusted with the
tyranny of the Union, while his apprehensions of
more serious trouble yet to follow made the low,
monotonous undertone of Martin Treworthy's speech
seem like the far off thunders of a coming judgment.

Could he have overheard a conversation that was
going on meanwhile in one of the basement saloons
at which the new mayor, in due respect to his Masonic vows, had found it convenient to wink, it
would only have darkened his musings.

Beside a table covered with green cloth, each with
a glass of beer before him, sat two men. In the
features of one was a hint of Celtic extraction; he
had very white teeth that, when he smiled, seemed
to have the treacherous gleam of a wild beast's, was
graceful in person, and rather particular about his
dress—a kind of Americanized Robespierre. It is
not an enjoyable fact to ponder, but it is a fact
nevertheless, that we have in our midst men of the
same type with that blood-thirsty triumvirate who

ruled Paris in '93, though our American sun of freedom shines rather too brightly in their eyes, and
they generally burrow in the darkness of illicit
saloons and secret lodges.

The other man was coarse-featured, large-boned,
much given to profanity, and wore a Knight Templar's badge conspicuously displayed. The fumes
of their cigars mingled sociably together as they
sipped their beer and conversed in low and confi-
dential tones; and, in short, they answered very well
to that graphic description given by David in the
sixty-fourth psalm of the wicked "in secret counsel."

"Don't forget a good stiff glass of whisky all
round to prime 'em up for the job, Reynolds," said
the personage first described. At which reminder
the other only nodded as if he was in no danger of
neglecting so important a matter, while the first one
continued.

"That cranky fool, Newhall, must be made to hold
his tongue. All the opposition to the strike has
been stirred up by him."

"Not so easy; he's deep as a well."

"A knife for traitors," was the significant response. This laconic remark, however, was not
quite original, being in reality quoted from a late
speech of Herr Most.

"If you ain't a cool one, Gerrish!" exclaimed the
other with an oath, clapping his companion on the
shoulder. "You'd be a match for the devil himself."

"Bah!" was the scornful reply. "Keep that old

woman's talk to yourself. I don't believe in a devil no more than I do in a God. Men are what we've got to deal with in this age of the world."

Reynolds was used to being snubbed and lectured by his chief, and his only answer was to drain his glass and meekly wait further orders.

But of this precious pair, in whose creed dynamite and whisky were the leading articles of belief, we shall give the reader out of respect to his moral and religious scruples at being placed in such company, but the briefest possible glimpse. Reynolds was blacklisted—discharged for his own fault, but he represented himself as persecuted for belonging to the Union, and played the martyr role with such success that he found himself hoisted at once into a place of power and notoriety very much to his liking, and where he drew a salary larger than his lost wages. He was obliged to play second fiddle to Gerrish, however, for though not so much of a bully and a blackguard the latter was a born leader, and by far the more dangerous of the two. He had not been long in Jacksonville, and Nelson as well as many of his fellow-workmen were inclined to resent this dictatorial sway of one whose antecedents were so little known, quite forgetting that there was a slight inconsistency involved in such a state of feeling. Had they not sworn to obey all the rules and regulations of the Grand Lodge? thus virtually placing themselves under the complete despotic control of its chief—a man they knew as little about as they did of the Shah of Persia?

The variety of uses to which secrecy may be put is an important but neglected branch of knowledge among the great bulk of its simple-minded members. Missionaries in Africa tell us of secret societies among the natives, under whose wings of darkness, demon-worship, kidnapping and cannibalism are as freely practiced as more civilized crimes in the safe shelter of a lodge of Masons, Odd-fellows, or Knights of Pythias. How long before Christians in America will be as wise as their brethren in Africa and refuse to fellowship secretism in any form even when disguised in the holy garments of temperance? How long before temperance workers will understand that the cause of God and the cause of the devil cannot be fought with the same weapons; that in taking the vows of secrecy they are actually striking hands with all the Masonic saloon-keepers, brewers and distillers, as well as their Masonic allies in our courts and legislative halls? How long before honest workingmen will understand that when they join a secret trades union they are joined as one body to the dark, aristocratic, monarchial, antirepublican institution of Freemasonry; and through it with the Nihilist, the Socialist, the Ku Klux—men whose profession it is to stir up rebellion, revolution, anarchy; and who without the aid of liquor, labor's greatest enemy and curse, could not achieve half the triumphs they have in the past or will in the future unless God in his mercy opens the eyes of our nation to its danger?

There can be but one answer to such questions.

Society will never frown upon any evil that the church tolerates. Political action will never be taken against it till Christian voters and Christian statesmen demand such action. When Zion puts on her beautiful garments; when she casts out of her midst with scorn and loathing every thing that would defile her purity; when she shows herself "terrible as an army with banners" against every form of sin and iniquity, then the honest temperance worker and the hard-handed son of labor will no longer believe a lie; and evil men and seducers will have a foretaste of the coming terrors of that Judgment Day when they shall say to the rocks and to the mountains, "Fall on us and hide us from the wrath of the Lamb."

CHAPTER XII.

The yoke of fraternal love and duty fastened so long ago on Nelson's boyish shoulders by a mother's dying hand, had often been a fetter on the freedom of his personal action—on his *soul*, never. But when he ignorantly degraded his manhood to wear the yoke of a secret labor union, he found, like many another honest American working man, that he had sold his birthright of liberty for a mess of pottage. He had never been a very active member, but had contented himself for the most part with simply paying his dues, and cherishing the comfortable delusion that he was thereby helping to rear up a breakwater against the greed and tyranny of capital. Thus he was as ignorant as any outsider of the dark designs hatched in its secret conclaves; or how, little by little, through the operation of that law in lodgery, certain as any law in mechanics, (by which the unprincipled, unscrupulous element as surely rises to the top as the decent, virtuous, Christian element sinks to the bottom) a new class of leaders developed by the present crisis were coming to the front, whose regard for the laborer was like that of a wolf for a sheep

Nelson was slowly waking up to the consciousness

that their yoke was hard and their burden anything
but light.   His hope of a speedy marriage, his dream
of some quiet prairie farm where his life and
Martha's should glide away in rural peace, the dream
which had so often come to him in the heat and
grime of the workshop like a vision of cool waters—
all this he must put far away into the indefinite
future.   The faster Tom regained health and
strength the nearer came the time when he must
take up his old burden of anxiety.   And the worst
of it was he was powerless.   He could say some
very true and bitter things of the few leaders who,
to serve their own selfish ends, were willing to keep
three or four hundred men out of employment.   But
he must bear it, though the cords were already beginning to cut into the flesh.

Nelson Newhall was not a physical or moral
coward to be afraid of men he despised—and yet he
was afraid. · We bespeak for him the reader's charity, however, as well as for the minister whom one
or two Masons or Odd-fellows in his congregation
can intimidate so effectually; not that they wield as
individuals more influence than others, but the whole
lodge power stands behind them—that subtle, mysterious, Satanic force of which Revelation is full of
dim hints; that backs up every popular iniquity;
that cannot be grasped, or measured, or analyzed;
that sways politicians, controls legislatures, gags the
pulpit, persecutes the saints; and which to resist
means in short either more courage or more faith in
God than most men possess.

But matters were coming to a crisis. The dangerous, vicious element among the strikers was as wax in the hands of the leaders; and in fact Mr. Gerrish, who was a professional labor agitator, had instigated more than one riot and directed more than one assassination while engaged in that congenial field among the Molly Maguires of the coal regions.

The day the non-unionists were expected to arrive passed off quietly, though an extra force of police had been engaged in anticipation of trouble. But the following night the watchman, in his tour of inspection through the works, discovered a suspicious-looking parcel, which, on examination, was found to be an infernal machine containing enough dynamite to wreck the entire building. That the perpetrators of the act designed to destroy life as well as property there could be no doubt. Jacksonville was thrown into a fever of excitement over the diabolical attempt; the papers chronicled it in startling headlines; men and women discussed it with blanched faces; and those astute gentlemen, the detectives, hastened to the spot, made an examination of the premises, looked wise, and stated to the satisfaction of all inquisitive interviewers that they had found a clue, but did not wish at present to give further information.

Stephen Howland, with the sturdy yeoman blood in his veins that had loved justice and hated tyranny since the day it wrested Magna Charta from an unwilling king, could not but feel a keen interest in the struggle, despite his horror of such lawless methods of warfare on the part of the laborers.

"What a pity," he said to Mr. Basset, "that working men can't be made to see that when a third party with interests diametrically opposite to either, steps in between them and their employers, it must only lengthen and make more deadly this unnatural strife between labor and capital. They are robbed on three sides—by the selfishness of rich men, the ambition of designing leaders, and the grog-shop. Such is the terrible triumvirate that the American laborer has to face to-day; and if Christian people cannot force something like Christian action on our government in relation to these evils, we must expect a reign of socialism sooner or later."

"That's so," returned Mr. Basset, in his easy way of agreeing or seeming to agree with everybody he happened to be talking with that Stephen found at times secretly exasperating. He had begun to feel, without exactly knowing why, that Mr. Basset was not exactly his ideal of a reformer.

"The grog-shop is the worst of the three," he continued, thoughtfully. "The passions excited by their real or fancied wrongs it sets on fire of hell. And as for high license here in Jacksonville, it has worked just as I thought it would. It has only been a temptation to evade the law and increase the number of unlicensed saloons. Still there is nothing like seeing a thing tried to convince people, and the women are certainly doing a grand work in pushing on public sentiment in this matter."

"Oh, we never could get along without them—they are so earnest and devoted—always to the front when there's any good work going on," galiantly responded Mr. Basset. For though that gentleman had never actually given them a cent's worth of real aid, he was after all not very different from many politicians, noted and unnoted, to whom, if flattering words and promises could be made to take the place of down-right honest help, the women of the W. C. T. U. ought to be everlastingly grateful.

A few fanatics like Martin Treworthy had the hardihood to suggest that the package with its terrible contents was never placed there by the prime movers of the plot, but by men whose secret lodge oath of unquestioning obedience made them fit tools in the hands of communistic leaders to do their unpleasant or dangerous work; and unless the secret societies which hatched such conspiracies were suppressed, and that speedily, by the stern hand of law, dynamite outrages would become as frequent in America as in Europe.

"I've put in considerable money into the Union," said Nelson, "but I never put in a cent to buy dynamite with, or to clothe in soft raiment men lazy and unprincipled enough to want to live off the earnings of honest labor. It is time this thing was stopped. We are forfeiting what the laborer can least afford to lose—all public sympathy and respect. But we can't handle communists in America just as Bismarck handles them in Germany."

"Masonic Congressmen can't anyway," retorted

Martin, dryly. "It would be too much like passing sentence of hanging on a family relation. Look at the way they've done in Utah—how they've let this foul thing, polygamy, spread and spread, and why? Because the only way to stop polygamous marriages is to suppress the secret oaths of the Endowment House, and Congress would no more put its hand to a bill to do *that* than it would take a poker by the hot end. Your average politician hates to burn his fingers. And it is with dynamiters exactly as it is with Mormons, they don't dare to lay the axe at the root of the tree. Touch one secret order and the whole Masonic Grand Lodge would come tumbling down about their ears like the temple of Dagon on the Philistine lords—and they know it."

"But there is this terrible grog-shop question to be settled first," said Nelson. "I hold to taking one thing at a time."

"Just what the Anti-masons said in 1835 when the slavery question came up. And so they stopped fighting the lodge to fight slavery. And what was the result? The lodge sneaked South in the Morgan uprising, laid the egg of treason and brooded it thirty years till in '61 the full-grown viper crawled out to plant its fangs in the nation's heart. And all the while slavery kept growing more powerful, getting a stronger hold on the government, and all the business interests of the country, till it was strong enough for rebellion. Masonry stood behind it just as it stands behind the saloon now, getting up secret temperance orders to do the bidding of the Masonic

Grand Lodge—the very bulwark of the dram-shop. Dispose of this question and let some other one come up, and it will skulk behind that—and so on; and the end of it all would take a wiser man than I am to foresee."

To this speech, delivered with Martin Treworthy's usual vigor of utterance, Nelson could think of no better answering argument than this:

"Anyway, the saloon in its immediate effects is worse than the lodge. I've suffered enough from the rum curse to be sure of that. Of course I don't know anything about slavery, but I should say it was a rather worse evil than Masonry."

Martin Treworthy stopped in his walk up and down the room.

"Don't you suppose *I* know what slavery is? Look there."

He tore off his jacket, and disclosed his bare shoulders, ridged and seamed with terrible scars.

Nelson stood aghast at the sight.

"Why, Mr. Treworthy, what does that mean?"

Martin smiled grimly.

"It only means that when you was a little shaver not out of long clothes, I was finding out what slavery was. Those are the marks of a whipping that I took at the hands of slave hunters thirty years ago for refusing to tell them the hiding-place of a fugitive; and why the ruffians didn't finish off with a bullet through my brains I never could tell, unless they thought it unlikely I should ever come to after such usage."

"Terrible," said Nelson. "You suffered all this to give liberty to a fellow-being, and yet this is the first I ever knew of it. You are a strange man, Mr. Treworthy."

"I have had no call to tell of it before," said Martin, coolly, "though every single one of these scars I am prouder of than I should be of the stars of a Major General. I only want you to know that I have made about as intimate acquaintance with the devil of slavery as you have with the devil of the whisky jug, and for my part I would rather have fetters on my body than on my soul."

A momentary silence fell between them, and then Nelson said with a sigh,—

"I really believe if it weren't for Tom I would go away from here. Even hiring out on a farm would be better. I could at least sell my labor at my own price without anybody's else dictation."

And at that Martin was wise enough to be satisfied with the advantage gained, and held his peace.

*   *   *   *   *   *   *   *   *   *

Meanwhile the sagacious detectives before mentioned had unriddled their clue—a piece of paper with some writing on it dropped near the place where the dynamite had been deposited, along with other bits of circumstantial evidence needless to particularize here; and in their Solomon-like wisdom were not simply suspicious but absolutely certain that Nelson Newhall was the real perpetrator of the attempted outrage.

CHAPTER XIII.

Nelson's arrest caused much excitement in Mrs. McGowan's quiet boarding house, and fell on Martha like a thunderbolt. But if she was not exactly a heroine, she had the stuff in her of which heroines are made, and she neither wept nor fainted when Martin Treworthy told her the news, but exclaimed indignantly:

"It is all a wicked plot. His opposition to the strike has made him enemies among the workmen, and they have laid this scheme to revenge themselves on him, and turn off suspicion from the real criminal."

"But, you see Nelson has been fool enough to join a secret clan, and from *their* point of view the wretches, who actually put the dynamite in the building and perilled scores of lives, were guilty of nothing worse than 'imprudence' and have got to be 'shielded from the consequences' some way or other. Nelson has incurred their hate by opposing the strike and opposing the leaders, and he can fill up the gap as well as any other innocent man; under the circumstances maybe a little better."

"Oh, can it be that God will let Nelson suffer un-

der such a wicked accusation—so absurdly false on
its very face!" burst out Martha. Whereat Martin
Treworthy cut short his growling, and essayed to
comfort her with that kind of advice which, however
trite and commonplace it may seem, has comforted
people in trouble in all ages.

"Keep fast hold on your trust in God. Don't let
that slip. Anchor your heart right on to his promise, 'He shall bring forth thy righteousness like the
light, and thy judgment like the noonday.' That is
the best way to do now. It is all coming out right.
Why, bless you, there ain't anybody believes him
guilty. The only witness against him whose testimony amounts to anything is a worthless fellow
who would sell his soul for a drink of whisky. That
young Howland says there ain't a jury in the land
would indict him on such evidence. He'll come out
all clear from this—but—"Martin Treworthy spoke
the last words in the slow way in which he always
uttered his strange half-prophecies that were the
more impressive from the fact of their being so
often couched in Scriptural language—"the end is
not yet."

To Martha they sounded like the echo of her own
unvoiced forebodings, and struck a chill to her very
heart. But she asked no questions.

Stephen Howland had felt more than a passing interest in the young workman who had been his first
client in Jacksonville, and undertook his defence
with much ardor as a case even better suited to his
chivalrous temper than prosecuting rumsellers.

The torn fragment of paper found where the dynamite was deposited was a part of a letter with Nelson's name attached; but Stephen's quick, judicial sense saw at once that all this "circumstantial evidence" if it proved anything proved too much, as the real criminal would in all probability have covered up his tracks better; while under his sharp cross examination the miserable fellow who had been hired to perjure himself became involved in hopeless contradictions, and finally broke down at a point where he testified to having recognized Nelson on a certain occasion, the hour being late in the evening, by the light of the moon; a statement which the almanac failed to verify, as Stephen, after due examination of that important authority, quietly informed the jury.

Nothing now remained but to sum up in one brief and powerful argument all the facts in the case, which proved a conspiracy to criminate his client on the part of some members of the Union who were dissatisfied with his course in relation to the strike. The evidence was so overwhelming that Nelson was triumphantly cleared of the charge without the jury leaving their seats.

In the course of his speech Stephen incidentally remarked, "I believe fully in the right of laboring men to organize for their own better protection, but when these secret organizations become engines of intimidation and terrorism, and fetter personal liberty, they are a nuisance to the world and the greatest possible curse to labor;" and in doing so he merely expressed an opinion which he supposed would be shared as a matter of course by every good, intelligent citizen. In his own mind it really seemed like a very innocent and well-turned sentence, and decidedly apropos to the defence, but Mr. Basset, who had dropped in to hear the proceedings of the court, as soon as it was over made him aware of his mistake.

"It won't do now to condemn the secret trades unions for the rash acts of a few. It will be likely to hurt your practice if you say such things. So many Masons and Odd-fellows belong to these societies that there's a *kind* of connection, you see. And besides you are likely, unaware, to hurt the feelings of a brother, and so go contrary to that rule of charity which is such a fundamental principle with all true Odd-fellows."

It did not occur to Stephen that if he fully carried out this rule and never said or did anything that could by any possibility hurt the feelings of Masons or Odd-fellows, it would effectually prevent him from making another speech against the saloon business as long as he lived. But Mr. Basset's glorification of his favorite order upon all possible occasions had begun to slightly pall upon his taste, and it *did* strike him as an unpleasant idea that there should be any link between him and dynamiters—which he was on the point of dryly observing when he saw Martin Treworthy a little distance off, his rugged features in a glow of delight, and turned away rather abruptly to shake hands with him.

The old soldier with his odd mingling of various and seemingly opposite characters, who had fought and suffered for the cause of human liberty, in those days already as much a part of history to the generation to which Stephen belonged as Bunker Hill or Valley Forge, had made a strong impression upon his fancy on the occasion of the former trial, and he was glad of this opportunity to renew his acquaintance. But the greeting he received from the old border hero was decidedly more confusing than Mr. Basset's.

"That was good—the way you come down on these unions. God bless you, and give you the chance to hit the whole brood of secret orders a good many such raps."

Poor Stephen felt himself in an awkward dilemma, but the Howland honesty came to his rescue, and he said, while the blood rushed uncomfortably to his face, "I fear you misunderstood me, Mr. Treworthy. My remark was not intended to condemn all secret societies, or even the trades unions further than their tyrannical abuse of power. I am an Oddfellow," he added hesitatingly, "but I trust I am a good citizen for all that. I no more believe in any society which tries the dynamite argument, or restricts personal liberty, than I do in rum-selling, and should feel that it was just as much my duty to fight it."

This was decidedly an opening for Martin Treworthy, who had enough of the wisdom of the serpent not to speak his real chagrin at the unexpected revelation. He only muttered, "I might have known they would rope you in, my fine fellow;" and then, taking advantage of the unsuspecting Stephen, said:

"Well, you *have* fought the saloons like a young Jephthah, as though you'd been regularly raised to the business, but somehow we hain't got rid of the Ammonites yet."

"The fact is, Mr. Treworthy, saloon-keepers are the very hardest kind of fish to catch. In the first place all kinds of obstacles are thrown in the way of procuring evidence, and when evidence is obtained there is the difficulty of convicting. The jury fail to agree, or there is a loophole in the statute book. It is really discouraging."

"Well, I remember going on a hunt once after mail robbers," said Martin, in the slow, ruminative fashion in which he used to begin his stories of border experience. "They belonged to a gang that had kept the whole country in terror for years. They'd ride into a town with their revolvers cocked right in open day, and take whatever they wanted. Sometimes, out of sheer cussedness, they would amuse themselves by picking a quarrel with some poor fellow in one of the stores or restaurants shoot him dead, and then ride off without anybody's daring to move a finger to stop 'em no more'n as if they had the numb palsy."

"That was a pretty state of affairs," commented Stephen, whose Eastern ideas were much shocked. "I hope you caught the villains and hung them to the nearest tree."

"We rode miles and miles through the brush-wood," continued Martin, "and at last we sighted the rascals—were, in fact, nearly within pistol range, when I seen one of the fellows raise himself in his saddle, fling up his arms and then let them drop down to his side. And after that 'there was no more luck about the house' as the old song says. It was really queer what accidents happened to put us back, till finally we lost the trail altogether. I didn't understand the matter as I did afterwards. The fellow give the Masonic sign of distress; the leader of our party was a Mason himself, and worked it so as not to have them captured."

Stephen felt as if a calcium light had been flashed on sundry puzzling points encountered in his legal practice, but its chief effect just then was to give him a sense of discomfort like the light let too suddenly in on eyes that have been long bandaged. So he only said, "Aha," while Martin wound up with a moral to his tale as follows:

"They say sauce that is good for the goose is good for the gander, and if secret signs and grips are good for thieves and murderers, they are good for rumsellers; and if they are good for that kind of gentry they are good for dynamiters. Better stick a pin in there. It may come handy to refer to next time you have a liquor case to try."

And Martin Treworthy, with a curious smile on his face, strode away, and left the young attorney to recover as well as he could from the effects of "more light" than had been flashed upon his understanding by any degree of Odd-fellowship which he had yet taken.

The Union denied emphatically any knowledge of or sympathy with the dynamite plot, and there were plenty of unthinking, good people who never stopped to consider that though this might be true of the brotherhood as a body, there could easily be a wheel within a wheel—a lodge of dynamiters inside of a seemingly innocent trades union, bound together by the same secret covenant to shield "imprudent" members.

The scheme of blowing up the works and then fastening the guilt on Nelson had been planned by Mr. Gerrish as a fine piece of double revenge: first on manufacturers who had failed to appreciate his office and titles as he deemed they deserved; and secondly on the young workman, who from first to last as a recognized leader of the better element among the operatives was regarded by him much as Haman regarded Mordecai. The task of seeing it carried out by trusty underlings into whom he had talked his own atheistic and communistic ideas he handed over to Reynolds, according to his usual plan of furnishing the brains, and letting some obsequious tool do the labor. He had not counted on the egregious failure of both schemes, and when his subordinate held another secret conference with the chief, he found him in anything but an amiable mood. He stormed and swore at his unfortunate aid-de-camp, and told him that "he had managed the job like a —— ——." The concluding noun and adjective we

forbear to give, though really very just and applic-
able to their subject It had the effect, however, of
making Reynold's eye flash and his countenance red-
den, as if there was some limit to his endurance.

"That ain't hardly safe talk, let me tell you, to a
man that could have you arrested by dropping a little hint to the police."

Gerrish did not, as might have been expected,
break out into oaths and curses at this threat. He
only smiled—that tigerish smile before which Reynolds, with all his superior bulk, shrank as it is said
even lions will shrink before the hyena; and with an
almost imperceptible motion of his hand towards
the glittering dirk concealed in his bosom, he hissed
slowly between his teeth:

"Remember the penalty of a traitor."

The two glared at each other for a second, and
then Reynolds said with an uneasy laugh:

"Come, what is the use of all this? I think we
had better attend to business."

"So do I," was the laconic response of his chief.
And the worthy pair who had quarrelled before, and
knew that in all probability they would again, made
up after the fashion of their peculiar species—that
is to say, they smoked a couple of cigars together,
and indulged in considerable profanity while they
discussed the general situation of affairs. There
was no ignoring the fact that the strike was every
day growing more unpopular, and as their power
over the workmen must be in some way retained,
they came to the united conclusion that to appear in

the *role* of peacemakers, bound to have a pacific settlement of the difficulties, would be decidedly more
for their interest than to keep up the agitation.   But
when the tiger is once unchained it is not always an
easy matter to get him back into his den—a fact on
which Gerrish and Reynolds failed to count.

Comparative quiet, however, had reigned since the
discovery of the dynamite plot, owing to the refusal
of the frightened "scabs," as the strikers called
those who had taken their places, to go back to work
until there had been a thorough examination of all
the premises.   But under the calm were strange
elements of fierceness and fury.   It was the ominous quiet that precedes the cyclone.

Nelson was popular with the best class of the
workmen.   They greeted him with cheers as he
came out of the court-room, and altogether he was
considerably more of a hero after his unpleasant experience than he had been before.   The sight of
their honest faces, and the real joy which they
showed at his release, touched him.

"How I wish I could get all the workmen together
and talk a little common-sense into them.   I think I
could," he said to Martin Treworthy, who had accompanied him to his lodgings for a little conversation over the day's events.

Martin only gave a low grunt, which, if it expressed anything, expressed skepticism.   And Nelson so understood it, for he continued eagerly:

"They are under bad leaders, and they don't know
it.   Even that faction among the workmen who have

a grudge against me I do not feel like greatly blaming. They are so ignorant, and they have real wrongs. These men who claim to represent them, and don't represent them no more than wolves represent a flock of sheep, hold them in a state of the most complete vassalage. This strike has opened my eyes to a good many things, and one is that some new form of organization on a free, open democratic basis would be a great deal better for working men than these secret labor unions which afford such dangerous facilities of leadership for mere adventurers and deadbeats and blacklegs. I have been a fool, Mr. Treworthy. I dare say you enjoy the confession."

"Mightily," chuckled Martin. "I knew you'd cut your wisdom teeth after a while. But we ain't through with trouble yet. They are going to try starting up the works again to-morrow. The men have got pretty much over their scare now and can't afford to loaf round, but as the strikers can't play the dynamite game over twice, a riot will most likely be the next thing in order. Last night I happened to be going past when one of them Socialist fellows was holding forth, and I thought I would just turn to and listen a while. The chap stole a sight of his talk from Ingersoll, and forgot to put in his quotation marks every time. And he could quote the Bible, too—told them it would only be 'spoiling the Egyptians' as the Israelites did, if they should rase to their foundations a few of the fine houses of the rich, and take all they could lay their hands on.

The rabble he was talking to cheered like mad when he said that. They were just primed for a riot."

"A good part of the crowd that gather to hear such talk," said Nelson, "is supplied from a class outside of the workmen. The increasing number of no-license towns ·has brought into Jacksonville more of the saloon element than ever before. There are always plenty of that kind of fish round where there is any labor disturbance. These Socialist chaps can swill down beer by the hogshead, and bluster and rant; but that is about all they can do. Their bark is terrific, but their bite is of small account. It is these liquor saloons, these underground doggeries at every street corner that are going to play the mischief. I believe that without their inspiration Socialism, at least here in America, would be as harmless as a viper with its head cut off. But we've dethroned King Cotton and put up King Whisky, and the end will be—nobody knows what. Take foreigners, now, like many of the workmen here in Jacksonville, ignorant of the first principle of free government, self-government; take our rich capitalists, caring for nothing but to get rich faster; take these Socialist firebrands, and then add the liquor element, and we certainly have the material for riots, dynamite explosions, or everything else of a lawless nature."

And, as it happened, Nelson was just then, like all of us at times, more of a prophet than he thought.

CHAPTER XIV.

Matthew Densler, the chief proprietor of the works, had begun life himself as a common operative, had amassed his large fortune by a combination of shrewdness and diligence, and had also developed in his early struggles with adversity a temper as unbending as his own iron and steel. He had no unkindly feeling towards the class from which he had risen, but he made very little allowance for their peculiar weaknesses; in fact, he was rather inclined to look with a slight contempt on the laboring man who had not been able to do as well as he had himself. Trade unions he hated above everything else on the face of the earth, and all his stubborn powers of resistance were brought into play by the present crisis.

He made a point of visiting the works himself in person, and thus trying to infuse something of his own feeling into the new hands, who were in truth a rather cowed looking set. To have to be escorted back and forth from their work by policemen, and be subjected to a course of terrorizing and intimidation harder to bear than open violence, were not things especially inspiriting, and the majority heartily wished themselves back where they came from.

The day passed quietly, but groups of strikers had been slowly gathering on the street, and when the non-unionists left off work at night, they had to pass through a gauntlet of foes, yelling, shouting all manner of derisive epithets, and armed with stones and clubs—a few with concealed knives.

But at the very commencement of the melee, a tall figure in a workingman's garb stepped forth from one of those groups, and mounting on an empty barrel called out in a clear commanding voice, which for an instant silenced the rioters.

"Fellow workmen, I want to speak to you."

It was Nelson Newhall.

His audacious movement had taken the mob completely by surprise. A man thoroughly in earnest always possesses a strange magnetic power over others, and in that instant of astonished, startled silence, both the attacked and the attacking parties waited, curious to hear what would come next.

"I want to talk to you for five minutes as one intelligent working man may talk to another. Is it any worse for the capitalist to oppress and ill-treat you than for you to oppress and ill-treat your brother workmen? By what right do you forbid them to earn their daily bread? Is it the right of the strongest? That is the right the capitalist pleads. How long will you handle this two-edged sword? How long will you imagine that one wrong can right another? that riots and strikes and unlawful violence will ever alter cause and effect, or change your condition one iota except for the worse?

"But now I want to talk to you about the chief cause of all this trouble. Run it right down to the roots. What causes strikes? Low wages. And what causes low wages? Dull times. And what causes dull times? I will tell you in a few words. You pay away your money for beer and tobacco instead of bread. You go to the saloon, order a drink, and pay your dime over the counter. One dime paid over the counter of the two hundred and fifty thousand dramshops, licensed and unlicensed, in these United States amounts to twenty-five thousand dollars in one day. In a year it would amount to over a million and a half. This is only the price of one drink daily, remember. Multiply this by the actual number of drinks sold and the sum goes into the hundred millions. Supposing these hundred millions went to buy the things the world needs and wants, would anybody lack employment? How quick every iron and cotton and woolen mill would start up all over the country. Now when times are dull, there are always fools enough to say, 'It is all owing to over-production,' when the fact is there can't be too much to eat or to wear, or too much of anything, in short, which goes to make human beings happier or more comfortable. It is all owing to under-consumption. People get along without things they want, or with less of them, because, to put it in plain words, these two hundred and fifty thousand dramshops have taken the money. I don't deny that in our land to-day there are men who have made big fortunes by grinding the faces of the poor." Cries of "That's so," greeted Nelson at this juncture, and a voice, thickened by heavy potations of beer or something stronger, shouted out savagely, "String the rascals up to the lamp-posts." The young workman was dealing with turbulent material, but he took no notice of these interruptions except to calmly continue.

"While you are cursing capitalists, just remember that the liquor dealers and distillers whom you support by your money and your votes are capitalists too, and the amount of their united capital is over one billion of dollars. Now this vast sum invested in honest manufactures would give work at good wages to every laboring man in the United States. These are hard facts, but you won't hear them from politicians dependent on the rum vote, and you won't hear them from men who counsel murder and arson and pillage as a remedy for the wrongs of labor. Suppose the late plot to blow up the source of our daily bread here in Jacksonville had succeeded, would you have been any better off to-day? The fact is, we working men don't know where our real power lies. With one stamp of our feet we could put down this miserable dramshop business that has more to do with low wages and dull times than all other causes combined. By a system of intelligent co-operation we could make every monopolist shake in his shoes from Maine to California. By voting in our own interests instead of the interests of whisky politicians, we could make our hand felt where it needs to be felt—on the wheels of government. Instead of sending millionaires to Congress, whose first thought will be when this or that measure comes up for consideration, 'How is it going to affect my stocks or my bonds?' we could send men from our own ranks whose first thought will be, 'How is it going to affect the working classes?' Now the great iron and woolen interests are represented in Congress because they are backed up by the money power behind them, and labor, without which those interests would be valueless, ought to find full as efficient a backer in its millions of votes—thrown away every election because one half of you don't understand the intelligent use of the ballot and the other half are bound to sustain a party because some office-seeking demagogue tells you that the whole country will go to rack and ruin if you don't."

Now this speech was not exactly "made on the spur of the moment." It had been thought out in his hours of respite from toil. It had been as a fire shut up in his bones through all the long weary days of the strike, and now that he had an opportunity to let it forth, his burning, trenchant sentences came like the rush of many waters. The electric fire with which his whole being was charged even passed to a few of the more sober and thoughtful part of his audience. They began to cheer.

Nelson might have finished his speech in good order and had the satisfaction of quelling the incipient riot in its first stages, but two untoward things prevented. For in the first place scattered through the crowd of workmen were numbers of that loose, floating class of whom he had spoken to Martin Trc-worthy, and who were not at all suited by any such tame ending of affairs. They had joined the mob for the fun of seeing a riot, and a riot they meant to have. And in the second place his scathing arraignment of the saloon as the chief source of their ills was not agreeable to those of the workmen who had imbibed the theories of Socialistic speakers. They were accustomed to hearing all the blame laid on the shoulders of the manufacturers, and preferred decidedly that solution of their difficulties. Such wild and lawless elements were not to be controlled, though they might receive a momentary check by the array of statistics and argument in the young workman's speech. To the majority of the rabble it had only been, to use the words of Jeremiah, "like a very lovely song of one that hath a pleasant voice and can play well on an instrument." The novelty over, the reckless, rioting spirit again began to manifest itself.

"Come, dry up now. We've heard enough of your talk. You are the feller that's been standing up all along for these rich, lazy, lollypops of manufacturers. And that's what I think"—here followed an expression rather too emphatic for these pages, while a brickbat whizzed uncomfortably close to Nelson's head, and struck against the walls of the building behind him—"of you or any other working man who will take the part of bloated aristocrats, and go agin his own flesh and blood."

"That was a weighty but not a convincing argument," said Nelson coolly and sarcastically as he dodged the missile. "The friend who just interrupted me must take surer aim next time if he wants to shut my mouth. This wild, communistic talk may do for Europe, but God help us working men of America should we ever make assassination and dynamite the weapons of our warfare, for then hate will rise up to answer to hate, passion to passion, and I warn you the contest will be a very unequal one. Bad leaders and bad liquor do the cause of labor more harm than all the 'bloated aristocrats' in the land."

"If the rich uns mought 'ev their wine, the poor uns mought 'ev their beer," shouted out a brawny Cornish man, whose Vulcan-like strength was only to be surpassed by the ugliness of his temper when too full of his favorite dram. While another chimed in derisively:

"I'll be bound old Densler keeps plenty of the real stuff in his cellar. Maybe we'll make a visit there to-night and find out."

The mob laughed and shouted at this piece of bravado.

Nelson opened his mouth to reply. A stone struck him squarely on the jaw. The spirit of riot had once more taken possession of the crowd, and there was only time for the heartsick feeling that he was indeed a prophet without honor to rush over him in a bitter wave, before the necessity of looking out for his own personal safety became pressingly apparent. In vain the policemen used their clubs. Stones and brickbats flew promiscuously.

Nelson was agile and quick in expedients. He turned down an alley with half a dozen of the rioters at his heels, intent on giving him rough usage if they should succeed in getting their hands on him, then darted through an open doorway, the door kindly shutting to behind him and interposing a strong barricade of bolts and bars against his baffled pursuers, who hung around it for awhile like enraged wasps, and then left him alone with his deliverer, who was no other than our old friend Pat Murphy. Ever since casting his vote for the W. C. T. U. Pat had stood fairly by his newly discovered principles, considering all the temptations to do otherwise which were in his way. It must be remarked, however, that the women of the W. C. T. U. have a habit (inconvenient for liquor sellers and their political allies) of not abating a whit of their fervor and zeal when election day is over, and their lines of effort are wonderfully varied. Mrs. Judge Haviland herself had sent flowers and hot-house grapes to his daughter slowly dying of consumption, and baskets of warm clothing for the younger children; and it cannot be denied that such ministrations in the saloon-cursed homes of Jacksonville had, to illogical minds like Pat's, a peculiarly convincing power. Anyway he held "the temperance women" in high regard, and had they been veritable canonized saints could not have spoken of them on all occasions with more reverential respect.

Pat knew Nelson and liked him.

"Och, Misther Newhall, but ye're safe now. Bad luck to the murtherin' villains."

"I wish I could see Mr. Densler," said Nelson, after he had duly thanked his rescuer. "I wonder if he has left his office yet."

"The boss?"—and Pat grinned—"He come here about tin minutes ago in about as big a hurry as yerself. Ye'll foind him in that little room beyant, but och, he's cross as a bear with a sore head."

Nelson started in very natural surprise to find that his retreat was shared by his employer, but the fact was Matthew Densler enjoyed the distinction of being the best-hated manufacturer in Jacksonville. He had left his office by a back way, but when he saw that the rioters had full possession of the street he would have to traverse in order to reach his home, he concluded that it would be more prudent to seek some place of safety and wait, either till the disturbance was over, or a guard of policemen could be summoned to escort him. At present those officials had their hands full, and all that the dis-comforted manufacturer could do was to watch the progress of affairs from the cobweb-curtained win-dow of his retreat—a rough, unfinished room used for purposes of general storage.

He was, as Pat had informed Nelson, in a decid-edly bearish frame of mind, and gave only a surly nod to the latter, who now, that the excitement was over, felt both weary and heartsick. He had cast his pearls before swine. Was it strange that they should turn again and rend him? But the heart of the young workman throbbed too deeply in pity and sorrow for his misguided brethren to feel altogether sympathetic towards his irate employer.

"The mob is threatening to sack your house, Mr. Densler," he said. "They would not attempt such a thing till night, of course, and they may not attempt it at all, but I think it would be wise to set a guard over it."

Nelson received but small thanks for his information.

"A pretty pass things have got to when an honest citizen has to seek the protection of the civil authorities in his own home! But they needn't think to frighten me into giving in. No; not while my name is Matthew Densler."

Nelson had spoken his mind to the riotous workmen. Here was an excellent chance, often longed for, to speak his mind to the other side.

"Mr. Densler, I want to say a word."

"Say on," was the gruff response.

"Supposing you manufacturers all went by the Golden Rule, and treated your employes exactly as you would like to be treated yourselves, do you think there would be all this strife and violence?"

"Yes;" was the furious response. "While they have their Grand Worthy Something or other, like that Gerrish—I can't remember all the fellow's titles —to come between and stir it up. Curse their confounded impudence! The other manufacturers may give in. They'll find I am made of sterner stuff."

"I think myself," said Nelson, steadily, "that these secret labor unions are not for the good of either side, though I myself belong to one. But, Mr. Densler, if I mistake not, you yourself belong to a Board of Trade whose only object is to so control the market as to add to the already colossal fortunes of its members. While you capitalists combine together to inflate or depress prices at your own will, can you blame working men for combining too? Can you set them an example of selfishness and greed and not expect that they will follow it?"

Some men rather like a blunt presentation of the truth. Matthew Densler was one of that class. He smiled grimly.

"Go on. You are just the kind of a chap I like to hear talk, and if I had had two or three like you to treat with in the beginning of the fuss there might not have been any at all."

"I have but one thing more to say, Mr. Densler. The working man's enemy is yours. When drink steals away his brains he is ready for riots—ready to kill and burn and destroy. But you manufacturers think too much of your business, your comfort, or your convenience, to attend the caucusses and primaries, and look out for what the saloon interest is doing. If you allow it to bribe, to corrupt, to control, do not wonder when you reap the bitter fruits of your own sowing."

Matthew Densler called himself a temperance man, and in one sense this was true. He did not drink liquor himself, nor did he offer it to others, and if the mob carried out their threat of visiting his house they would have been likely to be disappointed in the contents of his cellar. But at the same time he had never taken any strong ground for prohibition. A political measure was of interest to him merely as it might injure or benefit his business. Prohibitionists and reformers generally he was a little inclined to despise—they did not know how to make money.

We take pleasure in sketching Matthew Densler's portrait thus minutely, not that he has much to do with our story, but because he represents very fairly a class of "penny-wise, pound-foolish" manufacturers who are quite too common. But this much must in justice be said of him. If he was a hard, obstinate, irrascible man, he was at least an honest one. He had the Anglo-Saxon instinct for fair play and no favor, and was not at all displeased with the young workman for this frank statement of his opinions.

"Go on," he said, with the same grim smile. "You seem to have taken it upon you to set my sins in order before me, and as it happens I haven't anything to do just now but to listen."

"Mr. Densler," said Nelson, flushing, "my remarks were not intended to have a personal bearing. I believe you are full as just as the average, but while you rich manufacturers care more for making money than for the bodies or souls of your workmen, these foreign anarchists and socialists will find a fair field among them. Not a third of the hands are concerned in this riot, but of that third beer and whisky are the leaders. If you persist in ignoring the greatest issue of the age, why, look out. The time *may* come when you will have to call for armed soldiers to defend your property instead of a few policemen."

But even as the last words left Nelson's lips an unwonted sound for the streets of Jacksonville caused them both to start. Above the roar and yells of the mob came the sharp and simultaneous report of firearms. In the melee one of the strikers had drawn his knife, seriously stabbing a policeman, and the men of law, tired of using their clubs, had at last opened fire on the rioters.

Matthew Densler was not an unfeeling man. With a pallor in his face and a shiver through his limbs he turned to Nelson.

"You've come down on me hard, but I don't think any the worse of you for it. God knows I would have given my right hand not to have this happen."

"I believe it, Mr. Densler," said Nelson, earnestly.

At that moment employer and employed had a much better understanding of each other than ever before.

The riot was soon over. The mob melted away in confusion, leaving two of their number prostrate on the pavement—one stone dead, the other breathing faintly, but shot through a vital part.

They carried him into the works, it was the nearest place, and made him as comfortable as possible for the few hours of life which remained to him.

The streets were soon quiet—abnormally quiet. Business and pleasure were alike suspended. All sorts of wild stories were flying about, rumors of wholesale incendiarism were in the air, and many of the citizens formed themselves into armed bands to patrol the streets till daybreak. Lodge-ruled and saloon-ridden Jacksonville was beginning to eat the fruit of her own doings.

Just as Nelson, seeing that the danger was over for the present, was about to leave his place of re-fuge, a summons came for him to hasten with all speed to the side of the dying man.

"His name is Schumacher," said the messenger, in response to Nelson's inquiry. "He's seemed awful restless and uneasy—'pears to have something on his mind like."

Socialist and infidel though he was, Nelson had always felt a certain liking for Schumacher as a man capable of better things, and he felt shocked and grieved.

He found him lying on his hastily improvised couch, with his eyes closed and the pallor of death upon his face; but when Nelson approached he opened them and said faintly:

"I want to see you alone."

The standers-by respected his wish and withdrew. In the presence of this soul going into eternity, even curiosity to know what he had to say to him grew dormant in Nelson's mind. The rough room, the dimly-burning lamp, which happened to be so placed that his own figure was cast in grotesque outlines on the wall, all seemed to waver and shift before him like the figures in a dream, while with straining ears he listened to the dying man, who spoke in faint but distinct whispers.

"I made that machine for blowing up the works. I didn't put it in the building. I don't know who did. But I never thought of their accusing you. On my soul I didn't."

"Let that all go," said Neson, soothingly; for on the whole he was not much surprised at the revelation. "Had you meant to injure me I should have forgiven you all the same, for I hope I am a Christian, and as it is there is nothing to forgive. It is against God and your fellow-men that you have sinned."

"But I *had* to do it. I must tell you that. We were detailed. Each one had his share in the job, and if we had refused or let on, it would have been death."

Horror-struck, Nelson listened. He had read of the Nihilists, Invincibles, and Black Hand, but always with a faint and far-off kind of interest as something that did not and never would directly concern him. Yet right here in Jacksonville there was, according to Schumacher's statement, a secret organization which, whatever might be its name, was modelled after them, both in purpose and methods of working.

"That isn't all," he added, speaking with a strange, feverish energy. "We've got our list of marked men—obstructionists, we call them. Matthew Dens-

ler is one; you are another. Last night we held a
meeting and drew lots. We don't go by our own
names, we go by numbers. The red paper with
your name on it was drawn by No. 10. I am
No. 10."

Nelson gasped for breath. He felt a horrible
sense of suffocation, and then a sudden wave, half
of pity, half of increduility, rolled away the nightmare feeling sufficiently for him to speak.

"You never would have taken my life, Schumacher. I don't—I can't believe it."

"I was bound by my oath to do it or be killed myself. That's a kind of a tight place to put a man
into. But now you must go away from Jacksonville; there's no other way. I couldn't die without
warning you. You must go—go—*quick.*"

The dying man sank back exhausted by the effort
of speaking. Nelson hastily summoned the physician and watchers. A stimulant was administered
and he partially revived, but his mind seemed to
wander. The words he uttered were not coherent,
only one several times repeated sounded like
"mother." He was back in his childhood's home
with his parents, simple, Bible-loving German Christians, who never dreamed when the old Lutheran
pastor sprinkled the baptismal drops on his infant
brow that their only son would be left to wander in
the dark mazes of infidelity.

And how did it come about? Through association with the atheistic, communistic leaders of a
secret labor union. And the same process is going

on all over our land to day; the subtle poison is being silently injected through the myriad Christ-excluding lodge worships that are paraded in the newspapers and defended by unthinking, Christian people as nothing but harmless benefit societies. Poor Schumacher had only become a convert to the universal religion of Masonry that puts the Bible, the Koran and the Vedas on the same level; and if to him Christ was only a great spiritualist medium, a mere man, of wonderful powers but perfectly to be accounted for, let not that minister or church member who offers strange fire at altars where the very mention of that Holy Name by which he is called is forbidden, cast the first stone at this bewildered and deceived workingman who simply followed out to their logical conclusions the doctrines taught in every Masonic or Odd-fellow lodge.

Suddenly he opened his eyes with a gleam of consciousness.

"It is dark," he muttered, *"dark*, DARK!"

"Do you want a minister sent for?" inquired the doctor, who thought it about the right thing to propose, though he had no great faith in ministers, being himself a believer in the same "universal religion."

But he shook his head, and his eye fell on Nelson with a look of supplication. Over that sandy foundation of negatives on which he had built his faith, or rather no faith, were fast rushing the cold waters of death—fierce, inexorable, hungry for their prey.

Nelson was a Christian man; he knew that imploring glance was directed to him.   He must say something.   Slowly and distinctly he repeated that precious text, which, while the world stands, shall be as a beacon light flashing far out over the dark sea of eternity:

"God so loved the world"—Nelson's heart was tender with his own recent practicing of the God-like grace of pity, and perhaps for that reason he threw into the familiar words, all unconsciously to himself, a deeper pathos and power—"God so loved the world that he gave his only begotten Son, that whosoever believeth in him should not perish, but have everlasting life."

Over the face of the dying stole a strange calm: whether the calm of dissolving nature or the peace which passeth all understanding, who shall say?

A moment's labored breathing, and Schumacher, infidel and socialist, lay dead.

CHAPTER XV.

A MODERN PUBLICAN.

We will now visit quieter scenes.

Fairfield is rejoicing in a flourishing Farmer's Grange, and though Israel Deming's trial of "the machine" had not been altogether satisfactory, none of the sanguinary results which Uncle Zeb's comparison had seemed to dimly predict have yet happened. As for Dora, she has found the grange precisely what she wanted and. expected—a field for new conquests over the hearts of her rustic admirers, as well as a most advantageous theater for the display of her pretty features, and all those general feminine bewitchments which ever since the Fall have beguiled the foolish Adams of our race.

Uncle Zeb sometimes slyly inquired with an inward chuckle "if the machine was working well."

"Beautifully," broke in Dora on one of these occasions, addingly saucily, "You needn't ask father. He hasn't got his mind made up yet."

Mr. Deming laughed and gave her rosy cheek a playful pinch.

"I believe a good frolic is all you young folks care about."

"We were all young ourselves once," sagaciously observed Uncle Zeb. "I remember the husking parties I used to go to when I was a boy amost as well as though the last one only happened yesterday. And I remember the hogsheads of New England rum they used to tap whenever there was a bee or a raising or anything of that kind. How the times *have* altered. It does beat all. Our minister used to preach rousing sermons on election and foreordination and the eternal sovereignty, and I re'ly think he was a good man, but he used to like his glass of toddy as well as anybody, and it's a fact now—I've known him in his parish visits to take so much at the different places he went to that when he come to go home he couldn't walk straight. Talking about that makes me think of what Deacon Wetherby told me to-day about Snyder that keeps that doggery over to the east part. He's got converted."

"You don't say so," responded Mr. Deming. "Well, well; that's good news, if it is true," he added with a little touch of doubtfulness, which perhaps he ought not to have felt, considering how many times he had read the story of Zaccheus the publican.

"Oh, there ain't a bit of doubt," briskly responded Uncle Zeb, who could gossip about anything, a conversion or a revival as soon as a marriage or a death. "Deacon Wetherby says it makes him think of Saul of Tarsus to hear him a praisin' and a prayin'. And you know he was one of the lowest kind of critters before. And sez I, 'Deacon, that shows we ain't to despair of the most miserable sinner that walks the earth. The Lord's mercy ain't straitened.' And the Deacon, he jest grasped my hand and sez he, 'Uncle Zeb, I feel like goin' around and singin' "Amazin' grace" all the time since I he'erd on't.'"

Dora had slipped away while this conversation was in progress. We must confess the truth— neither temperance nor religion were to this young damsel very attractive themes. She hated the sight and smell of rum, and as for rumsellers, they were a miserable, degraded set, and drunkards' wives and children—why, they were to be pitied of course. But as she generally ended by putting all such thoughts out of her head as soon as possible, the reader will perceive that no very great drafts were made on her sympathies. She was glad in a general way that that wretched Snyder was going to quit rumselling and lead a better life. Why couldn't everybody be good and respectable? It would be so much easier for themselves and better all round.

The deep, solemn problems of human existence, that mystery of sin and misery under whose weight creation groans and travails, she either passed over entirely or touched with the same ignorant lightness with which a butterfly might be supposed to sun its wings alit on a page of mathematical diagrams.

This modern publican was no other than Peter Snyder, who, since he was cast out from Jacksonville, had wandered through dry places seeking rest, and finding an empty shanty in a part of Fairfield where he could ply his trade without much risk of

molestation, he had taken possession thereof and set
up what was ostensibly a small grocery store, but
where the initiated could obtain at any hour of the
day or night the very vilest brand of liquor in the
market.

It is decidedly pleasant to look upon one's self as
persecuted in a good cause. Peter Snyder considered himself a martyr to the doctrine of personal
liberty, but we must confess that he showed very little of the martyr meekness. If, during his stay in
Jacksonville, he had seemed possessed of an evil
spirit to seduce and destroy, like the man in the parable, that evil spirit had returned to him since he
settled in Fairfield intensified sevenfold. He had
always sold rum for a living and he meant to sell it;
and every bothering, fanatical fool, who, as he
pathetically expressed it, "was trying to ruin a poor
man's business," he consigned in no gracious terms
to the adversary of God and men, with whom, judging
from the frequency and freedom with which he used
his name, Mr. Peter Snyder seemed to be on very
intimate terms.

But why should the candid reader utterly condemn
this poor, nineteenth-century publican for his resolution.   He had the government permit to sell liquor.
Why shouldn't he sell it? We are told in Holy
Writ that earthly governments are God's viceroys;
and if, standing in the place of Eternal Justice,
Eternal Purity, Eternal Love, they *dare* to license
that which is the cup of death to soul and body, to
put bitter for sweet and sweet for bitter, darkness

for light and light for darkness, is it strange that in the minds of the governed, especially that class who, like Mr. Peter Snyder, are not in the habit of making nice moral distinctions, there should exist some confusion of ideas. Why is it right for the nation to sell rum, and wrong for the individual? And if rumselling is right, why may not some other things be right too? It is from the class of minds thus taught to question that the socialist will always make the readiest converts to his doctrine of dagger and dynamite. Congressmen, legislators, and "all in authority" from the Chief Executive to the local magistrate, can you afford to run the fearful risk that every government must run which makes right and wrong mere rhetorical terms by licensing iniquity, and then joining as an active partner by taking to itself ninety per cent of the profit? Is it not warming in its own bosom the serpent's eggs which in time will hatch the cockatrice of anarchy and revolution?

But to return to our publican. He was low and despised. Decent and respectable society would have shuddered at the very idea of admitting him within its pale; but was there in his heart some latent seed of good, or did the prayers of his long-sainted Methodist mother come up in remembrance before God, or was it that sublime, inscrutable purpose of Jehovah to have mercy on whom he will have mercy that wrought the miracle? For while theologians dispute over the nature and laws of miracles and look askance on cases of faith healing as a superstition of weak and simple minds, the work of the supernatural goes on in the same grandly immutable fashion with which the sun shines and the rain falls and the seasons come and go and ask no leave of any theological school.

Mr. Peter Snyder had moments when his conscience was not at ease, and like the troubled sea when it cannot rest, it cast up mire and dirt. It was at these periodical seasons that he swore the loudest and declaimed most violently against "hypocrites," under which comprehensive term he meant to include in a general way everybody who made any pretensions to be better than himself. For it must be explained that Mr. Snyder decidedly resented being classed among the world's off-scourings—its pariahs and its Ishmaels. In his own opinion he was no worse than the professing Christian who, for the sake of gain, rents his property to a saloonist, or the politician who, for the sake of securing votes, caters to the saloon interest, or the public official who winks at violations of the law in his Masonic brethren; and on the whole, looking at the subject from an unprejudiced point of view, we are inclined to think him in the right.

So when it was reported that a series of revival meetings were going to be held in the neighborhood, Mr. Snyder had considerable to say on the subject, but we will not take the trouble of transcribing his remarks as the reader can easily imagine their general drift and tenor,

"They say Elder Wood is a goin' to come down

on the Masons red hot. That'll suit *you*, Snyder,"
chuckled Jack Bender, who, with several other red-
nosed and bloated specimens of humanity, was
lounging round the bar-room stove, discussing the
forthcoming meetings in that free and liberal style
with which such matters are generally argued under the inspiration of an atmosphere reeking with
oaths and tobacco smoke.

"You don't say so," responded the worthy proprietor of the establishment; and after an instant's
reflection he brought his fist down on the counter
and roared out with a tremendous oath:

"*Then I'll go to hear him.*"

Jack laughed.

"Did ye hear that, boys? Snyder is willing to go
to hear the water saint jist for the fun of hearing
him blow up the Masons. If that ain't about the
nighest to cutting off yer nose to spite yer face as
anything *I* ever hearn on."

But Mr. Snyder's resolution was not of a kind to
be shaken by a little harmless chaffing.

"I don't care if it is," he responded fiercely. "I've
said I'll go, and I *will* go. And now jist look here.
Any on ye as goes to acting off shines on the
preacher will have me agin him square. I give ye
fair warning."   .   ·

This was not altogether an idle threat, as Mr. Snyder had been in former days a pugilist of considerable local renown. Even now he was a match for
three rowdies like Jack Bender.

Good Elder Wood had no idea that the rough,

hardened-looking man who took his station close to
the platform and listened with such edifying attention was really playing the part of a protecting
angel; still less of the strange leadings through
which God was about to glorify his name by one of
those signal triumphs of redeeming grace which in
the biographies of a Bunyan or a Newton seem to
show us as by a lightning flash the unsearchable
depths in that love which passeth knowledge.

Neither was any such thought in the mind of
Peter Snyder when he went to hear this anti-rum,
anti-tobacco, anti-lodge apostle. His anger against
the Masons had burned with a steady flame ever
since they refused him admission into their "ancient
and honorable fraternity." He understood the reasons
for this refusal perfectly well. It was not because
he sold rum. It was not because he was a profane,
hardened sinner. He knew that the lodge took in
others as profane and hardened as himself; that
being a brewer, distiller, or dealer in alcoholic
liquors was never in itself a bar to membership.
But a low, illiterate, and altogether disreputable
rumseller could be no honor to the craft; and so the
lodge simply acted with a keen eye to its own credit
in thus turning upon him, as we have seen, the cold
shoulder, and treating him in the same manner, in
short, in which it treats women, fools, cripples,
negroes, minors, and old men in their dotage.

He waited with a satisfied smile on his face to
hear the elder begin on the subject of Masonry.
The most scathing exposure of lodge hypocrisy and

fraud would have been as nectar to Peter Snyder's soul.   But suddenly, with the power of a two-edged sword dividing the joints and marrow, God's truth struck him, transfixed him in an agony.   He forgot what he came to the meeting for.   He forgot everything but one terrible fact—that he was a sinner. It seemed as if he heard the very hissing of the unquenchable flames, and felt their breath in his face. He shivered, his features worked convulsively, and then with one despairing groan he fell forward in front of the preacher's stand and lay as one from whom the life had departed.

The early history of Methodism, both in England and America, abounds with instances of strong conviction inducing a kind of cataleptic state, especially in rough, uneducated natures, as if the body lay for the time a bound and helpless captive to the spirit over which it has so long held brutal domination. They belong for the most part to a religious era that has passed away, but now and then a similar combination of causes will produce a similar effect. And whether struck down by a supernatural power directly exerted, or as modern materialism would explain it, by intense excitement causing temporary paralysis of the great nerve centers, the result in Peter Snyder's case could not have been seriously altered by either conclusion.   He always averred that while lying in that strange trance he saw the Lord, and those who knew him before his conversion never felt inclined to doubt the statement.

He came to himself no longer a swearing rough,

but meek and gentle as a little child, and the first thing he did to attest the depth and genuineness of his conversion was to roll out every cask of liquor in his shanty and empty their contents into the creek which ran back of his dwelling.

He happened to be engaged in this employment when Dennis O'Sullivan, a regular *habitue* of his establishment, came to get his black demijohn filled. He gazed on the frightful waste too spellbound with horror to utter even an exclamation, till he saw him knock out the head of the last cask. Then he could contain himself no longer. He rushed forward in the vain hope of saving it from the general destruction, but already half its contents had mingled with the waters of the creek, and gone to poison the fishes. He made a maddened grab to catch some of the precious liquid, cursing himself meanwhile for bringing a demijohn instead of a dipper. But he was too late, and with a howl of rage and disappointment he turned and fled, as he honestly believed, from the presence of a lunatic, astonishing Mrs. O'Sullivan by the unheard-of phenomenon of his return home at an early hour with his demijohn unfilled, and perfectly sober.

The news of Peter Snyder's conversion spread far and wide through the region. He was as strong an Anti-mason as before, though from very different motives. His opinion of the lodge from his new standpoint he one day expressed to Deacon Weatherby, who rejoiced over this brand plucked from the burning, as only saints and angels can rejoice.

"A long time ago," said he, "I wanted to jine the Masons, and I felt dreadfully cut up because they blackballed me. Now I've he'erd some folks say that the lodge was as good as the church, but jist see the difference. Has Masonry got a word of kindness for the poor wretch that everybody despises? When he's sinking in the miry clay of his sin will it go to him and try to help lift him out? Will it show him the Lord Jesus as *I* see him a hangin' on the cross with the nails in his hands and feet, and say, 'There, poor sinner; you've hated the only One that kin save you, but there he is a dyin' that you may live.' When Masonry will do that it may call itself as good as the church, but till it does it is a swindle, a cheat, and a devil's lie."

But as Peter Snyder is to reappear again in our story, we will leave him for the present and go back to Jacksonville.

CHAPTER XVI.

DRIVEN FORTH.

"You must leave Jacksonville," said Martin Treworthy, decidedly, as he paced up and down the hermitage. "If you stay here your life won't be worth insuring."

"But Tom—what will he do without me?"

"Oh, that's settled easily enough. I can take charge of him for awhile. Tom and I are good friends."

"But it will be too much trouble for you," said Nelson, doubtfully.

"I never expected to live without trouble," answered Martin, dryly; "and anybody that does will be amazingly disappointed."

Nelson was silent a moment, doing meanwhile a good deal of painful thinking. It was to him a bitter cup to be thus driven forth to a new field of combat, and all because he had sought too faithfully the welfare of his class, and fought too bravely against the anti-Christian forces that were seeking to drag them all to one common, brutish level of the beasts that perish. And if he had voiced his own thought at that instant it would have been to utter the wail of the old Hebrew prophet, "My people are destroyed for lack of knowledge."

"Yes," he said, "I will go. And after all it is for Tom's sake."

Martha and her aunt lived in the immediate neighborhood of the riot. They had passed a troubled and anxious night, and when in the early morning there came a tap at the door, Martha hastened to open it with a premonition of coming ill. Nelson stood there, his face blackened and bruised where the rioters' missiles had struck him, and haggard with want of rest. She suppressed a slight scream, and in a few brief words he explained the situation.

"Yes, you must go," she said firmly, but with pallid lips, "for Tom's sake—and mine."

"I know I can find work of some kind somewhere else," responded Nelson, thinking how just like Martha it was to put herself last. "Tom, poor fellow, has taken it into his head that I am going off to find the farm I have talked to him so much about, and I let him keep the idea. I didn't know but it might make him happier and more contented. He will miss me sadly."

"Well," answered Martha, her bright, brave woman's nature asserting itself, "let us take a lesson in child-like trust from Tom. Between the stores on Mr. Treworthy's medicine shelf, and the dainty dishes I shall compound up to tempt his appetite, we will work wonders. But you must not stay," she added with a slight shiver. "You must go. God bless and keep you, Nelson."

And so Nelson turned his back on Jacksonville, and went forth not knowing whither he went.

He had laid Schumacher's information promptly before the mayor, but the latter had been disposed to receive it rather incredulously. Like too many aspirants to public service, he liked office but hated trouble, and so far the coveted mayorality had not brought him much of anything else. The temperance agitators would not let him alone, but kept reminding him by implication, if not in plainer terms, of his unfulfilled promises. The strike had added another element of uneasiness to his overflowing cup, and now here was a secret society of Anarchists to ferret out. It is a disagreeable necessity to have to fight one's own kith and kin. Let us pity Jacksonville's unfortunate mayor.

"This is an extraordinary statement—most extraordinary in fact," he said, as he nervously fingered his watch-chain, which was so heavily weighted with the various mystic insignia of the different secret orders to which he belonged as to be quite a marvel to the uninitiated. He was a little man, rather fussy and important, the sort who bustle about on days of processions and displays as if in their native element, but are mere nonentities, or worse, when any sudden crisis calls for energetic action. "Of course we shall look into this matter, but we can't arrest without knowing the place of meeting or the names of some of the members. I don't see as the law can do much till they actually commit some overt act and so furnish us with some kind of a clue."

Whether Schumacher would have made a fuller revelation had death delayed the stroke a moment

longer was a question that Nelson never quite answered to his own satisfaction. To know that such
an organization existed among the workmen, and
that he himself was one of the predestined victims,
filled him not so much with emotions of personal
fear as with a kind of horror in which individual
feelings had no share. No. 10 had gone before a
tribunal where all secret oaths taken in darkness and
ignorance are null and void, but it had not yet occurred to him to wonder who would take the place
of No. 10. He had been irritated by the mayor's
want of backbone on the liquor question, and as he
started for the door could not forbear giving him
this one sharp thrust.

"A simultaneous raid on all the unlicensed liquor
dens of Jacksonville would, in my opinion, discover
both the leaders and their place of meeting without
waiting for some life to be sacrificed first. It is in
these dens that this Socialist mischief is brewed.
The screens that hide one iniquity are just as convenient to hide another. I have told all I know in
regard to this matter, and now it remains for the
authorities to act—and act promptly."

Jacksonville's chief functionary was unused to
such a vigorous style of address from a common
workman, and the reader will not probably wonder
that he did not like it over much. It must be acknowledged that Nelson in his rough garb and his
stern, rebuking speech might have passed with a
very little stretch of fancy on the mayor's part for
an incarnation of all those disturbing social ques-

tions which nowadays make official pathways so dis-
agreeably thorny.

Matthew Densler read the note of warning which
Nelson contrived to dispatch to him with a face as
imperturbable as if it had been a report on the condition of the money market.   The hard-handed and
hard-headed millionaire was made of very unimpres-
sionable material, and shared to some extent that
Napoleonic belief in fate which is rather common in
men who, without much faith in the guiding hand of
a higher Power, have carved out their own destinies.
If it was his fate to die by bullet or dynamite, why,
he should, and nothing could avert it.   It was disagreeable to contemplate, but so was death in any
form.   Meanwhile, to Matthew Densler's shrewd
mind, trained to forecast chances in the financial
world to a hair's breadth, and not without considerable keenness of sight at reading the signs of the
times politically, this was a very threatening and
dangerous state of affairs.   Anarchy was in the air.
This discontent, this spirit of rebellion and revolt
everywhere meant something—something ominous,
something dread.   But he comforted himself as did
Hezekiah of old, and Louis XIV. in more modern
times, by reflecting that the social earthquake which
these things portended would not be likely to come
in his day.   And then he took ink and paper and
rapidly wrote two checks, each for a considerable
amount, and the next day sent them to the families
of the men who had been killed in the riot.

Martin Treworthy, when he heard of it, only shook

his grizzly head with the characteristic remark, "He's rung truer than most of 'em would, but there's fire under all this smoke, and its *justice*, not alms-giving, that's going to put it out."

CHAPTER XVII.

KILKENNY CATS.

As organized secrecy appeals to nearly every passion of the human heart, it is not strange that it should draw into its net fish of every kind. With Schumacher the governing idea had grown to be this: that the laboring classes were wronged, that they by no means had their rightful share in the distribution of that wealth which their hands created. And as the best wine makes the sharpest vinegar, so that constitutional hatred of oppression which might under other circumstances have made him a patriot, under the atheistic, anti-republican influence of the secret lodge system made him a conspirator. For Mr. Gerrish we cannot say as much. Born and bred in the Roman Catholic church, his rebound from its restraints had been accompanied by a fierce, unreasoning hate of all law, ecclesiastical or civil. He possessed naturally the qualities for a conspirator, the coolness, the adroitness, the mixture of boldness and craft; and under no circumstances would he have been anything else. The other members were chiefly foreigners, whose future labor millennium was a social revolution in which all property lines should be obliterated, all obstructionists destroyed, and everybody be as good as another.

Exactly how this state of affairs was to be brought about they did not know, but they had great faith in what their leaders told them, that it was going to be accomplished some way, and they were not of a class to be much troubled with any philosophic or moral doubts.

The tidings of Schumacher's revelation spread like wild fire. Jacksonville stood aghast at this discovery of a society of modern Thugs in her midst, and very reasonably; but is it possible that the good people who talked it over and exclaimed, "Awful! terrible! What *is* the world coming to!" were ignorant of the fact that a secret order comprising half a million members known as Free and Accepted Masons, scattered over the country and meeting nightly on their high places, were bound by oath to obey every summons of their leaders, and shield every brother right or wrong, under no less a penalty than throat-cutting, disembowelling, and a burial in the sea at ~~high~~ water-mark where the tide ebbs and flows once in twenty-four hours?—oaths of which that uncompromising old statesman, John Quincy Adams, once wrote that "a cannibal ought to be ashamed?" But as we happen to know that some of these good people had taken those very oaths themselves, while others had accepted without examination the witness of friends and acquaintances that "Masonry is a good thing," the theory of ignorance is not exactly tenable, and we can only find a reason for their bitter denunciations of a handful of Socialist workmen who were only putting their own Masonic principles into practice, on that broad and general ground of human inconsistency which accounts for so many strange things.

The order of the Brothers of the Red Mark was thrown into consternation. They could not be sure how much or how little was known to the authorities. But one thing was certain, Nelson Newhall was with Schumacher in his last moments, and soon after he had suddenly and quietly left Jacksonville. The warning that he was "spotted" must have come from No. 10; but death had stepped between, and all the vengeance they could wreak on the traitor was to pass a resolution, when they next met in secret conclave, consigning his memory to everlasting disgrace and infamy among all true and worthy brothers.

The meeting was a stormy and excited one—Pandemonium on a small scale. Some of the members had really shrank with horror from the plans of the organization as slowly unfolded before them, but fear of the consequences should they divulge anything, and also something of the same regard for their oath that Herod felt when he beheaded John the Baptist, had kept them quiet. But now they saw a way out. And so the brotherhood was broken up into two separate factions, one proposing to disband till a more favorable time for carrying out their peculiar scheme of social amelioration, the other denouncing all cessation of warfare as a cowardly compromise with robber capitalists and moneyed despots.

Some of these poor laborers had begun to realize in dim fashion that they had been robbed of time, wages, manhood, and self-respect; that the conspiracy against society into which they had been inveigled had only made public sentiment their enemy, and now threatened to turn against them the sword of law; and furthermore, that all this mattered very little to such leaders as Mr. Patrick Gerrish, whose chief concern at this critical juncture appeared to be concentrated on the one point of escaping himself out of the imbroglio with a whole skin. Reynolds, to do him justice, had been to a certain degree sincere in his advocacy of the laborer's rights. He had acted the part of a sycophant and a toady, but, as we have seen, not without some stormy interludes between him and his chief.

But we will give the reader for another, and, we are happy to add, the last time, a free ticket of admission into the beer saloon which was their chosen place of meeting.

"Brothers of the Red Mark," shouted No. 5, a fiery little German radical, the power of whose lungs seemed to be in inverse ratio to his size; "the tocsin of liberty shall one day resound through the length and breadth of the land, and the banners of the Social Revolution be planted on every church and public building. Let us bide our time, but keep to our motto: Down with tyrant capitalists, down with priestcraft; down with law, down with government —they are allies of both; but in secret let us agitate, organize, plan, till the time is ripe for open revolt.

All who counsel submission are traitors, and ought
to be treated as traitors."

This speech of No. 5, delivered with a foreign ac-
cent which we have not tried to reproduce, caused a
most uproarious and tumultuous scene between the
opposing factions, one side feeling themselves personally branded with this opprobrious title, the
other taunting them with its justice till fierce re-
criminations, dire threats and shaking of fists, added
to too much liquor in their brains, culminated at
last in a free fight.

The unpleasant passage between the two leaders
mentioned in a former chapter had caused a breach
which was not healed over. Reynolds feared Gerrish; Gerrish distrusted Reynolds. The latter had
outwardly acquiesced in the plan of the former for
ending the strike by arbitration, but reflection convinced even his rather obtuse mind of two facts.
While he himself had not the smallest hope of being
reinstated in his old place, and was therefore interested to have the strike continue as long as possible,
the case with the other one was widely different.
That gentleman was, as we have stated before, a
labor agitator by profession. It was his usual policy
to stay long enough in a place to stir up all the
trouble he could between workmen and their employers, but never to prolong a strike beyond the
point when it ceased to be for his personal advantage to do so.

On the whole Reynolds had some reason to feel
dissatisfied with his reward for the cat's-paw part he

had played, and in the contest he now took sides with the opposite faction and boldly accused his quondam leader with a cowardly desertion of their cause. Gerrish retorted with laconic sarcasm.

"Look out," answered Reynolds, angrily, "I can tell a story that would send you to the gallows."

Perhaps there was more swagger than real truth in this statement, but to a man conscious that his past life had been full of ugly episodes, the threat could not fail to have a disagreeable sound.

"Liar!" hissed the one.

"Traitor!" thundered the other.

And in the confusion, nobody saw just when or how, Gerrish gave Reynolds a deadly stab. He managed to stagger out into the street with a cry of murder which brought the police to the spot. They made a few arrests, which did not, however, include the principal actor in the tragedy.

At this point, very much to our relief, and doubtless to our readers, Mr. Patrick Gerrish fades from our story. At present he figures as an Irish dynamiter, a line of business for which his talents peculiarly fit him.

And so the Brotherhood gave up the ghost in a drunken brawl and was heard of no more. And as the Grand Union refused to sustain the strike any longer, the deceived and betrayed workmen were only too glad to resume work at the former prices.

Stephen Howland sent a copy of the Jacksonville *Patriot* to the old couple who were thinking of him and praying for him in that far-off village among

the New Hampshire hills, with a lengthy article in
it bearing these headlines: STARTLING REVELATIONS!
*A secret society of Ku Klux among the laborers un-
earthed by a murder in a saloon.   A manufacturer and
a young workman on the marked list.   The latter
leaves the place to save his life.*

"Jacksonville must be awfully wicked," observed
Mr. Josiah Howland, after reading it over carefully
to his wife who heard it in silence.   "I kinder wish
Stephen *could* have made up his mind to stay East.

Mrs. Phœbe, in her mother's yearning after her
first born, had often been tempted to wish the same
thing, but she always changed it to a prayer: "De-
liver him, O Lord, from the temptation that is about
him, and bring him safe into thy heavenly kingdom."   So she only answered, quietly:

"Well, I don't know, father.   If the Lord lead
him there it must be for some good purpose.   Let
us wait and see."

Mrs. Phœbe's whole life was a blessed waiting
time.   She loved, and prayed, and worked; and
when she reached the limit of the possible in human
action, she let the threads go without a careful or
anxious thought.   She had done her part.   Another
would perfect the web.

"All this agitating, and shaking, and overturning,
only seems to me like one of the signs of the end,"
she added.   "Men's hearts failing them for fear and
for looking for those things which shall come upon
the earth."

For Mrs. Phœbe, to a New England matron's

clearness of mind and keen grasp of all common, every-day subjects, added a mystical side—a delight in the mysterious, the sublime, the incomprehensible. And it was in keeping with this part of her nature that she should joy in the thought of the Second Advent, and see in all the portentous signs of the political and social heavens but the omens of His near approach who will judge the earth in righteousness, and whose coming will be with burning and fuel of fire.

"I can't see," said Mr. Josiah Howland, "why people are not more awake to the dangers of secret societies. Mason and Odd-fellow and Good Templar's lodges are fairly eating out the life of the churches. I've been seeing it this good while though I hain't said much, not perhaps as much as I ought to. We wonder there ain't no revivals, and we labor and pray, and have meetings, and try to get up an interest—only to have the lodge steal away our converts. 'If such things are done in a green tree, what shall be done in the dry?' If ministers see no harm in secret societies, why should ignorant working-men? I take it that the church must be purified first before the world will grow much better."

"'And if the salt have lost its savor, wherewith shall it be seasoned,'" softly repeated Mrs. Phœbe Howland.

CHAPTER XVIII.

NABOTH.

Despite Nelson's fears, Martin Treworthy did not find Tom a troublesome charge. He was as ready to be amused as a child, and gentle even in his rare fits of refractoriness. Sometimes he would take strange whims into his head, but they were usually of a harmless sort. Nelson had always managed him easily, and Martin, from being so much with him during his sickness, had gained an influence over him only second to his brother's.

Martha, true to her promise, allowed scarcely a day to pass without looking in upon the two, and bringing some little delicacy to tempt the invalid's rather feeble and capricious appetite.

"Mr. Treworthy," she said on one of these occasions, as she placed on the table the bowl of sage broth she had brought, and looked up into his rough, kindly face, with her clear, earnest eyes, "I have always told Nelson I would help him keep the promise he made his mother to take care of Tom—that I never would think of him as a burden, or to be ashamed of in any way, but love him and do for him as if I was his very own sister. And I am glad I can begin now."

If Martin Treworthy had spoken his exact thought

just then, it would have been to say that at last he
had seen the woman whom he deemed fit to clasp
hands as a peer and equal with her who was sleeping in her maiden beauty under the prairie roses.
But he had been trained in a school of knighthood
that was prolific in deeds by which to prove its chivalry and very sparing in words.

So he only said, as he emptied the broth into a
tin kettle and set it on the stove—competent housekeeper as he was in his small domain—

"It ain't one woman in ten thousand that would
come up to the mark like that, though I needn't tell
you of it—you know it as well as I do. But now,"
he added, answering the mute inquiry in Martha's
face, "we needn't expect to hear from Nelson yet
awhile. He won't want to write till he finds a place
and has something to write about. I don't think his
going away was a mistake. Maybe there wouldn't
be any danger now in his coming back, and maybe
there would. To my mind there's no saying about
that. Matters are quiet now, and it don't look as if
there was going to be any more trouble. But we
can't tell. He has roused a double enemy—a snake
with two heads. The saloon men don't forget what
he did last fall, and when they owe a grudge they
know how to stir up the evil passions that are in
human nature nearly as well as the lodge knows
how to plot to carry them out. He's stayed long
enough in Jacksonville—that's my opinion. The
Lord didn't make man as he did the trees and vege-
tables, to stay in one place all the time. It will do

him good to get away for awhile and enlarge his
ideas a trifle. They'll bear it. He don't know
everything yet."

At the very moment when Martin Treworthy was
pronouncing this dictum, Nelson, in a small river
town about forty miles distant, was "enlarging his
ideas" very considerably on one or two important
subjects—a process that is sometimes a disagreeable
and painful one, like cutting teeth, especially when
it involves some matter about which we have hereto-
fore obstinately refused to be enlightened.

He had not left Jacksonville without a definite
plan in his head—a plan he had thought of before,
and which only the seeming impossibility of leaving
Tom for a sufficient length of time had prevented
him from carrying into execution. The spring was
opening, the sap was beginning to stir in the trees
and patches of green to show by the wayside. He
would hire out on a farm for the summer, and make
such arrangements as would permit him to have
Tom with him. The country air and country living
would be better than doctor's drugs, or even Martin
Treworthy's treasury of roots and herbs. On the
whole he might have rather enjoyed this unexpected
opportunity to pursue a course he had so often had
in mind if it had not seemed to his brave nature too
much like a cowardly flight. But how could he
keep the promise made to his dying mother unless
he guarded the life so precious to Tom? He knew
too well the bitter hatred felt by many of the
workmen—a hatred which had its basis in igno-

rance, and as Martin Treworthy truly conjectured, had been fostered and fed in low liquor saloons whose proprietors kept the fact in remembrance that Nelson's prompt and successful proceedings against Snyder was the first shell fired into their camp, the initial step in the warfare that was now threatening their destruction.

The conversation which was having this satisfactory effect on Nelson's ideas, he was holding with a man dressed in blue jean trousers tucked into boots that were a marvel of the cordwainer's art. His hair, which was abundant though much streaked with gray, he wore long; his beard was likewise of patriarchal length, but bore marks of careful trimming. Indeed, there was about his whole dress and person a singular mixture of neatness and slovenliness, carelessness and refinement; and his speech was something on the same order, for while strongly seasoned with the rustic *patois* of the southwest, he was evidently a man who had at least the rudiments of education, and when he thought it worth the trouble could express himself in good grammatical English.

The surroundings were in keeping: the four walls of a rough cabin; a rifle, with powder, shot and gamebag stacked in one corner; a rude bed made of leaves; a table which was nothing but a board laid over a flour-barrel; a rusty stove, a teakettle, a skillet, and much unclassified rubbish, completed a picture to which Martin Treworthy's hermitage was the height of civilization.

"Come from fur away, did ye, stranger?"

"Not from outside the State," answered Nelson, indirectly.

. "Wall, ye *look* honest enough," continued the man, eying him with a scrutinizing glance, "but for all I know ye may be the biggest rogue in these parts."

"And for all *I* know you may be the captain of some robber gang who make your cabin their head-quarters," retorted Nelson, coolly. "I am not sure as it is safe for me to stand here talking with you."

The man burst into a horse laugh, evidently delighted with this prompt payment in his own coin. And then he sobered suddenly; a fierce, vindictive glitter came into his gray eyes, and a singular look overspread his whole face.

"I say, stranger, did ye ever read the story of Naboth?"

"Yes," was Nelson's answer to this abrupt and rather startling question. "Why do you ask?"

"Because there's a right smart heap of Naboths in the world," was the laconic reply.

Nelson saw he had hold of an odd character.

"I am sorry if it is so," he said, eying his interlocutor rather curiously, "for that would seem to prove that there must be a good many Ahabs in the world, and I want to think better of human nature."

"Maybe you want to think better of it than the Lord does," responded the other, shortly. "You see I'm one of the Naboths."

"That's bad," said Nelson; "but it would be a great deal worse to be on the other side."

"I reckon you are about right, stranger," said the man, giving Nelson another scrutinizing look. "Now if you'll excuse me for 'quirin', Be you a Mason?"

Nelson replied in the negative, and he went on, talking in a rapid, excited fashion.

"Then I'll tell you my story. My name is Jesse Dukes; I was born and raised in Tennessee. I come here and I bought a farm—two hundred acres of good bottom land, the best there was in the county. I paid down my money in good faith, hard cash, and then it turned out that there was something wrong about the papers. Ahab wanted my vineyard and he got it. My wife was sickly and the worry killed her. Our two boys we buried before we left Tennessee. I lost heart. I didn't care for anything. I don't now, only to come across the rascal that swindled me out of all I had in the world just once" —and he clenched his hard hand—"see if I wouldn't give him his deserts, law or no law, for he won't never get 'em any other way. I made a hard fight, and if it could only have been a fair fight—but *he* was a Mason, a high Mason, and the lawyers were Masons, and so was most of the jury and the very judge on the bench. And it was all a gone case from the start. Now you'll 'low, stranger, that must ha' come mighty hard on a man."

Nelson had heard Martin Treworthy relate such instances of Masonic justice in our courts of law, but it was another thing to stand face to face with one who had felt the iron enter into his soul, and hear him tell the tale.

"Indeed it was hard," he said. "And more than that—it was iniquitous."

Mr. Dukes went on.

"You was inquirin', stranger, if this was a no-license town. Wall, lawfully nobody kin sell a drop, but bless yer soul, what's law to a man that by jest raisin' his hands to his head and lettin' 'em drop down agin by his side *so*"—and Mr. Dukes went through a pantomimic representation of a Mason in distressed circumstances appealing to a lodge bro-ther—"kin put every constable on the wrong scent. Now I was raised among the mountains where they manufactur'd a smart lot of moonshine whisky. Nigh every one among the farmers was in the busi-ness, or else knew consider'ble about it. They had their secret oaths and grips and false names to call each other by; and they jest defied all guv'nment could do to break 'em up. Our nighest neighbor, Colonel Barker, was head of the gang, and he was Deputy United States Marshal; and of his two right-hand men, one was Moses Kittle, a deacon in the church, and the other was Marion Hawkins, circuit judge. When there was any arrests made, there was the jury made up of Masons and members of the gang, and Hawkins himself on the bench, and in course they'd be discharged."

Rejected truths have a curious faculty of bewild-ering us by their sudden reappearance in all manner of unexpected ways and places. Nelson had stub-bornly shut his eyes to the fact that there could ex-ist any such alliance offensive and defensive between

Masonry and the liquor traffic. He had said with thousands of unthinking prohibitionists, "The lodge and the dramshop are separate issues," and refused to believe that they were in reality Siamese twins. But if one could so successfully protect the other in a lonely mountain region of Tennessee, why not in Jacksonville? why not anywhere else?

Jesse Dukes was a true mountaineer. He had that spirit of retaliation and vindictiveness which has made his race famous in the history of family and border feuds; he had also their gracious instincts of hospitality as shown by the way in which he pressed Nelson to come in and share his humble fare and lodgings. The latter was much too hungry to refuse the first, which he found excellent; and too weary not to be able to put up with the latter, in spite of the utter lack of all civilized appliances; and naturally he improved the opportunity to learn more about his host.

On losing his property, Dukes had taken up the trade of a trapper and built him a rude cabin by the edge of the river, and while he attended to his traps, or smoked his pipe in his low cabin door through the long, dreamy, summer afternoons, he nursed in his heart dreams of vengeance. This modern Naboth was by no means an ideal Christian, who could forgive until seventy times seven; on the contrary he was a very good specimen of an unregenerate man. For the lodge under whose protecting shield he had been swindled out of his all he cherished that feeling of sullen, helpless wrath with which

wronged and outraged men regard institutions too
powerful for them to combat, and on which they can
only heap smothered curses.

Seated by the fire after they had eaten their
homely supper, for the evening had closed in chill
and frosty, Jesse Dukes entertained his guest with
a series of anecdotes, showing the singular majesty
of the law under Masonic rule.

"I 'member now a treasurer in a bank, a high
Mason, that spekilated with the bank's money to the
tune of thirty thousand dollars," he said, while the
dim light played over his features and threw the
corners of the cabin into deeper shadow, giving a
Rembrandt-like touch to both. "Wal, they 'rested
him and put him under bonds for trial. One o' the
bondsmen was a high Mason, too, and doggoned ef
the sneakin' varmint didn't contrive to put all his
property out of his hands, so that when the treasurer took leg-bail and run off to Canady, he didn't
hev to fork over a red cent; the rest hed to pay it
all. One on 'em it completely ruined—that was my
old neighbor, Ben Barksdill. Jist cleaned him out
of everything he hed. Ben was a stout, strong man,
but he was too far along in life to ever reckon on
scrapin' enough together to git back the home and
the farm all clear of incumbrance that hed to go under the hammer afore he could pay his part o' the
surety. Arter that happened he sorter went inter a
decline and died. The doctors called his disease by
one of their larn'd names, but they needn't tell me.
I watched with him the night he died, and I tell ye,

stranger, that man died of a broken heart. A few years afterward the treasurer come back spick and span and smilin', and the justices let him go free—never laid a finger on him. But they took up a poor boy that never had any eddication or bringin' up whatsomever, and sent him to jail for five years jist for stealin' an old watch; and it wa'n't re'ly proved agin him, nuther.

"And I 'member a case meaner nor that of a man that was treasurer for a town, and stole a right smart lot o' the town's money. He was a Mason, and what should he do but go out to the barn, git a rope and tie himself up, so's to make it appear as if it was all the work of robbers. He made up a good story, a re'l thrillin' one, fit to go intèr a novel, and some believed it and some didn't. When the case come to trial, the sheriff, right afore judge and jury, took a piece of rope and tied his own hands in exactly the same kind o' knots, and showed the court jist how easy it could be done. Now what would a been your verdict, stranger, ef you'd been sittin' on that ar jury?"

"I don't see but one conclusion, Mr. Dukes," said Nelson. "I should think no better proof could have been given that the treasurer stole the money himself and hit on this ingenious plan to evade detection. He certainly was not acquitted?"

"He sartinly was, stranger, with all that evidence right afore 'em. And I kin tell you of meaner things nor *that*. We hed some onpleasantness at a 'lection, and Dick Mosely, a sandy-haired chap that never happened to hev jined the lodge, got mixed up in the fracas, and was 'rested on the charge of flourishin' a revolver round a leetle too promiskus like. He swore he didn't hev one about him, others swore he did, and he was sent up for four years. And not long aterward a feller that *was* a Mason picked a quarrel with a man he hed a grudge aginst, whipped out his revolver and fired, jist barely missin' his head, and the court fined him ten dollars.

"And I kin tell you meaner things nor *that*," continued Jesse Dukes, taking up his climacteric refrain. "I know'd a Masonic sheriff that was sent to 'rest a man on a double charge of forgery and bigamy, but he kept puttin' it off till the raskill made tracks for Mexico. Now I want to tell ye how that same sheriff did by poor Job Muzzy. Doggoned ef it don't rile me up when I git to thinkin' on't. Job was as honest a feller as ever breathed, but he'd been unfortunit—sickness in his family, and then he wa'n't re'ly one o' the forehanded sort, he nor his pap afore. But he did one thing and another— teamed some and so managed to rub along. I come across him one morning, and he seemed oncommonly chipper. 'I'm goin' off to work at lumberin',' sez he, 'for awhile. I've jist bought a wagon, and I've mortgaged my hosses as part payment on't, and I'm kalkerlatin' to make a fresh start in the spring.' And he spoke of how he hated to leave his family, and his little gal in perticler. He was jist bound up in that child, Lil her name was, and no wonder, for she was the cutest, peartest thing; and I 'member while we stood there a talkin', her a runnin' out in her white sunbunnit and her curly hair, yaller as gold, callin' 'pappy' in her putty baby way. Job went off tellin' everybody the same straight story that he told to me, and what did that Masonic sheriff do but send a special deputy arter him to bring him back on pretense that he was goin' off to evade payin' the debt, and lodge him in jail where he lay three or four weeks without the shader of proof agin him. And that wa'n't the wust on't. While he was there in jail his little Lil took sick and died, acryin' in her last minutes for her pappy. And they sed it was enough to melt a stone to hear poor Job Muzzy take on when he come out, and found only a little grave and one of her yaller curls left him of his darlin'. I tell ye, stranger, things like them burn inter a man's heart. I ain't a Christian, nor one that's hed much schoolin', but I kin read and I kin think, and I know that in the Book they swear on in every court room there are heaps of sich texts as this: 'Woe to them that decree unrighteous decrees to turn aside the needy from judgment, and to take away the right from the poor.' And it's better than meat and drink to me to read them ar passages and think the Lord Almighty has got a day of reckoning comin'."

And the trapper's eyes kindled with a fierce, sinister gleam, as if already his imagination saw that day dawning. This rough mountaineer, sitting in his lonely cabin and pouring forth his terrible indictments of that Secret Empire which holds in its

invisible clutches the life and property of American
citizens, seemed like a confirming angel who had
suddenly started up to bear witness to the truth
which from Martin Treworthy's lips Nelson had so
often treated with that apathetic indifference which
is more than half skepticism.

It was in Jesse Dukes' cabin that he wrote his
first letter after his flight from Jacksonville, but
through some unfortunate accident it was delayed,
and Martha, in the lack of all tidings from her betrothed, began to feel an anxiety secretly shared by
Martin Treworthy, to whom Nelson was as the son
of his old age.

CHAPTER XIX.

THE GOOD SAMARITAN.

Tom's idea that Nelson had gone to buy the much talked-of farm proved at first very convenient. It kept him in a child's state of amused expectancy, but like a child his feeble mind soon grew impatient at the delay, and a deep-seated longing after the one human being who had loved and cared for him with a self-sacrificing devotion more motherly than fraternal took possession of his soul. Hour after hour he would sit gazing dully into vacancy, but there were other times, as we have before stated, when he took into his head the strangest and most unaccountable freaks; really periods of semi-derangement when his weak brain became the prey of some crazy fancy, the pursuit of which seemed to have the effect for the time being of wakening it into an abnormal activity.

There had been of late a very decided improvement, so that even Martin Treworthy, who knew so well the deceitful nature of his disease, could not believe that in spite of his apparent increase in strength he was actually failing. But after Nelson went away he began to pine—but so imperceptibly that the fact was not realized by his two friends and watchers. He would eat a few mouthfuls of Martha's carefully prepared jellies and broths, and then, with the caprice of the consumptive invalid, want no more, but he refused no medicine however nauseous, and his great, blue, vacant eyes kept fast the secret of that longing which was consuming his life's already flickering taper.

He liked and was even fond of Martin Treworthy, but he had something of the instinct which leads an animal to forsake new and strange quarters from which it misses the familiar hand that has always fed it. One thought he brooded over, but concealed with a cunning he only showed when one of these half-insane fits was on him: and that was to steal away and find Nelson.

There came a warm, almost summer-like afternoon when Martin Treworthy ventured to leave his charge, as he supposed, quietly sleeping. The south wind, the sunshine, and the scents of early spring stealing in through the half-closed door, combined to excite more than ever Tom's restless notion to wander off; and with many furtive glances to the right and left to make sure that he was not watched and followed, he opened the door still wider, and stole out with noiseless footfall and heart as exultant as the child's who sets out to run after the rainbow. The world was wide, but Nelson was somewhere in it, and if he walked on and on—poor Tom's fancy made no more allowance for possible obstacles than the minds of other dreamers—he should certainly find him.

The fever that was burning in his veins buoyed him up with a strange, fictitious strength. In half an hour he had left Jacksonville behind him, and guided by some dim, undefined instinct he took the road that lead due west and directly towards Fairfield. It seemed to him that the farm Nelson had gone to buy must lay somewhere within that circle of golden light, and so he pressed on—on with his face set towards those purple and amethyst splendors, those gates of pearl and opal behind which must lay the Paradise he sought.

When at length the road deviated to a more southerly direction, he quitted it and took a straight course across the fields. It was not easy travelling. His feet sank in the brown, ploughed earth, sharp pains came with every breath he drew, but the strange impulse was on him still. He stopped at a house where some children were playing, and inquired if they had seen Nelson. A woman came to the door, but she thought him only a crazy tramp, and his inquiry elicited merely a pitiful comment which he did not understand. He turned away and went on. The light grew paler, till but one long, golden bar remained. The night fell darkling with all its mystery of silence and shadow and starlight. Terribly weary and chilled to the bone he finally crept unnoticed into a barn whose doors stood hospitably open, and found warmth and shelter, like any other vagrant, in the hay.

It happened to be a barn on Mr. Deming's estate, to whose household we will pay another visit, while

poor Tom sleeps on, blessedly forgetful for the time
being of the wild notion that has taken possession
of his weak brain, and Martin Treworthy, in a state
bordering on distraction, has engaged the police in
an active search after the missing boy.

Mr. Israel Deming was discoursing with Uncle
Zeb on various matters: the prospect of a war in
Europe, the state of the grain market, and the peculiar disadvantages under which American farmers
labored. Dora was standing at the window looking
dreamily out to the still faintly glowing west, and
thinking—but Dora's secret dreams and visions are
her own, and though in a sense they are far more
foolish than Tom's, we will not meddle therewith.
Mrs. Deming, as usual, was not so far distant but
that she could put in her word on occasion.

"I s'pose now," remarked Uncle Zeb, "a war in
Europe would raise the price of breadstuffs and
make business livelier, but then in the long run I
don't know about it. War is a bad thing, look at it
any way you will."

"I know it will take more than a brush among the
nations on the other side of the globe to cure our
hard times," said Mr. Deming, decidedly. "It is a
rascally shame the way public affairs are managed.
Just look at it a minute. More wheat raised last
year than we know what to do with, and here are the
Indians starving on their reservations, and thousands of unemployed workmen whose families don't
know where their next meal of victuals is coming
from. The power is all slipping into the hands of

the few. We used to send brains to Congress and no money; now we send money to Congress and no brains."

Dora was sorry for anybody who had to starve. It must be dreadful, but then it was nothing that she could help. She didn't vote nor make the laws. And as for the ballot for woman, *she* had all the rights she wanted already. Why should she concern her head about politics? Such ideas we may hear daily from the lips of charming creatures who, secure in the affection of husbands and fathers, can embroider lambrequins and crazy quilts, and read the latest society novel all day long if they choose, and never a thought for that great army of sad-eyed, patient women from whom the rum traffic is draining the life-blood drop by drop, while they stand selfishly in the way to keep from the hands of their less fortunate sisters the only weapon that can redress their wrongs. So don't be too severe on our little Dora, who could be pitiful enough to any case of individual distress brought directly under her notice, but whose sensibilities distress in the gross, represented by figures—so many starving Indians, or so many victims of the dramshop—did not greatly affect.

"Arter all, farmers have the best on't when there comes a pinch," said Uncle Zeb. "Got that machine in running order yet, Mr. Deming?"

Mr. Deming had a feeling that Uncle Zeb saw through his disappointment in the grange, and was slyly laughing at him. But he did not choose to confess that the machine had not so far paid expenses. His wife was in hearing distance, and he dreaded her keen opinion much more than he did Uncle Zeb's inward chuckle.

"There's a good deal about it that I don't see the use in," he said, cautiously. "But then it suits the young people, and if it gives them a taste for the soil and a little innocent amusement besides, why, it's a good thing so far as it goes. I don't suppose it is really time yet to pass judgment on it fairly."

"Well, when is it time, Mr. Deming?" put in his spouse. "After you've got your fingers cut? And as for the young people, it is my opinion that the grange will teach them as much of farming as the Good Templars did of temperance, and not a thimbleful of either one."

Uncle Zeb chuckled in silence while Mr. Deming laughed, it being the only answer he could make under the circumstances. He had begun to find out that the grange was a rather costly machine, and could not help inwardly acknowledging that for the agricultural classes who had so little ready money, the simple and despised farmer's club had its points of advantage. But it did not occur to his mind, strangely enough, that he was himself helping on the transfer of power from the many to the few by paying away his money to a secret organization, to go in turn into the hands of unknown leaders, thus supplying the means for that very corruption and demagogism he inveighed against so bitterly. But Mr. Deming was perhaps as consistent as most men.

The limit of our vision which forbids us to see both sides of a sphere at once has its analogy and counterpart in the moral world.

To Dora there were some things about the grange which made it more attractive than Good Templarism. She liked the mixture of flowery sentimentality in the lectures; she liked to join in the harvest dance—even her mother could not object to a pleasant, social recreation not lasting more than five minutes—and she enjoyed immensely the distinction accorded her as an acknowledged beauty, of personating one of the three heathen goddesses who are the presiding geniuses of the grange. All these were among the things in which Mr. Deming "saw no use," but a young and pretty girl intent on making conquests, and a hard-headed old farmer who is chiefly interested in the management of stock and the various kinds of fertilizers, might naturally be supposed to regard such a subject from widely differ ent standpoints.

Dora happened to visit the barn early in the morning. She saw a supposed tramp asleep on the hay, and fled for the house with a wild scream that roused Tom and frightened him even more than his sudden apparition had alarmed his sister. He scrambled out of his hiding place, and when Dora had reached the shelter of the kitchen porch and turned to look once more she saw the object of her terror crossing the fields on a curious, staggering run. He must have been drinking. How lucky he hadn't set fire to the barn or done some other dreadful thing!

Dora had a mortal and certainly a very excusable horror of a drunken man.

Tom, in his feverish sleep, had dreamed of Nelson's farm. He thought they were both there together and everything was so beautiful and bright, and he was perfectly happy. Even in the shock of his waking up there still remained a shattered remnant of the beatific vision. The sun was rising full and glorious. Royally unclosed those golden gateways of the east for the monarch's triumphal passage. But above stretched a low-lying, ominous bank of slaty-colored clouds, and as he rose higher and higher they spread over him their pall-like mantle. The wind grew chill and keen and piercing, and a few drops of rain began to fall—not many, but enough to chill poor Tom to the very marrow.

He had taken once more to the high road. A passer-by eyed him curiously, but his staggering gait was against him and wakened suspicion in other minds besides Dora's that he had been drinking.

At last, unable to go further, he sank down utterly exhausted by the roadside. He seemed to have no consciousness but of such utter weariness that it seemed like a bottomless abyss in which even pain was swallowed up.

Dennis O'Sullivan, at that particular moment, was standing in the door of his shanty and calculating the chances for a rainy day, with a thought of his unfilled demijohn. The walk to Jacksonville, the nearest point at which he could procure liquor since Peter Snyder had abandoned the business, was considerably longer than he cared to take unless the cravings of appetite grew unendurable.

By way of assisting his mental conclusions he lighted his old clay pipe, apostrophizing meanwhile an aged goat which was allowed free run of the O'Sullivan mansion, and over which he unfortunately stumbled in his efforts to find a match. The animal really looked patriarchal enough with his long beard to have a certain mythological suggestiveness as if he might be some kind of household Lares.

Dennis, in his sober moments, had sufficient sense to know and acknowledge that he and his family had been better off since the day that Peter Snyder emptied his casks of rum into the creek. But he had given place to the devil of strong drink quite too long for the mere fact that he had now to go several miles instead of a few rods after it to work a thorough reformation. If the strongest advocate of moral as opposed to legal suasion would but make a practical test of his theory on Dennis O'Sullivan as he stands at this moment, a poor, ignorant Irishman, ready to sell soul and body for a glass— no, for a drop of the fiery poison that has nearly burned up will and conscience in its fierce flame, he might confess that there are cases in which it proves a broken reed, and the need of something stronger grows very imperative.

Dennis smoked away for a few moments. The clouds gathered thicker, the rain fell in larger drops, but that empty demijohn must be filled. He took it from the shelf and with hat slouched over his eyes started forth with a feeling that was partly shame, partly a fierce determination to have it or perish, and partly the involuntary impulse of the passion within him.

At the very same moment Peter Snyder was setting forth on a vastly different errand. From the moment he had surrendered himself to his divine Captor, one thought, one desire had possessed his soul—the thought, the desire that possessed Saul of Tarsus. Oh, to be allowed to do as much good as he had hitherto done evil! And so he had been led irresistibly to tell his experience wherever he could find anyone to hear it; and as this is just what the world of sinning, suffering men and women want, he had begun—not to preach exactly, in his humility he would have been the first one to disclaim a preacher's title—but to tell the story at temperance and revival meetings of how the Lord had met him, shown him Himself, granted him mercy, hardened wretch though he was, and how that same mercy must then be for everyone. Only the simple, ever-new story of One who calls not the righteous but sinners to repentance. But from Peter Snyder's lips it had a strange power, and as we have said he was often called upon to tell it in an uncultured but earnest, almost inspired fashion that sent many to weeping and praying who had never wept or prayed before.

They both took the same road. Peter Snyder had a few moments the precedence, and thus he came soonest on the prostrate form of Tom.

"Sleeping off a spree, most likely," was his first thought; as it appeared to be also of another man who rode by on horseback, then reined in his horse and rode back.

"He ought to be taken to the lockup, but we haven't a constable worth the name in Fairfield," and with this expression of contempt for Fairfield's rural police the man rode on, leaving Mr. Snyder to deal with the case as he best might, and also to some meditations on Masonic charity—for he knew the man to be a prominent Mason—that were not flattering to the much-vaunted benevolence of the order.

He bent over Tom, examined him carefully and saw at once the truth. He was in a fainting fit from exhaustion. The face he had certainly seen before. It was Nelson Newhall's feeble-minded brother, and rushing back on his mind came the memory of the wrong he had done or allowed to be done him, and the swift and righteous punishment which had been visited on his head. Mr. Snyder regarded that punishment now in a very different light, as all just and right, and not the thousandth part of what he deserved. He was about to try alone to bear the unconscious Tom to a place of shelter when Dennis O'Sullivan came up, but did not pass by, Levite like, as did the other; but stopped, his compassionate Irish heart prompting him to aid all he could.

Mr. Snyder's eye caught sight of the demijohn.

"The Lord didn't mean you should get that filled to-day, Dennis. Here is a boy that is sick; we must get him in somewhere out of the rain."

Dennis threw down his demijohn very willingly, and together they lifted up Tom and carried him to shelter. Dennis had never been quite able to get over his doubts of Mr. Snyder's sanity, but he had a feeling that he was going to do a very foolish thing which he would rue on the morrow, and it seemed even to his ignorant heart as if heaven had had pity on his weakness and stopped him from his errand to Jacksonville.

Mr. Snyder, on this subject, had no doubts whatever. He had been stopped from giving his testimony at the meeting to which he was bound. But what matter? He had now other work to do: perhaps the undoing in some measure of former evil; at least the trying to, which in the Lord's sight might count for as much.

CHAPTER XX.

It was some time before Tom recovered animation, and then he developed symptoms so serious that Dennis O'Sullivan was dispatched for a physician. This was not simply for the reason that he was close at hand; but Peter Snyder was now as earnest to be his brother's keeper as hitherto to be his destroyer, and it was with a determination to help Providence keep the demijohn empty for one day at least that he sent him on the errand, having first fortified him against his alcoholic cravings with a cup of strong coffee.

"An' shure, Mr. Snyder," said Dennis, when he was told to go for one who lived four miles away, "I moight foind ye a doctor nigher'n the Forks."

Mr. Snyder (for it is a singular proof of the power of Christianity to uplift a man socially as well as morally that even his old cronies no longer addressed him in their old, familiar fashion) glanced up from the helpless form over which he was working, chafing the cold hands and feet and applying restoratives, and hesitated an instant, but only an instant. Then he answered decidedly:

"I know you could, but I've got my reasons. If

it was a dozen miles instead of four I wouldn't have the other one."

The doctor "nigher than the Forks" happened to be one of those medical practioners with whom a free prescription of whisky seems to be the one re- source when, as not infrequently happens, their knowledge is at fault and their *materia medica* ex- hausted. Peter knew that the first thing he would be likely to do would be to order alcoholic stimu- lants in some form, and this repentant rumseller was determined by the grace of God that he would never again be even an accessory to putting the bottle to his neighbor's lips. That the doctor in question was also a Freemason may have somewhat affected his decision, but before the reader accuses Peter Snyder of unfairness and bigotry, let us present the case.

The bright and shining example of Masonic char- ity to which he had just been a witness was in itself an argument strong enough to appeal to obtuser minds than his. He had read the story of the Good Samaritan, or rather had managed to spell it out with much difficulty, but his narrow range of literary attainments did not incapacitate him from judging for himself which carried out most fully both the letter and spirit of the parable: he and Dennis.O'Sul- livan who had never enjoyed the benefit of lodge in- structions on the subject; or the man of the square and compass who could coolly turn away and leave a fellow-being lying by the roadside, exposed to the pitiless storm, with the hasty surmise that it was all that fellow-being's fault! Supposing he had been right. Were the thieves who lay in wait between Jericho and Jerusalem, and who only took a man's purse and bodily ill-treated him, half as bad as the modern thieves who lay in wait to rob and murder him soul and body, and then shield their crime under a government license? Peter Snyder thought not, and it must be acknowledged that he had both logic and Scripture truth on his side. Furthermore, the chances were ten to one that the Masonic doctor would forget to come. He had this convenient habit of forgetfulness when his patients were from a lower strata in society than he cared to attend: and sometimes—for he disproved the assertion that doctors never take their own drugs by a free use of his own alcoholic prescriptions—he was not in a condition to remember anything.

Martin Treworthy, when he heard that Tom had been found and where he was, may be pardoned if he entertained at first some disagreeable suspicions. He had not heard anything of Peter Snyder since he left Jacksonville, and the name suggested only a human spider whose custom was to catch and devour all the foolish human flies he could inveigle into his trap; though, of course, had the question been fairly put to him, "Can there be saving grace with the Eternal for such a wretch?" Martin, who held firmly to all the cardinal points of evangelical doctrine, would have answered, "Yes," most emphatically. Still, as I said before, let us forgive him if such a thing as Peter Snyder's conversion had not yet occurred to him as among the possibilities. But upon his arrival he looked in upon a scene very different from what he had imagined.

Tom lay very quiet. All his vital powers exhausted, his feeble mind, still more enfeebled by disease, was only conscious of having been terribly tired and terribly cold, and being suddenly lifted into an atmosphere of warmth and rest. There were bright, red drops on the coarse napkin with which Mr. Snyder at intervals tenderly wiped his mouth and lips, but his eyes were closed and he breathed as softly and evenly as a sleeping child. The vision of Nelson and the farm no longer danced before his bewildered brain, but in place of it had come a feeling of delicious assurance that it was all coming true by and by, only he would have to wait a little while longer.

Some have advanced the theory that in the resurrection state, a certain subtle atmosphere emanating from and enveloping us with a mantle of personal individuality as strong and unmistakable as the physical habits or the bodily features which belong to us in our mortal existence, may form the basis of spiritual recognition. And Martin Treworthy had now an experience slightly similar. This was Peter Snyder, but over him had passed a change—that miraculous making over of the entire man when a new heart and a new spirit is put within him, and a new song in his mouth, even praise to Him who hath redeemed him to God by His blood and made him in the glory and mystery of salvation a king and priest forever. Such a wonderful thing to happen to him!

There were moments when Peter Snyder stood dazed with the strangeness of it—that it should really be given to *him*—the new name and the white stone, and the ineffable blessedness of pardon, and most wonderful thing of all that he could actually begin his life over again and live an existence as different and as utterly separate from his former one as an angel's from a fiend's.

He rose hesitatingly when Martin Treworthy entered. Something of the shame of his old misdeeds clung about this new life still, like a kind of husk which would never quite drop away; and perhaps it was best that it should not, for it was a healthy shame and had its own mission to perform in making him a better man.

"I s'pose you remember me for a poor, miserable, God-forsaken critter, Mr. Treworthy," he said humbly; "but you won't see any rum bar'ls round here, nor smell any tobaccy, nor hear any swearing. I've knocked clean off from them things and I want folks to know it, and that Jesus Christ has stood by and helped me all along, and if I ain't what I was once all the praise and glory is his. I want *you* to know it special"—Peter Snyder paused an instant, and then he went on in a tone that, while still humble and even appealing, had a certain manly dignity: "Maybe you'd prefer to find this sick boy of yourn in other hands, and I can't say I blame ye for the feeling, but I found him layin' by the roadside in a dead faint, and I've done all for him I know'd how.

And if you are a Christian, and somehow I take it you are, you'll feel as the Lord does—glad to give me a chance even if I don't deserve it."

Perhaps there was a little touch of—what shall we call it?—not defiance, not resentment, but the natural feeling of a converted publican who is conscious that his former life has given his fellow-men great reason to mistrust him, and yet in whom the unspeakable "kindness and love of God our Saviour" has wakened a strange longing to be trusted.

Martin Treworthy's spiritual intuitions were quick. He had come with the feeling that he could not even bear the idea of Tom's being touched by the man to whom his present condition was in so large a degree owing, but when he realized the truth, Peter Snyder's speech did not seem a strange or impertinent one. Why should not this poor publican, if he had truly repented, be allowed to bring forth fruits meet for repentance? Why should he, as he himself put it, be grudged the chance to undo some of his evil work.

Martin Treworthy held out his hand, and the bright drops stood in his eyes.

"The Lord bless you, brother; and may he forgive me for an old Pharisee that I am."

"But," answered Peter Snyder, his coarse, uncomely features half covered with a straggling, red beard, not very dissimilar to that bestowed by old Venetian painters on his apostolic namesake, irradiated with a smile both humble and sweet, "I said nothing of the kind. I said I didn't blame ye for any feelin' ye might have, and no more I don't. It's only nateral ye should feel so."

"That don't make any difference," said Martin. "I've found that the best thing to do when the coat fits is not to get mad about it, or to make believe it don't fit, but to pray the Lord to fill us so full of grace that our souls will grow too big for wearin' on't comfortable. And now about this poor fellow here; I must take him home as soon as I can."

"But I ought to tell ye"—Peter Snyder stopped for an instant as if it was a little difficult to go on— "I've had the doctor to him. I thought it wouldn't do no hurt, and he says—but then doctors don't allus tell right—that his wandering off so, and the fatigue and exposure and everything has only brought the end nearer that wa'n't a great way off anyhow. We've done all we could, but if there's anybody that ought to be telegraphed to it had better be done right away."

By "we" Peter Snyder meant to include his wife. She was a small, pale, broken-down, slatternly woman, with little education, but womanly enough to have known times when she was thankful for the three short graves that covered all her maternal hopes. Her husband had not always been kind to her—quite the reverse—but she had adapted herself to her lot with a resignation as complete as it was hopeless; so very complete, in fact, that she did not respond readily to the most earnest and well-directed efforts on his part to lift her up to the same moral and spiritual elevation he had himself reached.

Theoretically this should not have been. She ought to have risen at once to the height of her new opportunity, but theories and facts are not always reconcilable. Will a flower, beaten to the ground by a week of hard rain, lift itself immediately on its stalk when the rain is over, and the sun comes forth to create a new world out of twinkling grassblades and shimmering leaves, and all the myriad of dimpling, flashing, wayside pools? Then why expect it of a miserable, degraded womanhood, made miserable and degraded by circumstances and associations not of her choosing? And I boldly put it to the good sisters of the W. C. T. U., if our hearts should not oftener go out in prayer for the wives of our two hundred thousand rumsellers. It is a bitter cup many of these women drink. God only knows how bitter.

Martin Treworthy felt his brain reel. Mechanically he went to Tom's side and sat down. If he was only sure where Nelson was and could dispatch a telegram! But he did not think of a more subtle telegraphy, an electric wire hidden deep in the mysteries of being, over which messages are sometimes strangely flashed to the soul, though philosophy as yet can only class it with the long list of mental and spiritual phenomena about which we may only presume to conjecture.

Tom knew him, for he smiled, stroked his hand, and said something rambling and but half coherent, of which the only intelligible words were "Nelson" and "the farm."

They watched beside him, one as tenderly as the other, all that day and the next, Martin Treworthy almost feeling his whole being dissolve as it were in the intensity of his one constant petition that Nelson might return before the flickering lamp of Tom's life went out.

*　　*　　*　　*　　*　　*　　*　　*　　*　　*

The sun was going down in a glorious sweep of golden light that reflected itself in the tranquil waters of the creek like some dual existence, half dreams and half reality, but one so like the other that the dream seems a reality and the reality seems a dream.

Tom had been restless much of the time, and now he wanted to be lifted up and look out. The window stood wide open to give more air to his exhausted lungs, but the day had been one of those unusually mild ones which have such a singular charm, as if the spring, in a fit of coquetry, was trying on some of the matronly airs of summer. The thermometer had registered 75 in the shade. A slight haze from the smoke of far-distant burning prairies gave a dreamy softness to the horizon like a thin veil drawn over glories too bright for mortal view.

What was passing through his mind, which had seemed too dull and imbecile almost to have thoughts? I think nothing beyond a general sense of calm contentment. The state of partial delirium was over, and he only remembered his strange escapade like a bad dream from which it is pleasant to wake. But suddenly his eyes brightened. He seemed to hear something unnoted by either of the watchers at his bedside. It is a sound of horse's hoofs. They are coming nearer and nearer, and he knows by some strange intuition that they will stop at the door, that the rider will fling himself off in hot haste, and that rider will be—Nelson.

It is even so. Tom is again folded in those strong arms, and the scalding tears are falling on his face, and he wonders why when he is so happy. Does there come before his weak brain the image of a Love mightier than a brother's?—of sunshine falling on green fields in some far-off blissful clime brighter than all his dreamings, where that love shall enfold him forever and all his miserable heritage of weakness, mental, moral, and physical, drop away and leave him what God and nature meant he should be; restoring to him the heritage of which he had been despoiled without hope of redress? Though our Christian faith bids us believe that to such unfortunates the deficiencies of their earthly lot will be balanced in another world, can any such consideration diminish aught of the sin and crime of depriving them of their birthright here? Do not the highest scientific authorities unite in telling us that the great majority of the feeble-minded children who fill our various asylums are made such by the intemperate habits of parents? Yet to increase the revenue, and give more power to corrupt politicians, we allow the traffic to go on! On whom shall the blame be put? Who is responsible? Christian voters, answer.

The mysterious change came over Tom's face. Nelson saw it, and it checked his sobs with an impulse of foreshadowing awe. He lay back on the pillow panting for breath, his eyes wide open and fixed on a warm, golden gleam that shot across the roughly plastered wall opposite.

"Sing," he said, wearily.

And Nelson sung the hymn which for some unexplained reason Tom had always seemed to like the best:—

> "On Jordan's stormy banks I stand
>   And cast a wishful eye,
> To Canaan's fair and happy land
>   Where my possessions lie."

Nelson had always wondered why Tom should fancy it, being perfectly certain that his understanding was not equal to any real grasping of the sentiment of the hymn; but it suddenly flashed on his mind that he had perhaps connected the words in some dim fashion with their old air castle destined to have no earthly realization.

The thought made it hard for Nelson to go on, but he would not let himself falter.

And even as his voice rang out sweet and true in the closing lines, Tom fell asleep.

*   *   *   *   *   *   *   *   *   *

"It was that night in Jesse Dukes' cabin. I had just laid down when I seemed to hear Tom's voice and started up broad awake, but everything was still, and there was nothing to be seen only the stars shining down through a chink in the logs; and I fell asleep again after awhile for I was tired. But I

couldn't get it out of my head that Tom wanted me,
and the impression, on my mind kept growing
stronger every day, for I stayed round in the neighborhood thinking I should get a letter right off, and
when none came I made up my mind to go back to
Tom, and never leave him again."

This was in substance the explanation which Nelson gave of his startling reappearance to Martin
Treworthy, who was blaming himself for a miserable
counsellor and heaping on himself many undeserved
reproaches for having urged him to leave Jacksonville at all.

"My dear old friend," said Nelson, affectionately
taking his hand, "this won't do. You counselled according to your light. It seemed best at the time
that I should go away and seek another home for
both of us. And who shall say it was not best so
long as God ordered it. I thought if I could only
put Tom where he would be *safe*, where not the
shadow of temptation could touch him! And the
Lord has done just that thing—so much better than
I could do it."

And Nelson once more bowed himself over the
unconscious dead, dimly wondering if Tom had met
their mother, and what they would say to each other
as the golden doors of the new life closed behind
them. As he stood there he was conscious of a
hand touching his arm, and a voice that said
brokenly:

"If I could give my own life in his place, and ye
could have him back again, I'd do it in a minit, but

when a man has been weaving the devil's web most all his life, undoing the threads comes hard. If ye can only forgive me for the Lord's sake for my share in bringin' this trouble on ye."

Nelson's feelings towards Peter Snyder, so far as he thought of him at all, had not been unlike Martin Treworthy's. Still, his anger against the system itself on which he felt his brother's death to be directly chargeable burned with too fierce a flame to leave much to spare in any merely personal direction. The moments in which he stood there were not simply moments of communion with his beloved dead, still less of mere indulging in his grief. He was passing through a mighty baptism in great waters, and while he shivered in their chill embrace he felt not only the divine strength that is born of sorrow but that tenderness which comes to the heart when a great grief has smitten it. So he did what six months before he could hardly have imagined himself as doing—took Peter Snyder's hand in a friendly grasp and said solemnly:

· "If the Lord has granted you forgiveness, what am I, a mortal man, that I should withhold mine."

But though Nelson forgave Peter Snyder from his heart, and himself turned comforter to Martin Treworthy, he did not choose to send any word to Dora of her brother's death. He believed, and we must acknowledge he was not far out of the way, that Dora in her new relations had so far forgotten the old as not to care to be reminded of them, and furthermore would be far more likely to be ashamed of the fact that she had an imbecile brother, than to feel any special affliction at his loss. I am afraid he felt a little hard to Dora, perhaps harder than the real facts warranted. But among other indictments of the drink system, which standing by Tom's dead form he had vowed to battle heart and soul all his life through, he might have very truthfully brought this—that it had robbed him of a sister.

Uncle Zeb, who was, as we have before said, the general news-carrier, casually mentioned the next day "that the poor crazy chap he had hearn was dead, that had been picked up over to the east part."

"It's wonderful now how that Peter Snyder is changed," he continued. "They say he took him in and sent for a doctor and cared for him like a brother o' mercy. And I wouldn't wonder if it was him that Dora saw tother morning asleep on the hay in the barn."

Dora thought very likely it was, and she wished she had not been such a goose as to be frightened at the poor fellow. But beyond vague regrets Dora's reflections on the matter did not go.

MARTHA AND NELSON.

The motive which had led Nelson to leave Jacksonville no longer existed. The recent labor troubles had driven off many of the old hands, and new ones had been taken on, so that there was practically an almost entire change of the working force. The men for the present had enough of cutthroat organizations, and it was not likely that the Order of the Red Mark would meet with a speedy resurrection.

Martha, seated at her work-table with Nelson at her side, felt almost as if the past few weeks had been an ugly dream. Only in her visions of their future home there would ever be one form missing; unless, indeed, he came as a gentle ghost whose impalpable hands should drop unseen benisons, sweetening their united lives as with perfumes of Paradise.

Nelson took up Martha's scissors and began to toy with them in rather absent fashion. He had some news to tell her. At last it came abruptly.

"Matthew Densler has offered me the foreman's place at the works, and I have accepted it."

Martha did not speak at once; her emotions at the announcement were somewhat divided. She kept on with her work but her hands trembled, for Martha had her weaknesses like other women where those she loved were concerned, and the terrible scenes of the riot were still vivid in her mind.

"I left Jacksonville," continued Nelson, with perhaps an intuitive perception of what she was thinking, "because it was more to my taste to decamp quietly for a season than to be forced to go about with a concealed dirk or revolver ready to use on my fellow-man. But as you well know, my chief thought was Tom—to get him out of the neighborhood of the saloons, and rid myself of the constant worrying fear that when he got well—I never thought there could be any other ending"—and Nelson caught his breath with a half sob—"his slumbering appetite for drink would again be awakened, and I should have a repetition of all the old misery and trouble. I remember so well how I felt the first time Tom came home to me intoxicated, and I realized the terrible truth—that there was a double curse on him. And yet it wasn't his fault, poor boy, that wretches in the semblance of men should decoy him into saloons and make him drunk for their amusement."

"Nelson," said Martha, earnestly, "try to look away from human wickedness and cruelty to the dear Lord's compassion in thus taking Tom to himself, and so mercifully restraining his appetite all through those long months of his illness, that you only remember what a sweet, loving, gentle soul he was."

"I do try to, but my heart aches so to see him back in his old place; and then the thought that I shall never minister to his comfort again, never tell him stories or sing him songs, comes surging over me like a great black wave, and leaves me feeling so sore and empty. I know it is selfish; that I ought to be glad he is safe, but it is hard."

"God knows it is," said Martha, with a sympathetic tremble in her voice.

"Most people would wonder I felt so," said Nelson bitterly. "They would say I was only rid of a burden. Little they know about it."

"Average human nature is coarse-grained," said Martha, soothingly. "We must make some allowances. You know I don't feel in that way, nor does Martin Treworthy. Dear old man! I believe you are just like a son to him."

"I dare say I shall feel differently when I get more used to not having Tom to think of and care for. But it is like ravelling out a part of my life, and I really think it is better for me, all things considered, that I should come back and take my old place at the works. I have always hated the noise and heat and grime of the shop, and naturally I have a great love for the soil, and for all the sights and sounds connected with a farm, but just now I couldn't bear them. Densler is really more just than the average of the manufacturers, and I am hoping that since his late experience he will see the reasonableness of adopting a more liberal and conciliatory policy with his workmen. And there is another thing. I don't want to forego taking a freeman's part in the next election. I think we shall have an exciting time, when every righteous vote will be needed. Martha, the prophets of our day may cry, 'peace, peace!' but there can be no peace till these great questions that are pressing to the front and clamoring for an answer are settled. And it is American working men, not millionaires, nor the scum and riffraff cast by the old world on our shores who have got to settle them. By God's grace I will be one to stand at my post and fire my ballot whenever and wherever I see a wrong to hit."

Martha dropped her work, and her eyes were full of those unshed tears that only rise in moments of solemn gladness.

"Oh, Nelson, I will help you to be strong and true! You shall never falter because I am weak. We will work together, pray together for the good time coming when Christ shall reign over our nation —and everywhere."

And was it strange that Nelson, looking into her glowing, earnest face, should feel himself elevated to the height of prophecy, though it only took the form of a familiar Scriptural quotation, at which Martha smiled and blushed, but seemed in no wise offended.

"*The heart of her husband doth safely trust in her so that he hath no need of spoil. She will do him good and not evil all the days of her life.*"

CHAPTER XXII

UNCLE ZEB TRIES A MASONIC EXPERIMENT AND MEETS WITH UNLOOKED-FOR SUCCESS.

The current of our story bears us once more to Fairfield. It is a summer day, the exact counterpart of the one on which we made our first visit to Israel Deming's farm a year ago. Nothing has altered; that is to say, there is the same aspect of careful thrift, the same abundance of creature comforts. There is only the hidden, impalpable change which goes on in all our human lives as unconsciously as the change of particles in our physical frames.

Dora has felt in the last few months the dim and hitherto unknown stirrings of her undeveloped woman's nature, and begun to vaguely realize that her free and happy estate of girlhood cannot last forever. All very salutary knowledge so far as it goes, but in Dora's case it has only gone far enough to produce a misty glamour in which neither the present nor the future assume exactly their right proportions.

Uncle Zeb and Mr. Deming are discussing matters and things with their usual freedom and familiarity, the topic of their conversation being a recent sermon preached by Elder Wood from the text, "In secret have I said nothing." Fairfield was not used to anti-secret sermons, or indeed reform sermons of any kind, and if it excited anger and hard speeches in many quarters, it gave at least a new theme for general discussion, and considered in this light was quite a god-send to Uncle Zeb, who sometimes found his stock subjects of gossip worn very threadbare.

Probably one of the very best ways of finding out the various points of view from which anything is regarded in the community at large is to hear the matter freely talked over in the domestic privacy of an average household; and for this reason we will join unseen the group in the back porch precisely at the moment that Uncle Zeb is delivering himself as follows:

"*I* like a preacher that'll keep folks awake, and that's one reason why I'm allus on hand when I hear Elder Wood is goin' to preach. He's got a master way of kinder takin' up things and flashing Gospel truth onto 'em till they look as different as night and morning. Naterally a man don't like to change his mind arter he's got it once made up, but then that don't alter right and wrong. Whatever a minister thinks he ought to say without fear or favor, let it hit as it will. That's my doctrine." .

"Why, Uncle Zeb; I thought you was a good Mason," said Mr. Deming, half jocularly.

There was the slightest perceptible shrug of Uncle Zeb's shoulders as if this might be a doubtful point.

"Maybe I am and maybe I ain't. Anyhow I know too much to give myself away as some on 'em are doing. It's real redikerlous—all this talk about rotten-egging the Elder and riding him on a rail, jest for standing up and speaking what he thinks is the truth, as if this wa'n't a free country where every man has got a right to free speech. That's what I stickle for. I stand by the Constitution and the Declaration of Independence."

And Uncle Zeb ended with a rather triumphant inflection of his voice as if conscious that he was holding a position at once patriotic and unassailable. In truth Uncle Zeb's Masonry sat as loosely on him as the liberal theology of the present day on some of its supporters; but this latitudinarianism of opinion was naturally and easily accounted for by the fact that though he had once joined the order and paid dues, nobody knew when, he had long ceased to be numbered with the membership of any particular lodge.

"I shouldn't have minded so much his hitting Masonry," said Mr. Deming; "but it seemed to me that when he included the grange, as though that wa'n't much better, it was going a little too far."

"So, ho!" chuckled Uncle Zeb. "Mustn't throw stones at *your* winders it seems. Might hit that machine inside and put some of the gearing out of kilter."

Mr. Deming mentally winced, but he remembered that for Uncle Zeb to have his joke was as fixed as any fact in nature, and he would not have cared were it not for the consciousness that he had indeed "given himself away" much more freely than he meant. A year ago he would have indorsed every

word of Elder Wood's sermon, but joining the
grange had converted this honest American farmer
into a tacit apologist for the whole secret system.
It is indeed remarkable how a very small admixture
of error in our mental lens will make us color blind.

Dora sat in unusual silence. To her the sermon
would have been an agreeable variety for its novel
subject, if for nothing else, had the preacher's attacks been confined entirely to Masonry, against
which she entertained a truly feminine prejudice;
but Elder Wood, while he looked upon the latter as
the old mother serpent, saw no reason why he should
not bring down his club of spiritual truth and logic
with stunning force on the smallest member of the
family that happened to wriggle across his path.
So the grange, with other minor orders, received
special mention as a system plainly emanating from
Masonry, with the same Christless ritual, the same
sham benevolence and morality, and the same offer
of final salvation; to all of which Dora listened without feeling any particular force in the argument.

There is nothing in the world more impervious to
religious truth than that shell of complacency in
which a young and careless soul wraps itself,
when secure in youth and health and beauty it feels
no need of anything higher, or deeper, or more satisfying; but repels every offer, every promise, every
appeal by saying as did the old Laodicean church,
"I am rich and increased with goods *and have need
of nothing.*" But when the Elder referred to the
paganism of the grange, and asked how many Chris-

tian women would willingly personate its three presiding heathen goddesses, Ceres, Pomona, and Flora,
after knowing the characters which they severally
bore, Dora began to feel a new interest, for had she
not been chosen to enact the part of Flora?
and did she not at their last meeting wear roses in
her dark hair, and roses at her bosom and belt, and
look as bewitching and sweet as if she had been a
veritable rose herself? And it came with a sudden
shock to her self-satisfaction to know that she was
personating one of the vile and shameless women of
antiquity, whose hand she would on no account have
touched had she been a character of the present
day.

Poor Dora! She was vain and foolish, yet pure
of heart and intention, and she shrank from the very
thought of any connection with impurity and shame
as from the touch of red-hot iron. She felt per-
versely inclined to be angry with the white-haired
old minister for telling these homely truths. Why
couldn't he have kept silent on that particular point?
for she felt certain that she could never again act
the part of Flora in the grange without a scathing
remembrance that would make her cheeks burn.

Mrs. Deming was setting up the heel of a stock-
ing, and necessarily occupied in counting stitches,
so that she had as yet taken no part in the conversation. But it was not because her mind was not
fully made up on the subject, for she now spoke out
decidedly:

"I believe every word of that sermon was Gospel

truth, and I wish there were more ministers like
Elder Wood. He's got the real martyr spirit in
him. Think how wonderfully that Peter Snyder
was converted under his preaching! It seemed almost as it was in the days of the apostles; and for
my part I think the warnings of such a man ought
to be regarded. It did me good to hear him say
right out what I've thought and said myself ever so
many times about Masonry's protecting the saloons,
and encouraging drinking and all that sort of thing."

Now to know that some good and noble soul
whom we have reason to look up to with reverence
thinks just as we do is certainly one of the best possible reasons for holding on to our belief that can
be adduced outside of divine inspiration; and Mrs.
Deming may be pardoned if she clicked her needles
with a conscious sense of superiority. Whether
Uncle Zeb cared enough for the institution to which
he nominally belonged to take up the cudgels in its
defence it is impossible to say, for at that moment
the appearance of a man riding by on a light sorrel
steed—in fact the identical horseman who not only
would have passed poor Tom by on the other side,
but worse even than the ancient Levite, would have
consigned him to the tender mercies of the police
and the lock-up—turned the current of the conversation into a slightly different channel.

"That Dacey now is a smart-appearing man, and I
suppose he's done a good deal in getting the grange
started. But it looks to me as though he'd got a
number of axes to grind with all them farming ma-

chines that they say he's agent for. But then," added Uncle Zeb philosophically, "the hull world is putty much like a big grindstone if you look at it in that light."

· Mr. Deming decidedly wished that these remarks had not been made in the hearing of his wife, but she had reached another intricate point in her knitting and was perhaps not paying much attention, and Uncle Zeb had such an innocent way of bringing out his inconvenient sayings that Mr. Deming in spite of his inward discomfort could not really believe that there was any malicious intent behind them.

The gentleman just now under discussion was a comparatively new comer in Fairfield, but he always dressed well, and seemed to have plenty of money, and in addition to these two prime points he was, as Uncle Zeb had expressed it, "a smart-appearing man." It was generally understood that he held certain agricultural patents in trust for interested parties, and there were some in Fairfield who, like Uncle Zeb, thought his activity in organizing the grange sufficiently accounted for by this latter fact. He was good-looking, and a fluent, entertaining talker, and nothing being positively known against him, Fairfield society generally pronounced him "charming." It is true there were a few prejudiced people who ventured to disagree with the popular verdict; who saw something sinister, even sharp, low and cunning, under his bland smile and undeniable good looks. But of this class was not the open-

hearted, choleric, unsuspicious Mr. Deming; nor
Dora, who was rather weary of her boyish admirers,
and having made Mr. Dacey's acquaintance at the
grange meetings had begun by thinking what an
agreeable contrast a mature man of forty, who had
traveled about and seen the world, presented to cal-
low youths of eighteen and twenty, who seemed to
know as little what to talk about as what to do with
their feet and hands; and she ended by thinking a
great deal more about him than was prudent.

Dora had an intuition that her mother would disapprove of any such match, and possibly her father
too; and she never meant to marry without their
consent, but what was the harm in such a very pleasant acquaintanceship that would never be likely to
go any farther? The moths who hover about candles are not always of the masculine persuasion.
Dora had not the smallest intention of singeing her
pretty wings. That was a thing that never occurred
to her in all her dreamings, but why did his next remark make her feel for the first time in her life inclined to be angry with kind old Uncle Zeb?

"Dacey looks some like a man I used to know in
Ohio. He come from some Eastern State, Connecti-
cut I think it was, and set up store. And he was
jest a going to marry one of the finest gals in the
neighborhood when who should come onto the scene
but his wife with two of her children! He'd spent
all her property and then run off and left her."

"He ought to have been hung," said Mrs. Deming,
rattling her needles with quick emphasis.

"So I say," echoed Israel Deming. "Such men ought not to be above ground."

"Fix it any way you've a mind to there'll allus be rogues jest as there'll allus be grasshoppers and weevils and potato-bugs," replied Uncle Zeb, sagely.

"There wouldn't be so many rogues if Masonry could be put down," said Mrs. Deming. "It stands to reason. Talk about there being good men in the lodge! So there is, but you put a dozen fools and one knave together, and I'll warrant that the knave will manage the fools."

"Well, I hain't been nigh the Masons for twenty years," said Uncle Zeb, when he had got through shaking with his little inward laugh. "I expect there's been changes since then."

"When I was a girl," said Mrs. Deming, "I used to hear them tell about raising the devil in the lodge and wonder how it was done. I don't believe that has all gone by yet."

"I've seen it done lots of times," returned Uncle Zeb, boldly. "They'd have to rap on the ceilin' and say over something in Latin, and then he'd come stalking through the room, hoofs and horns and all, lookin' as if he'd jest stepped out of one of the pic-ters in Pilgrim's Progress."

"Uncle Zeb, what do you mean by telling such yarns!" exclaimed Mrs. Deming, slightly scandalized. But Dora, who saw only an avenue for her youthful spirit of fun, sprang up from her seat and said in her prettiest and most coaxing fashion, "Oh, Uncle Zeb, show me how they did it. Now do, please."

It was in vain that he tried to parry this startling proposal with the plea that it was so long ago he had forgotten the precise form of incantation necessary to use.

Dora, in her young, bright wilfulness, was not easily turned off from the idea, and with his usual readiness to enter into a jest, Uncle Zeb finally consented. Mrs. Deming indeed rather disapproved of any such trifling with the invisible powers of evil, but the force of her protest was rather marred by her previous skepticism, and so amounted to little.

"I guess I'll try it out in that ere back room," said Uncle Zeb; "but there must only be we two. More might break the spell."

In great glee Dora led the way to an unfinished apartment where the rough work of the family was generally done. There was a good-sized loft above and an open stairway leading to it, while doors at either end opened—one on the barnyard, where Dora's favorite bantams cocked expectant eyes and waited for her to throw them their customary feed of corn; the other commanding a splendid outlook over a field of billowy wheat, which, as it met without a break the blue line of the horizon, gave that sealike sense of measureless distance which is so restful to earth-weary souls—like a thought of eternity.

Uncle Zeb began to knock with his cane in various places on the walls, muttering meanwhile a peculiar and self-invented lingo. It is needless to state that he had not the smallest idea of raising anything except echoes, but magicians, ever since the Witch of Endor's day, have sometimes done better than they expected, and Uncle Zeb was suddenly startled by an answering thump and clatter overhead, while to his horrified vision something that owned unmistakable hoofs and horns shot down the stairs and past him out at the door. We are sorry to be obliged to record it of Uncle Zeb, but he was a sad coward, and such unlooked-for success in his experiment put him to precipitate flight, followed by peals of convulsive laughter from Dora, who, when the first instant of half-petrified amazement was over, saw through the whole mystery.

"Why, mother, it was only the O'Sullivan goat," she explained between her bursts of merriment, as Mrs. Deming made her appearance with Mr. Deming close behind, just in time to be a witness to the denoument. "You know the Van Eycks who lived here before we did owned him first, and he has never forgotten his old quarters."

"I declare, wife, if that ain't the best joke I ever heard of. Uncle Zeb really thought he had raised the old Nick himself." And Mr. Deming also exploded in a fit of uncontrollable laughter joined in heartily by his spouse, while the unfortunate magician finally ventured back looking rather foolish.

"This is the fust time I ever tried a Masonic experiment, and I guess it will be my last. But Marthy Washington! I reckon it won't be the last I shall hear on't."

Uncle Zeb was correct.

CHAPTER XXIII.

A PECULIAR KIND OF MORALITY AND BENEVOLENCE.

We do not see how we can better apologize for the undignified ending of our last chapter than to give the reader a glance into the law office of Stephen Howland, whom we have neglected of late, while pursuing the fortunes of the other characters in our story. He set out in his profession as the reader knows with a very high aim, and all things considered, he has kept to that aim with commendable resolution. When a young, ardent soul throws itself with all the earnestness of its nature into the battle against an organized and powerful wrong, it receives as it were in the very act a kind of invisible guard and shield. This does not always prevent the man, as proved by one or two melancholy instances in our political history, from being captured by an ignoble self-interest, and made to grind in the prison-house of the very foes he once fought—a blind and shorn Sampson, an Ichabod from whom the glory has forever departed.

It is too early yet to reckon on Stephen Howland's future with perfect certitude, but for our part we have a great deal of faith in the prayers of that simple, hill-country couple—even more than we have

in his Puritan birth and training, powerful factors
though they are. And at the same time Stephen, in
spite of all these helping forces, visible and invisible, stands in a place where he needs all the support they can give him. We are told of lying spirits
going forth to bewilder and deceive, and there is
certainly one in our own day which has been even
known to air its falsehoods and blasphemies in
Christian pulpits; a spirit that substitutes mystery
for truth, shadow for substance; that strikes at the
heart of faith with the concealed dagger of a disguised infidelity; and would smirch the white robes
of the Bride of Christ herself in the vain attempt to
whitewash its own garments.

This spirit Stephen Howland is now confronting,
and it speaks from the lips of Mr. Felix Basset.

"We've missed you at the lodge meetings lately,"
began Mr. Basset with his easy, cordial smile, "and
last night especially. We had an installation, and
there were a good many visitors from neighboring
lodges—some notable ones. So it was really quite an
occasion, and if I had had a doubt of your being there
I should have called round. This lack of interest
among members hurts Odd-fellowship more than the
attacks of all the anti-secret fanatics. Now I was
looking over the reports of the Grand Lodge the
other day, and I find we are really losing ground in
spite of large accessions—so many members drop
away after the first year and neither attend nor keep
up their dues."

Stephen's eyes were by no means fully opened to

the evils of secrecy, but he had begun to feel a natural disgust for the reiterated mummeries of the
lodge room.   The principles taught might be all
right—might even be as Mr. Basset had so many
times averred, a perfect religious system, able in the
absence of any other guide to lead its devotees
straight to heaven; but Stephen had a strong dislike
to farce, and an equally strong dislike for inconsistency.   The Odd-fellow ritual, especially the coffin
scene, had not in the beginning recommended itself
to his common sense or his good taste; and worse
than that he had reason to fear that there existed a
deplorable laxity in practice among many of the
members of this "moral" order.   He had fully
meant at some convenient season to have a serious
talk with Mr. Basset, in the hope that these unpleasant doubts and suspicions might thereby be laid to
rest, and the present occasion seemed favorable.   So
he began, rather hurriedly and with a half wish that
the talk was safely over, for between his desire
neither to offend Mr. Basset nor compromise the
truth he was not likely to find very smooth sailing.

"I have been pretty busy of late with one or two
important cases, and the installation quite slipped
from my mind last night.   But now we are on the
subject, I must say that I have lately learned facts .
which have both surprised and pained me.   I find
there are quite a number in our lodge who are in
one way or another connected with the liquor business.   I am trying, as you know, to serve faithfully
the temperance people of this city who have done

me the honor, though young and unknown, of making me their special attorney. And it is embarrassing to feel that I am joined by lodge vows with men
who have a personal intérest in supporting the
traffic. I can well see how cases may, and no doubt
will, arise in which I shall have to act against a brother Odd-fellow or stultify my conscience: and I
have been seriously considering whether it would
not be better on the whole to procure a demit and
withdraw from the lodge entirely. I have nothing
against the order personally, and I know there are
good prohibitionists in it. But that has nothing to
do with the difficulty, for it is not with those that
my business as temperance attorney will be likely
to bring me into collision. Why, I know from un-
disputed authority that the saloon property which
pays the heaviest tax in Jacksonville is owned by
an Odd-fellow, a prominent member of our lodge."

"Oh, if you come to that," answered Mr. Basset,
whose countenance, after the first start of surprise,
settled back into its usual agreeable smile, "no social or even religious organization was ever perfect.
Look at the church! I can point out to you members in good standing who do that very thing. I
could count you off a dozen, to say the least, good
Methodists and Presbyterians, who rent their property to saloon-keepers. I don't excuse such inconsistency of course, but the lodge is really no worse
than the church when it comes to the point."

Stephen was silent. At heart he felt a thrill of
indignation, as if he had heard some courtesan with

painted cheeks compared to his mother. If it were
so; if he had been deceived all along in both; if one
were as good, or, to borrow Mr. Basset's expression,
no worse than the other, what better thing remained
for a man than to fall back on pantheism, positive-
ism, or even a refined paganism, and drift into the
unknown abyss with the motto of the old grovelling
heathen world of St. Paul's day on his lips, "Let us
eat and drink, for to-morrow we die." Not that
Stephen was really conscious of having any such
thought; he would have repudiated it at once had it
presented itself in honest fashion. He would have
said, "There *is* something better;" and clung to his
old faith with the tenacity of a soul that fears ship-
wreck. But the *unconscious* infidelity which is like
the microscopic germs that diffuse invisible poison
in the air we breathe and the water we drink, I know
of nothing that will guard against that but such a
baptism of the Holy Spirit as shall consume these
spiritual sporadic germs in its swift, down-rushing
fires that take the whole life for a sacrifice and the
whole heart for an altar. And it was just this that
Stephen lacked.

He was aware that what Mr. Basset had said was
sadly, unmistakably true. The churches in Jacksonville seemed to be engaged in a pretty even race
with the world, which begat the natural fruits: un-
seemly rivalries with each other, and spiritual deadness. They had oyster suppers, and fairs, and fes-
tivals, and entertainments of every description; and
now and then there was a spasmodic effort to "get

up a revival;" as useless, and perhaps to heavenly
eyes as painful and hideous as the attempt to gal-
vanize a corpse into seeming life. Was it strange
that this modern Sardis allowed to stand unquestioned on her membership roll the names of those
who "took the price of blood and the wages of iniquity?" or that there were even whispered reports
of scandalous sin on the part of some of her prominent professors? But why did it not occur to
Stephen, as a curious coincidence, to say the least,
that every professed Christian whom Mr. Basset
vauntingly pointed out as in complicity with the
liquor traffic was either a Mason or an Odd-fellow?
Why did he not think that union with unbelievers
who practiced secret works of darkness might be
just as disastrous to the purity of the church now
as in early times when such "unequal yoking" was
so strictly forbidden?

But Stephen, as we have said, was silent. His
silence, however, made no difference with Mr. Basset, who talked on.

"Now just think of all the benevolent work that
is being done by the order. I don't mean to say
anything to run down other organizations, but for
pure charity commend me to Odd-fellowship. Over
two million dollars was paid out for relief last year
—you can see it for yourself in the printed reports,
I believe I've got one in my pocket now. When
anybody says anything against Odd-fellowship,
there's a plump knock-down argument for 'em. I
just turn round and say, 'Why don't the churches do

this work?' and that generally shuts them up. Just picture to yourself how many widows and orphans have been made glad; how many desolate homes have been cheered; in short, what a munificent work of love and good-will has been accomplished by the judicious distribution of this immense sum! Whatever else we do, my dear young friend, don't let us circumscribe our charities. 'He that giveth to the poor lendeth unto the Lord.' "

Stephen colored. He was naturally generous and open-handed, and he could not bear the tacit imputation of meanness in his motives for leaving the lodge. But he only reached up to one of the pigeon-holes where he kept his papers, and drew out a letter.

"What you say, Mr. Basset, reminds me of a letter that I received to-day from the widow of a certain Jacob Strycker, a lately deceased member of our lodge. I should like to show it to you as it refers to an important matter that I think ought to be set right immediately."

"Jacob Strycker?—let me see," said Mr. Basset. "Oh, I remember now. Mr. Strycker died at Ft. Wayne, slightly in debt to the lodge at the time. That circumstance, you know, cancels all claim to a benefit."

"But hear what Mrs. Strycker says:—'I write to you, Mr. Howland, because you are a lawyer and know about such things. The lodge in Jacksonville to which my husband belonged, and of which I understand you are a member, has refused to give me the customary benefit on the ground that his dues were unpaid at the time of his death. This is not so. He mailed five dollars from Ft. Wayne the day before he died, which was received and credited, and left a small balance in his favor. I know my husband believed that I would be provided for. Will you please look into this matter, and see that justice is done to a poor widow and her fatherless children, though she can only pay you with her blessing and her prayers. LYDIA STRYCKER.'"

"Of course there must be some misunderstanding," remarked Stephen, as he folded the letter. "No lodge in the land, I hope, would take such mean and dishonest advantage of a mere technicality, as Mr. Strycker's money was of course on the road at the time of his death."

"Well, now, that don't seem right, does it? She has written a very touching letter. I declare, I am really very sorry for her. But then as a sensible woman she ought to understand that there can't be any rule devised that will not sometimes and in some cases bear hard. The rule of Odd-fellowship is, 'Pay in advance,' and of course there will always be some compelled by misfortune to violate it. In that case all they pay in is forfeited, but they enter with that understanding, so it is really all fair enough when one comes to look at it—only, as I said before, it comes hard in particular cases."

"But Mr. Strycker kept up his dues," interrupted Stephen, impatiently. "Lawfully that money belonged to the lodge as soon as it left his hands."

"Well, I think it would have been better to have stretched the point and handed over the benefit; decidedly I do. Such things give a handle to the anti-secret party if they leak out, and they are sure to. We might pass round a subscription paper for Mrs. Strycker. I don't doubt but you could collect a handsome sum from the members of our lodge by going privately to them and stating the unfortunate features of the case. I would be willing myself to put down five dollars."

"No," said Stephen, rather hotly. "Mrs. Strycker has not asked for charity but justice, and justice she shall have. There shall be an appeal made to the Grand Lodge."

Mr. Basset drummed lightly with his cane on the floor and—a rather strange thing for him—did not immediately reply. Clearly the young lawyer was not made of the most manageable material in the world, and would have to be dealt with carefully, or in other words, dosed liberally with that commodity vulgarly known as "soft soap," which, by the way, as the reader has doubtless perceived, Mr. Basset had a native gift for administering. He had no intention of letting so valuable a member as Stephen Howland slip out of the order. And here comes in the natural inquiry, what made him valuable? and why should Mr. Basset be so specially anxious to retain him?

The former of these two questions is very easily answered. Stephen, as a young and rising temperance lawyer, could give the lodge a moral prestige that would offset any number of Van Gilders. What could more effectually shut the mouth of anybody disposed to carp at the convivial origin of Odd-fellowship, or to intimate that while intoxicating liquors might be forbidden in the lodge room, it still kept up the traditions of its birthplace in an English ale-house by gathering in saloons after the meetings adjourned, or circulating pocket flasks privately in committee rooms to an accompaniment of tobacco smoke, vulgar stories and coarse jokes, than to point to Stephen Howland, attorney for the Law and Order League, as a member in good and regular standing? As acceptable material for the lodge, he ranked nearly equal in point of fact to a popular clergyman.

The second reason is not so easily given. Mr. Basset's love for Odd-fellowship proceeded from mixed motives that could be resolved into unmixed selfishness by a little close analysis. He had an ease-loving nature, and preferred, so to speak, a self-adjustable religion that would fit every phase of worldly requirement; that would have an elastic adaptation to anything doubtful in belief or dubious in practice; in short, something totally different from the tight-fitting Bible code which would expose his moral and spiritual infirmities by conscious twinges as a tight shoe discovers a bunion. This he found in Odd-fellowship. It made no difference that he was nominally a professor of the Christian religion. He could wear the livery of both; and perhaps in the great day of account it will be found that at least a part of the guilt of such hypocrisy must be laid at the doors of those churches that allow this double profession, and thus in effect put the Christless paganism of the lodge on a level with the soul-saving doctrines of the cross. He never consciously avowed to himself that he looked upon Odd-fellowship as a possible covert in case of criminal "imprudence," for he hoped on the contrary never to forfeit what he was very fond of—the good opinion of his fellow-men, by any outward act that would condemn him in the eyes of society. And yet all the while there existed in his mental background a dim shadowy consciousness that the protection clause in the Odd-fellow's obligation might make it a very convenient thing if—but Mr. Basset never carried his thoughts beyond that innocent little preposition.

Stephen, for his part, looked on Mr. Basset as a good-hearted, social kind of a man, though rather shallow. On the whole he liked him. He had a certain open way with him that is always taking to a frank nature, and any suspicion of selfish motives in the latter's evident anxiety to retain him in the lodge was as far as possible from Stephen's mind.

Mr. Basset, with all his seeming openness, had not a little diplomatic craft. So he did not tell Stephen that he was morally sure the Grand Lodge would render an adverse decision in Mrs. Strycker's case; or that he himself had been knowing to more than one similar instance where men had paid in hundreds of dollars, but happening to die slightly in debt to the lodge, the moral and charitable order they had so trustingly joined kept their money, but refused all benefit to the widows and orphans supposed to be the objects of its beneficent care. There was one screw, however, yet unturned, and like a good-natured inquisitor of olden times, he proceeded with an easy smile to make Stephen feel this power.

"Speaking about a demit now. Of course anybody is at liberty to leave the lodge, but you remember the closing part of the Odd-fellow's obligation: '*Should I be expelled, or voluntarily leave the order, I will consider this promise as binding out of it as in it.*' A demit makes no difference with the irrevocable nature of the vow."

Stephen felt as if suddenly caught in a vice. He had merely been turning the idea over in his mind of leaving the lodge without coming to any definite resolution, for he meant to take no hasty step; though he could not help acknowledging that he had been very hasty in joining a society which by its very constitution he was prevented from knowing anything about beforehand—he could easily slip his neck from under the noose when convinced that it was not a good thing. Now the idea of irrevocableness made the obligation which had before rested on him with the lightness of a silken thread press like a band of iron. But he was too proud to let Mr. Basset discern his mental wincings. So he only said quietly, "I haven't made up my mind whether to leave yet or not, and if I do, it will not be because I have any difficulty with the obligation as I understand it."

"Now that is a very important point—to understand it right," said Mr. Basset, catching eagerly at this latter clause in Stephen's remark. "Unprincipled men creep into Odd-fellowship. There's no denying that. I'm sorry it is so. But you must take it like everything else, the evil along with the good. This report, by the way, I'll leave with you, and you can look it over when you have leisure. You know we may reason and argue about a thing, but when it comes to convincing, facts and figures do the business."

And Mr. Basset departed with a smile so beaming in its friendly cheerfulness that he might have almost sat for the benevolent spirit of his favorite order personified.

Stephen, in an interval of leisure between the study of his law cases, took up the pamphlet and ran his eye over the figures. It was certainly true that Odd-fellow benevolence had mounted up the last year to over two millions. At the same time its collections had reached a sum of over *five* millions. Stephen's mathematical mind at once perceived that the lodge was very well paid for its "charity" by a margin of three-fifths of the receipts. Would not an insurance company that took 60 per cent to pay its running expenses be called an arrant swindle? And if the church should do so, would not lodgemen like Mr. Basset be the first to call her by even a worse name?

These questions Stephen revolved in his mind and half decided in his next letter home to confess his

folly—for folly he now considered it—and ask
counsel. But it would pain the old couple to find
out that he had taken such a step and kept it so
long a secret from them; and his mind, until Mr.
Basset had so coolly showed him that he was reckoning without his host, had clung hopefully to procuring a demit; for he flattered himself that then his
whole experience as an Odd-fellow would drop out
of his life so completely that it need never be referred to or thought of again.

CHAPTER XXIV.

The president of the W. C. T. U. in Jacksonville, like many another woman in the White Ribbon ranks, had known a time when she construed St. Paul with extreme literalness, and would have faced the cannon's mouth sooner than an average-sized audience. Yet she had conquered early prejudice and native timidity so far as to be not only an indefatigable temperance worker, but one of the most acceptable speakers in the organization, her glowing eloquence and forceful logic being only matched on the platform by the charm of her noble presence and sweet, womanly voice.

There is nothing more wonderful in this whole wonderful movement than the fact that it has developed—not one Deborah, that would be nothing remarkable—but hundreds of Deborahs, each one a host in herself, who have risen in their might "for God and home and native land," unmindful of the sneers or the misunderstandings of smaller and weaker souls. Thank God for the army of temperance Deborahs! Is it not fitting that by them he should judge the traffic which has made so many Rachels.

Martha, however, never thought of herself in this exalted light, for she was in her own humble estimate only one of the rank and file, though she taught a primary class in the Jacksonville Band of Hope; and so when Mrs. Judge Haviland made her an informal call one day, she was as agreeably surprised as one of Napoleon's subalterns might have been, unexpectedly honored by a visit from his commander-in-chief.

The weather was warm and close. Mrs. Haviland sank down in the easy chair Martha offered her with a look of weariness and exhaustion in her face that might have been attributed to the heat by any one who did not know that in the past six months the number of local Unions and Bands of Hope which she had organized, the addresses she had made to adults, and the talks she had given the children, to say nothing of the time and strength diffused through numberless minor channels, were more than enough to keep mind and body strained to their highest tension.

"I called to have a little talk with you," she said, "about our Band of Hope especially. I want to praise you, Miss Benson, for the admirable way in which you have trained those little midgets. I was quite surprised as well as delighted the other day to see how clearly they seemed to understand political economy in its relations to the drink traffic."

"I am a pupil, myself," replied Martha, modestly. "I have only lately begun to study these subjects. My first introduction to temperance work was when

I joined the Good Templars, and the drink question as related to economic or hygienic questions was never once discussed in the lodge to which I belonged; or even alluded to."

"I do not like to say anything against any society which professes to work for temperance," replied Mrs. Haviland, "but I find that these secret temperance lodges educate superficially if they educate at all, which I am sometimes inclined to doubt; and the result is a host of nominal laborers who may be well-trained in lodge work but no farther. I rejoice in the broadening scope of the W. C. T. U. Looked upon merely as a grand educational agency for woman, it is a most powerful force in the mental and spiritual development of our sex. By it God is training the future mothers of our Republic for who knows what duties, what responsibilities!"

Mrs. Haviland was silent for a moment—a silence Martha did not choose to break; and then she continued, her face lighting up with a strange radiance as she dwelt on the record of the past, "I was one of the Ohio crusaders. Perhaps our way was a wrong one, but it was the way God led us. Even now I hear people sneer at that first early movement as a mere craze, a folly, a mistake. Perhaps it was all that, but it was a great deal more. *God* was in our mistake, our folly, if such it was—guiding us, teaching us, leading us by a way that we knew not of. And better to blunder and have God with us, than not to blunder and walk without him."

"We were native-born American women, educated,

religious, home-loving, with all the deep-rooted, moral instincts that belong to such as their native birthright, yet we were bound and helpless. We had to stand by while the temperance laws were made a dead letter, and 'primaries' packed by ignorant, whisky-drinking foreigners governed the elections. And what could we do? We were desperate and the cry of the desperate is to God. In a week every saloon in the city where I lived was closed. We felt almost as if the millennial day had come. But the time was not yet ready for us to sing the song of Miriam. In less than a year those gates of hell that we thought we had closed forever were opened wider than before. We could not understand it. Would this have been if all the voters who professed temperance principle had stood by us at the polls? Could men who did not love the cause well enough to risk a little personal discomfort and inconvenience to themselves adequately represent women who would have gladly died for it? It was a crisis for us and our work, but in that crisis a great idea was born—the Woman's Christian Temperance Union. There are many things I believe in now that I did not believe in then. We had much fallow ground of ignorance and prejudice to break up; but we did it thoroughly, and we sowed seed—good seed. Who will reap the harvest?"

Mrs. Haviland paused an instant in her rapid retrospection, a shadow swept over her grand face, and she turned to Martha and clasped both her hands with a strangely eager, earnest pressure.

"It is to you we look—young, brave, earnest souls, to take our places when we fall in the battle. For we must fall. We are human; we want to see the end for which we have prayed and labored. But for many of us that cannot be. And we know it; I know it."

Her voice dropped lower, and the brief, detached sentences came slowly as if wrung out by the pressure of some inward suffering.

Martha looked up at her wonderingly.

"Dear Mrs. Haviland; don't talk of any one's filling your place, least of all one so humble as myself, without talents, or wealth, or social rank."

"Martha—Miss Benson, you do not know the place you may be filling twenty years from now. What American girl does?"

Martha colored slightly. Although she was a believer in woman's suffrage, she was a very unambitious little person. If Nelson ever rose to stations of public honor, she felt that nothing would make her prouder or happier than to shine herself in that reflected glory, but she remembered that Mrs. Haviland might not know anything about Nelson, and be even unaware of their engagement, in which case her words were of course quite innocent of any prophetic intent. She made no reply save to listen with eager, reverent attention as the sweet, low, impassioned voice sounded on like the notes of an ancient chorus, half wail, half triumph.

"I entered the warfare like many another woman, because I was forced into it by the presence of the

monster in my own home. I had only one child—
a son. Oh, how I loved him! How I tried to shield
him from every touch of evil! But a taste for drink
was hereditary in the Haviland blood, and I did not
know it till it was too late. Perhaps it would have
made no difference if I had known, for how could
my weak woman's arms shield him from the snare
set on every side? I did my best, and when I could
do no more—when my Henry was brought home to
me dead, killed by a fall from his horse after he had
been taking too much wine, I knelt down by his lifeless form, and I parted the curls away from his cold,
white brow, and kissed him over and over just as I
did when I hushed him to sleep on my bosom an innocent babe. Oh, it seemed so long ago I did it,
almost as though far away in some lost eternity—
and I vowed to God then and there never to cease
fighting the fiend that had slain my child. For what
was my son more than any other woman's son? more
than poor Bridget Maloney's, for instance, who gets
drunk on the vilest kind of whisky instead of sherry
and champagne? God made mothers' hearts alike.
The Democratic party wants the Irish whisky vote,
and the Republican party wants the German beer
vote, and politicians bid for it, and the work of
death goes on. Give these Irish and German women
who have suffered so much from the brutality of
their drinking husbands the ballot, and though many
of them drank themselves, they would all vote the
prohibition ticket. My heart sickens and my brain
reels when I think of all the hideous wrongs and

cruelties that have come under my notice while col-
lecting facts and statistics for the work—little helpless children beaten, frozen, starved, burned to
death, or made helpless cripples for life. They were
not my children; I never even saw them; but they
had mothers with mothers' hearts, and I feel like
crying, 'O Lord, how long!' *Must* wrong be forever
on the throne? Will the day never come when politicians shall cease to betray the helpless to advance
their own petty selfish interests?"

Mrs. Haviland paused, and then she said in a
changed tone and with her usual gentle smile:

"I am pouring out all this to you because it does
me good. I am a woman and must talk. And now,
my dear, as I am old enough to be your mother, allow me to congratulate you on your engagement with
so noble a young man as Nelson Newhall. I have
had my eye on him for some time. He is worthy of
you and you of him."

There are many prohibitionists like Mrs. Haviland
who are working, praying, suffering for the cause,
and "with brave hearts breaking slow" pass to their
rest in the midst of the struggle, and never see the
deadly enemy that continually betrays their best ef
forts. In proof whereof we will only say that there
was a Masonic reunion that very night which was
attended by the mayor of Jacksonville, several politicians of considerable local note, and a goodly number of saloon-keepers. And "they met upon the
level and parted on the square" in all that mutual
good-fellowship supposed to be peculiarly Masonic.

CHAPTER XXV.

TWO WAYS OF ASKING A QUESTION.

Both the prohibition and anti-prohibition sides were silently marshalling their forces; and, while the political sea remained outwardly calm, one at all familiar with that fickle and dangerous element would have heard and felt the distant groundswell that prophesied of another and still more closely contested conflict than the last.

"I hope all prohibitionists will unite in one solid party phalanx and not play at cross purposes any longer," said Stephen Howland. "People may talk about making temperance a non-partisan issue as much as they like; it won't alter the fact The prohibition question has got into politics fairly, and all the king's horses and all the king's men can't get it out."

These remarks were addressed to a Good Templar who did *not* vote the third party ticket at the previous election for reasons which make an interesting subject of inquiry. He was a staunch prohibitionist at heart, and had fully resolved to cast his ballot for Col. Hicks, till over the hidden wires that connect Masonic lodges and Grand Army posts with the secret temperance orders, flashed the word:

"Gen. Putney is a Mason and a Grand Army man, and you must vote for him."

Let not the unsuspecting reader suppose that this command was ever orally communicated to the assembled lodge. It is one of the blessed advantages of organized secrecy that no such vulgar and clumsy method need be employed. It is true that our Good Templar and the majority of his really "worthy" brethren cast their ballots exactly as their Masonic leaders told them to; and yet so gently was it insinuated by those same leaders that the idea of voting for a man they never expected to elect was too ridiculous for sensible men; so solemnly was it set before them as a patriotic duty, in a crisis like the present, to choose the least of two evils, that they marched to the polls and voted for the Republican candidate, honestly believing that they were following their own sober second thoughts instead of the cue thrown to their chiefs from Masonic headquarters. In fact, Stephen was answered with one of the very stock arguments that had been so successfully employed on himself the year previous.

"But you know to vote the third party ticket when there is no reasonable hope of electing it is simply playing into the hands of the Democrats."

"There is no hope just because prohibitionists don't unite," said Stephen, quickly. "And as to 'playing into the hands of the Democrats,' better open war than secret betrayal. I come of old Republican, anti-slavery stock, and I am proud of it, but the sceptre has passed into the hands of men who know not Joseph, leaders as stiff-necked and obstinate as Pharaoh ever was; and the question is whether we shall follow their leadership and be all destroyed together in a political Red Sea, or follow the Moses of prohibition even if it means a forty years wandering in the desert before we come to our promised land."

Stephen had been brought up on Old Testament history, and this Hebraistic illustration came naturally to his tongue. In his own mind Col. Gail · Hicks was the prohibition Moses, and he could by no means understand the pusillanimous half-heartedness of temperance men who would go back on such a leader. Why did the Good Templars first indorse Col. Hicks and then vote solidly against him? We have, however, presented the reader with a key to this enigma, and merely mentioning that the key in question will fit a great many other puzzles, social and political, we will leave him to apply it at his leisure.

A coming event which is about to startle Jacksonville already throws its shadow over our pages, and we must hasten on to the denouement.

Stephen did not procure a demit from the Oddfellows. He wanted to see first what could be done in Mrs. Strycker's case; and possibly—O vainest of vain delusions!—his leaving the lodge might tend to make it worse, for where was the purifying element to come from if all the virtuous members abandoned it? Would it not be giving a rich and powerful organization right over into the hands of the devil?

So questioned Stephen, forgetting that an organization which professed "to give rest to the soul," yet rejected that Holy One in whom alone satisfying peace is to be found, must be of the devil from the beginning; and that even where Satan is concerned it is always best to pursue a strictly honest policy, and if he can show the shadow of a claim to give him back his own straightway.

There is a temptation here to make a digression. What is this talk so common nowadays in certain circles about "purifying the stage," and making even the dance and the card-table serve the cause of religion and good morals by bringing them into the category of home amusements, but a plan to rob the devil of his own property—that which he can prove by affidavits dating thousands of years back has belonged to him from time immemorial? Fighting the devil is all right; it is grand enough work for an archangel, for Michael himself, diamond-panoplied, and wielding the lightning for his sword; but to cheat the devil, to drive Shylock bargains with him! —in the name of common honor and honesty let us have none of it.

The Rev. Theopilus Brassfield, to whose church Stephen naturally gravitated on joining the lodge, preached sermons of a very advanced type of theology; so much so, in fact, that he was not only a great ways ahead of Paul, but the cross itself loomed dimly through his flowery sentences like a beautiful but rather obsolete symbol of something that had happened a great while ago, but which the fashionable congregation to whom he preached was much too "advanced" to need. Eating husks when it is an altogether new thing may be endured a while for the sake of the novelty, and there are those who are spiritually and mentally enough like donkeys to feed patiently on a daily course of thistles; but Stephen after a time when a Sabbath proved rainy, or hot, or cold, or he had got tired by sitting up too late over a law case the night before, began to find that he could get as much good by reading a sermon alone to himself. And Mr. Basset, though a member of this same church, and superintendent of the Sunday-school, never took him too task on the subject as he had done for neglect of his lodge duties.

Stephen was still moral, upright and manly. These were inherited qualities, and like the color of his hair and the shape of his nose could only be changed to opposite ones by some violent and un-natural process. The hardy, virtuous yeoman race who "had put to flight the armies" of the Spanish "aliens" under Elizabeth, "subdued kingdoms" under Cromwell, and done more than that when it founded in the untrodden wilderness of the New World a theocratic Commonwealth which should be an ideal of free government for all succeeding generations, had left upon him their mental as well as their physical impress. His hatred of dissimulation, his scorn of a lie, his innate chivalry to the weak were inbred, and came from the same source to which he owed his six feet of stature, his firm health and supple sinews. But that New England

Hannah, whose life, ever since Stephen was born, had been a daily prayer that he might be worthy of sonship in Christ's eternal kingdom, knew that heavenly grace was no hereditary gift; that the kingdom of which she longed to have him an heir must be peopled by them "who are born not of blood nor of the will of the flesh, nor of the will of man, but of God." Some subtle, spiritual clairvoyance told her that all was not right with Stephen; that he was keeping back something, and often when writing to him she had half a mind to put the question directly, but always shrank from doing so with a feeling that she had no right to force even her son's confidence in a matter that perhaps lay only between himself and God.

Stephen parted from his Good Templar friend, and stepped out from his den to take an airing, and rest his head which ached with being all day in a hot, ill-ventilated court-room, where a case was on trial that should not have taken more than a few hours to decide; but, thanks to law technicalities, and the fact that the defendant and most of the jury were Masons, seemed likely to last as many days, with an excellent prospect of coming to nothing in the mazes of some higher court.

Passing the Jacksonville Bank he saw before it a crowd, mostly of the laboring class—a quiet, orderly crowd, and yet with painful excitement manifested in their faces and low-toned talk. What did it mean? Stephen was not long left in ignorance, for a passing acquaintance hailed him with the inquiry:

"Heard the news? The bank has suspended. They can't find the cashier nowhere, nor a hundred and fifty thousand dollars of the funds."

Stephen turned pale as death. He had not a cent invested in that bank or any other, and the news involved no personal loss to him—but the absconding cashier was no other than Mr. Felix Basset.

"It's bad business—will be for a good many, I am afraid," continued the other. "He's been falsifying his accounts a good while, and nobody suspected it."

Stephen's heart was heavy within him. He grew dizzy. It was like a moral earthquake. Could this be true of a man who had always *seemed* honest and upright, who had been so friendly to him, and whom he had trusted with the entire trust of a frank and unsuspecting nature? Yet there was the crowd, and a bank official on the steps talking to them, though it was cold comfort for these poor laboring men and women to be told that the law would do what it could to recover their stolen property, in the face of the bad success which had attended the law's efforts in so many similar cases.

Nelson Newhall was standing near. He turned round, saw Stephen, and nodded in recognition.

"I hope you are not one of the losers," said Stephen, forgetting Mr. Basset for a moment in pity for the many obliged to see the hard earnings of a lifetime swept away.

"All I have laid up was in that bank," was the quiet reply. "But those who have work and are able to work are not to be pitied. I know an aged couple whose all was invested there, and now they will have to eat the·bread of public charity, which will be bitterer to them than death; and I can tell you of other cases almost as sad. God pity them."

"Amen," said Stephen, and he moved away.

The next scrap of talk which reached his ears was this:

"Church members ain't a bit better than folks that ain't. Things have got to such a pass now that when I hear of a man's cutting up as Basset has done I begin to ask what Sunday-school he is superintendent of."

"Come now, there's a question more to the point than that," gruffly put in another voice which Stephen recognized as Martin Treworthy's. "Basset was an Odd-fellow, wan't he? I say, better ask what secret society he belongs to."

It is a curious fact that while the press will record of a noted defaulter—the secular part of it with great gusto—that he belongs to the church and teaches in the Sunday-school, he may belong to the Masons, Odd-fellows, or any other secret society, and not a word on the subject be breathed by those same respectable journals. And we ask in the name of common fairness, why proclaim the one fact, and be silent about the other?

CHAPTER XXVI

THE TRUE LIGHT SHINETH.

The crowd did not linger long around the bank when the uselessness of doing so became apparent. They dispersed quietly, and the building was left to itself, with its closely-drawn shutters, barred doors, and rifled vaults.

Stephen, in his first shocked bewilderment, had felt as if every prop of trust in his fellow-man had been knocked from beneath him. The facts proved to be that Mr. Basset had speculated on a large scale and under an assumed name, and when fortune turned against him he had to face two alternatives: discovery and the State's prison, or a lengthened exile in some country out of the reach of extradition laws, leaving discovery to come afterwards. Strictly speaking, however, there was but one alternative present in Mr. Basset's mind—the one last mentioned; and as in the words of the homely old proverb, "one might as well die for an old sheep as a lamb," why not crib enough of the bank's remaining funds to enable him to live comfortably in the strange land he must make his future home? But was Mr. Basset all those years during which he had passed in society for a Christian man and an honest citizen, a conscious hypocrite? By no means. He

had caught the fever which seems almost indigenous
to American life, to get rich suddenly, and had only
verified the words of inspiration that "he who
hasteth to be rich shall fall into a snare." He had
gravitated to Odd-fellowship from the natural instinct of a man of weak principle to seek alliance
with some system that in its "show of will worship,"
its teachings of a mere outward morality would flatter him with a sense of self-merit and prestige in the
eyes of the world; and at the same time give him
what a weak man always wants—an invisible advantage over others. "But did Odd-fellowship really
have much to do with his fall?" inquires the "candid
reader." We will try to be equally candid in our
answer.

The writer once heard it remarked on the death
of "the oldest Mason in the country"—one of that
ubiquitous race which the order is continually bury-
ing, and of whom we are obliged to record that he
had robbed the widow and cheated the fatherless,
not on so grand a scale as Mr. Basset, but in ordinary business ways through the greater part of his
life—that "Mr. H— would not have been such a
rascal if he had not belonged to the Masonic lodge;"
which remark has a true and a false side to it. "Mr.
H—" had a turn for sharp practices, and a heart
that was like the nether millstone when it was a
question of his beloved dollars, but with neither of
these two circumstances could the lodge be properly
chargeable. It *was* chargeable, however, with being
a secret, oath-bound organization, and as such afford-

ing just the right kind of covert for men to hide under who wanted to swindle helpless cowans, keep
saloons, or rob banks; an indictment by the way to
which every secret clan must answer sooner or later
at the bar of an enlightened Christian public.   I
once heard a physician express the opinion that the
common use of anæsthetics had a deterioriating influence on physical bravery.   The very knowledge
that an agent exists which will give perfect insensi-
bility to pain takes away the courage to bear severe
operations, and the same principle may account for
some other things.   People lament the prevailing
dishonesty, the frauds and peculations too common
even to excite surprise, and never stop to ask
whether the prevalence of secret societies, each with
their Masonic protection clause, may have anything
to do with this state of things.   Does not the fact
that such societies exist, bound to shield each other
against the consequences of "imprudent" acts, virtually tempt to the commission of such acts and
thus put a premium on crime?   We respectfully
submit to all the philanthropists, moralists and reformers in the land whether it is well for government to charter these institutions and then tax law-
abiding citizens with the enormous expense of following criminals through their secret labyrinths in a
vain attempt to bring them to justice.   More solemnly would we put the question to every pastor,
How far is the church responsible for the fact that
our most noted forgers and defaulters are almost
without exception nominal members of her fold?

The pulpit is silent while the young men of the country are being drawn into the countless lodge-traps which borrow their religion from the idolatries of ancient Egypt, and their laws from the despot-isms of the dark ages; it lifts no voice of warning, no announcement of future woe against "them who seek deep to hide their counsel·from the Lord, and their works are in the dark, and they say, Who seeth us? and who knoweth us?   Is it strange that her children fall an easy prey to the masked destroyer? that the clerk or the cashier becomes a Mason, an Odd-fellow, a Knight of Pythias, submits to their degrading ceremonies, adopts their "universal religion," and finally startles the community with some gross betrayal of public or private trust? Those readers who expect me to heap maledictions on the head of Mr. Felix Basset, and pursue him with scathing denunciations for his fraud and hypocrisy, will be disappointed.   I prefer to keep my excerations, richly though he may deserve them, for others more deserving than he—for those who proselyted him to the service of the lodge in his penniless young manhood to make him tenfold more the child of hell than themselves, and last, but not least, for the pastor who could, by officiating at its Christless altars, give the lie to all his pulpit ministrations.

Stephen had not yet come to the point where he saw these things clearly, but Martin Treworthy's brave defence of the church against the lodge gave him a new respect for the old soldier; and what did

him no harm, an added dissatisfaction with himself
who had lost his right to do the same.

He re-entered his office with the feeling that it
was a miserable kind of a world, shut his law books,
turned down the gas and went to bed. But refreshing sleep after such a mental shock was impossible.
He tossed restlessly about thinking over his first
meeting with Mr. Basset, how companionable and
kindly he had seemed, and how he had urged him
to become an Odd-fellow. He went over in memory
the initiation scene. He did not want to and strug-
gled against it; but in that half-sleeping, half-waking
state the will, like some captive Arabian genii, seems
the victim of a power that revels in setting it all
manner of grotesque tasks. As soon as he shut his
eyes he saw before him the grinning skeleton, the
lighted torches, the masked faces; and every time
they passed before him the thing seemed more and
more diabolical—like a dream of infernal regions.
And then he seemed to be again in the little hill-
country church of his fathers. It was communion
Sabbath, and the candidates for admission, himself
among them, were standing before the table on which
were displayed the simple emblems of our Lord's
broken body and shed blood. He saw the pastor at
the baptismal font as he pronounced the solemn
words, "I baptize thee in the name of the Father
and of the Son and of the Holy Ghost." And how
in its heavenly pureness that scene contrasted with
the other! Like the pearl and jasper glory of the
New Jerusalem with the sulphurous smoke of the pit.

He finally dropped into a troubled sleep and over-slept himself. And in the hurry of getting ready for the early train (for he was obliged to go away on some court business) he had no time to think of troublesome matters. And after all why should he be troubled? It was sad, it cut him to the heart that a man who had stood high in the esteem of the community should turn out a consummate rogue, but this was not the first experience of the kind, nor was it likely to be the last. Still he could not dis-miss from his mind a thing that everybody around him was discussing, and which formed the staple news of the morning papers. He could not help overhearing one stranger tell another of a shocking suicide in a neighboring town, the result of a mind unbalanced by the loss of property consequent on the bank's suspension. Of course it must have been a weak mind at the outset, with no strong supports in either philosophy or religion, but this tended to make the case only more pitiful.

"Basset's safe in Canada by this time," remarked one of the two strangers, both of whom had a decid-edly clerical look, and were in reality two D. Ds. returning home from a conference meeting.

"Yes," returned the other. "All our successful rogues will be likely to make Canada their place of retreat till we can have an extradition law that will reach them. But how a man enjoying so high a de-gree of public confidence and esteem could forfeit it all for wealth he can never properly enjoy is a mys-tery that even the power of a sudden and overwhelming temptation does not to my mind fully explain. I account for it rather on the ground of a general and widespread corruption, a kind of moral miasma that taints church and state. One of the unfailing signs of that national decadence which ends as in the French Revolution with the wreck of all law and government, is the lack of trust between man and man, which always follows where God is practically dethroned, as he certainly is in our American nation to-day. As a patriot and a Christian I tremble for my country. The public conscience needs a great arousing. We want a Pentecostal outpouring of the Spirit on our sleeping congregations. This nation must be brought back to the basis of the ten commandments, but then that will only be by the lever of a living church behind it."

His companion, who wore glasses, and had a mild Melancthon-like face, shook his head in sorrowful assent.

"You are right, brother. There is too little pungent preaching on the subject of common, everyday morals. We are puffed up with denominational pride when we ought rather to mourn our spiritual deadness. Oh, that the Lord would remember Zion and comfort again her waste places!"

These ministers were good men. They really felt what they said while they had not the smallest idea that they stood in imperative need themselves of "a great awakening" on one very important subject. Their churches swarmed with Masons and Odd-fellows, and though the reverend doctor with the face like Melancthon's hated secretism, he bore no testimony against it. The seal on his lips was partly ignorance. He did not know much about the secret orders and he did not want to know anything more about them. He believed, so he would tell you, if you hinted gently at his duty in this regard, in the expellant power of pure Gospel preaching. And while he preached the Gospel—and he certainly did preach it and live it—women filled his church, at the same time that their husbands and fathers and brothers were receiving a mock regeneration and new birth in Mason and Odd-fellow lodges. And yet he could mourn and mourn sincerely over the desolation of Zion!

But Stephen suddenly forgot their talk. Standing on the platform, ready for the northward bound express train, stood two men, one of whom carried a carpet-bag, and had a face so covered with huge red whiskers that scarcely a feature was distinguishable; and yet this one glimpse gave Stephen a curious feeling of having known him in some long ago period, as if they had met and become acquainted in some pre-existent state. It was not till hours afterwards that a strange suspicion flashed through his mind. *Could* this Esau-like stranger have been Felix Basset?

There was something peculiar in their parting. When the red-whiskered gentleman had taken his seat in the car he turned his face for an instant to the window with an uneasy glance after his comrade who, during the pause before the starting of the train, had walked up and down the platform with keen reconnoitering looks to the right and left, and now standing somewhat back from the crowd and thus out of the range of observation, with one single rapid motion he brought both arms together from a horizontal position and touched with the index finger of his right hand, the other fingers being doubled inward, the second knuckle joint of the thumb of his left. Stephen, we must confess, was not a very bright Odd-fellow, as, indeed, one cannot well be who has higher objects with which to occupy his mind than the remembering of signs and grips, and though he observed the action it was done so quickly that he failed to recognize it as—the Sign of Safety in the Degree of Friendship.

Mr. Basset had, in fact, gone off a few days before the situation was discovered, but it was only as far as the house of a lodge brother, where he had been all the time hidden; and now cleverly disguised and within a day's ride of the Canada line we will take our final leave of him. But in justice we must say that even with a fair prospect of successfully eluding the officers of justice who supposed him a thousand miles away, he was a very miserable and unhappy man. Public disgrace, which but a little while before had only loomed up in the farthest background of his mental visions as a dim possibility, was now a real thing—as real as the cold clutch of Death's fingers on a soul unprepared—and what vow of a secret fraternity could stand between him and the inward avenger?

But is not this an unfair representation of Odd-
fellowship? inquires the reader.   Because a few
members defend criminals and uphold liquor selling,
must it follow that the whole order is responsible
for their individual action?   Now this is precisely
the point we desire to come to.   An order that in-
serts in its obligation a protection clause, which can
be construed any way according to the moral sense
of the candidate, certainly lays itself open to grave
suspicion, and honest men will be in no haste to
clear it from the first charge till it tears down the
convenient screen between criminals and the law
which it has borrowed from its Masonic mother.   In
reference to the second charge, one single fact will
suffice.

In 1870 a petition was presented to the Grand
Lodge of the United States to enact a law allowing
State Grand Lodges to prohibit members of subordi-
nates under their respective jurisdictions from engaging in the traffic in intoxicating liquors.   The
petition was refused, it being decided that "it is contrary to the spirit and policy of our institution to
pass any law on the subject referred to, creating a
new test of membership in the order."   Thus we see
that Odd-fellowship presents no more bar to the admission of a rumseller than it does to a Mormon or
an infidel.   We have conclusive testimony from one
of their own standard writers: "No peculiarities of
religious belief or practice are requisite to admission
in the order, *and none disqualify.*"

In fact the views of the Grand Lodge on the tem-

perance question might even be accepted with very
slight changes as a part of the declaration against
"sumptuary laws" embodied in their political platform, as we may learn by another quotation from
that same standard authority: "Lodges cannot
abridge the liberty of the citizen nor dictate to him
what he shall eat nor what he shall drink . . . .
neither will the laws nor the principles of Odd-fellowship descend to the restriction nor the regulation
of the beverage of its members."

It is a coincidence worthy of note that the
Masonic Odd-fellow whom Mr. Basset, as related in
a prior chapter, had "warned of approaching danger," acting on the familiar proverb that "one good
turn deserves another," now played a chief part in
aiding and abetting the latter's escape from justice.
Attached to the fashionable hotel which he kept was
an elegant club room, where assembled every lodge
night the convivially inclined among the brethren,
who smoked and played cards till the small hours
of the morning, and amused each other, while sip-
ping their glasses of wine and punch, with the various neat fictions about "important lodge work" by
which they imposed on the credulity of their unsuspecting wives. Nor did this interchange of reciprocal obligations with a professed prohibitionist shock
him greatly in view of the fact that he knew more
than one in the lodge who talked as stoutly for prohibition as did Mr. Basset, while holding secret business relations all the while with the very traffic
whose existence they affected to deplore. Mr. Parker

of the Phœnix House might have listened silently to the praise of Odd-fellowship as a temperance order, and even as a matter of prudent policy gravely assented, but he would have certainly indulged himself in a good laugh behind his informant's back at the absurdity of the idea.

Odd-fellowship is Masonry's first born, made in her image, and if anybody wishes a conclusive proof that this is so let him attack Masonry and then note the filial readiness of the average Odd-fellow to spring to her relief.

Stephen Howland felt as every truly upright soul must over the fall of another, intensely sorrowful; and his trust in what the Rev. Theophilus Brassfield had so often styled "a complete system of morality" was sadly shaken. He was in exactly the mood of mind which has lead many a man into downright skepticism of all good. Such an experience must either drive the soul to take a firm foothold on the Rock of Ages, or to launch its little cockle-boat on that wide sea of doubt whose farthest shores are the Cimmerian land of blank atheism where hope is a myth, and faith a dream, and the whole universe a vast hollow Nothing.

The illness of a juror caused a temporary adjournment of the court. Stephen was trying to while away the time over a newspaper when the opposing counsel sauntered up.

He belonged to the Bohemian class of lawyers, and considered no case out of the legitimate line of his practice which involved a big fee, or even one of reasonable size. He considered Stephen's notions of professional honor and probity as decidedly Quixotic, but such men have sometimes a curious liking for their moral opposites; and though frequently pitted against each other, they were much better friends than one could suppose possible after listening to their savage sparring in court hours.

"It was a queer thing now that Basset should do as he did. It come like a thunder-clap, but there is an epidemic just now of defalcations and embezzlements and forgeries. Such things seem to have their regular periods like the seventeen-year locusts."

"It would be refreshing if we could have an epedemic of public honesty," returned Stephen, dryly.

"I think the same, my dear fellow—in the abstract, you know. But for us lawyers—phew!—it would be as bad as an epedemic of health to the doctors. Now you take this liquor trade; it is a confounded bad thing all through, but if it should be swept out of existence to-day I should lose half my practice. I defend rumsellers and you prosecute, but, bless you! they'd better fall into your clutches than mine. I bleed 'em well now, I tell you. I took a five hundred dollar fee from one the other day, and I don't believe he had enough left to start him in the boot-blacking business."

The lawyer stopped to laugh, and Stephen could not help laughing too.

"I have had curious things happen in the course of my legal practice," the former continued, "but nothing queerer than what happened once in this very court-house when I was defending two liquor sellers arrested for violation of the Sunday law. You know the old saying, 'There's no telling how a jury will flop.' If you will believe it, with exactly the same evidence in both cases one was acquitted and the other fined seventy-five dollars. I found out afterwards that the one acquitted belonged to some secret society—the Noble Order of Red Men, I think it was—and his friends managed to get a juror or two who belonged to the fraternity onto the bench. Six were Masons and Odd-fellows. The other rumseller was a poor devil of an Irishman, forbidden any such privilege under ban of his priest."

"It is a privilege that if often used to mock justice will bring in a reign of lynch law sooner or later," said Stephen, indignantly. "I believe in equal rights and fair play even for liquor sellers."

The other shrugged his shoulders.

"This secret order business is overdone. It is our American failing to overdo things. When I was first admitted to the bar I joined the Masons and the Odd-fellows and the Knights of Pythias, thinking that when I was in Rome I had better do as the Romans do. And I can walk in their processions, and wear their fol-de-rols, and have a chief seat at all their feasts and pow-wows generally—if I want to; but as a rule I contrive to find other fish to fry. Really now, between you and me—hark! what's that?"

It was a sound of fife and drum. Stephen, from his boyhood, had a passionate love for martial music, and the inspiring strains seemed for a moment like the wings of some strong archangel lifting him above all his trouble and darkness into a realm of which his only conscious thought was like Peter's on the mount—that it would be good to dwell there.

"A detachment of the Salvation Army, they say," carelessly remarked the other lawyer, after making due inquiry of one of the throng who were bending their steps in the direction of the music. "I'm going to hear 'em."

Stephen followed with a readiness that surprised himself, for he was somewhat of a stickler for regular methods; and, though he did not doubt that the Salvation Army had accomplished good in its peculiar way, he had looked on a conversion under such instrumentality a little as he might on a miraculous cure wrought by some practitioner outside of medical schools—rather as a phenomena than a precedent. But the stirring music, the odd and yet deeply devout appearance of the company, as in fine military order they marched through the street with waving banners, and defiled on to the common where a rude platform had been erected—even the unmannerly interruption of a few rowdies in the crowd, impressed Stephen with a deeper feeling than that of mere novelty. The effect of their warlike songs, their regular-drilled tread, their earnest faces, was something like that produced by the early Methodist movement. It seemed to sharpen and define the

lines which an ease-loving pulpit has allowed to
grow so dim and misty between the Lord's side and
the devil's side.   And to Stephen's positive nature
it was a relief to feel sure once more that there *were*
two sides, even though he was not equally sure of
being himself on the right one.

The preacher announced no text. Stephen noticed
that he seemed to be a very well developed specimen
of muscular Christianity, and was evidently an illiterate man; but after the first words fell on his ear
he felt that he was standing in the presence of one
of those rare orators made by grace and not by art
or nature, and ceased to feel any repugnance. Not
a suspicion, however, crossed his mind that this was
Peter Snyder, the converted rumseller, who had
joined the Salvationists because they afforded a
channel for free and effective Christian labor, which
he could never have found in the set lines of old and
respectable religious organizations. He had no cul-
tured taste to be shocked by their peculiar methods
of work, and they on their part did not mind his literary and theological deficiencies. But there was
no loud, ranting talk, only a deep, sweet earnestness, a perfect unconsciousness of himself that produced an effect like the highest pulpit art.

"I want to tell you folks about Jesus Christ," he
began. "You think you know about him already
Maybe some of you do, and if that is so, you bain't
no kind of business to be standing round here when
you ought to be telling other people about him. Or
hain't you got nothing to tell? Didn't he hang

bleeding on the cross with the nails in his feet and hands and the spear thrust through his side for *you?* I want to know.

"But as I said when I begun, it's t'other kind I'm a goin' to talk to. The Lord is coming with all his armies and riding on his swift chariots of salvation, and you resist him jest as I did, a heapin' up sin against sin to be fuel in that day which shall burn as an oven. But I ain't a goin' to talk to you about *my* sins, for the Lord has cast 'em all behind his back; and I ain't a goin' to talk to you about *your* sins. Maybe I shall come to 'em by and by. People like to tell what they know about. Now I know about the Lord Jesus *for I have seen him!*"

The speaker made a pause. A startled hush fell on the crowd. Stephen at first thought the man crazy, and was half inclined to walk off, but curiosity impelled him to stay.

"It was at a big meeting over to the Forks. The Lord was there in power, and he showed himself to *me*—a hardened, profane, swearing rumseller. That's jest what I was, and do you wonder that I am never tired of telling about his goodness? that I only wish I had a hundred tongues instead of one to praise him with? Now the Bible says the Lord is everywhere beholding the evil and the good, but he don't show himself where men revile and hate him, nor it ain't reasonable he should. Why, he is in lots of places to-day where you might wait till you were as old as Methusalah and never catch a glimpse of the hem of his garment. A man may be standing at a

bar or handling dirty cards and be converted. I
don't say such a thing hain't never happened, but I
do say there's a thousand times better chance of his
being struck by lightning. There's one place where
I never heard of a man's seeing the Lord—I don't
believe the angel Gabriel ever did—and that's the
lodge. Masons and Odd-fellows get converted
sometimes, but it's always outside of their lodges.
Now what's the reason? Why, the lodge hain't got
no Jesus Christ in it. It's death to darkness to let
in the light, and any lodge that should let him in
wouldn't live an hour. It would be changed into a
prayer meeting, and all the members would be singing, 'Glory, glory!' as loud as they could sing."

At this point a drunken Freemason made some
attempt at interruption, but before the disturbance
had time to spread, Captain Snyder—we will give
him his Salvation Army title—said quietly, "We
will sing it now," and signalling to the drummer
the army pealed forth one of their most stirring
choruses. The Salvationists have certainly this advantage, if their opponents can make noise they usually know how to make more. But so naturally was
it done that the greater part of the audience really
thought it only a part of the ordinary exercises. It
was a kind of tactics, however, that proved very successful, the would-be disturbers not caring to strain
their lungs in such an unequal contest.

Stephen saw through the ruse, and smiled. Certainly he thought, "music hath charms to soothe the
savage breast"—when there is enough of it.

"Maybe, now, you want to know what I went to that meeting for," the captain continued, wiping his forehead with a red cotton handkerchief. "I went to hear the preacher show up other folks' sins. I never dreamed he'd put his grappling hooks right into mine, fust thing. I knew my trade was a wrong one; I knew it was destroying my soul; and I had my times of feeling bad about it and promising myself—it was *myself*, not the Lord, mind ye—that I'd quit it jest as soon as I'd sold what stock I'd got on hand. But when that time come I was no more ready to quit it than the devil was to quit me. He'd stand at my elbow and say, 'Ain't Government in with you in this business, I want to know; and do you pretend to be any better'n Government?' Sometimes the devil speaks living truth. Rumsellers tempt men to drink: who tempts the rumseller? I'd like to ask some of our big men in Washington that question jest to see what they'd say. But the Lord had shet me up in too tight a place for even the devil to squeeze in and try to make me think I was better than I was. Some people say there ain't no sich place as hell. What do you think it is to be shet up where you can't see nothing but pictures of yourself—what you've been and what you are, the meanest, wickedest, most God-forsaken wretch that walks the earth—and know you've got to sit there and gaze, *gaze*, GAZE forever, and see no way out! What is it to see the faces of all the widows and orphans you've made rise up before you as cold and still as the face of the dead before a murderer; and

all the men who have drank themselves into delirium tremens at your bar, like avenging fiends laughing horribly at your misery!   Don't tell a man that's
been in sich a place as that there's no hell.   Oh,
there *is* sich a thing as the bottomless pit!   Don't
believe the ministers dressed out in fine broadcloth,
with gold rings on their fingers, who try to make
you believe there ain't; but oh, every poor, wretched
soul, living on in sin and despair, there's something
else that's bottomless, and that God's love to you.
And I've got jest the same right to tell you this that
I have to tell you the other thing.   A man that's
seen the Lord knows what God's 'so loved the world'
means.   Nobody else can.   It seemed to me then if
I could be shet out of my misery one second it
would be like the drop of water the rich man in hell
prayed for to cool the tip of his tongue.   There's a
mighty sight of difference between feeling you're a
sinner, and feeling you're a *lost* sinner.   I jest give
up.   The Almighty had hold of me, and who can
struggle with the Almighty?   And jest as soon as I
had done that the vision of my sins was gone, but
right in the place where I had seemed to see 'em all
pictured out, I see a cross, and One was hanging on
it, and there was the nails in his feet and hands.   I
could see 'em jest as plain.   And oh, how loving
and pitiful he looked at me!—*me*, that had hated
and reviled him all my days.   There he was a dying
for my sins.   Why, I felt as though I'd be glad to
go and be nailed on a cross beside him like the pen-
itent thief if that would show how sorry I felt for

'em. How long do you think I held on to my rum
kegs arter that? Oh, it is a look right into the face
of Jesus Christ that makes the rumseller give up
his bar, and the drunkard his cups, and the swearer
his oaths. How quick every one of you sinners
standing here would throw down your arms and surrender if you could *once* see the Lord! You may
not be bad in your own sight or other folks'. You
may not sell rum nor drink it; nor swear, nor cheat,
nor gamble, but if you've never seen the Lord Jesus
it is because some sin has stood in the way. *You*
know what that sin is and the Lord knows. I don't.
But oh, you poor sinner, throw away that weapon
with which you are fighting the Lord! It is the
spear you are thrusting into his side. When you
look on him whom you have pierced it'll be turned
against you. The Gospel trumpet is sounding for
recruits; bimeby it'll sound for judgment. Come to
the Lord and be saved. Come now.''

He proceeded for some time in the same strain of
earnest, homely eloquence. Stephen, after awhile,
assisted by a chance word from some one in the
crowd, had recognized Peter Snyder in the impassioned, ungrammatical preacher. But it scarcely
made any difference in the effect of the message.

What did it mean—this strange troubling of the
waters of his soul? Could it be that he had deceived himself? that he had never seen that glorious,
thorn-crowned Face? Or why did all his being go
out in a strange yearning after that Vision of celestial loveliness? Why this bitter longing as for a

treasure he had lost and never missed till now?

With drums beating and banners flying the Salvation Army marched back to their barracks, to meet an impediment by the way in the shape of zealous policemen who arrested the leader and several of the musicians for obstructing public travel—a vigilance truly edifying in the light of the immunity enjoyed by other violaters of the law, who did not indeed parade the streets beating drums or singing hymns, but who ran illicit saloons unmolested under the very eyes of these watchful public guardians.

Stephen offered his services in their defense, feeling justly indignant at what he considered an outrage on equal rights by the authorities who freely allowed public parades of firemen, military companies, and secret societies of all descriptions, and of course brought upon himself anew the name among his fellow lawyers of being a legal Quixote, besides causing "the whirligig of time" to bring round some curious "revenges." The man he had prosecuted for selling rum he was now defending for preaching the Gospel!

Stephen did not at first analyze his feelings, or ask why the light of God's Spirit had been so well-nigh extinguished in his heart. But there is a saying of Pascal's in his Provincial Letters which applies equally well to that system of error embodied in the lodge, as proved by the revulsion of feeling with which a member after he has been converted or received a new consecration of the Spirit, invariably regards it: "There are two things in the truths of our religion—a divine beauty which renders them lovely and a holy majesty which makes them venerable; and there are two peculiarities in error—an impiety which renders them horrible, and an impertinence which makes them ridiculous." Stephen was not exactly like Little Faith, robbed by force of his jewel of heavenly hope. He was more like the simple savage, who exchanges his pearl for a glass bead. He knew that his religious affections had grown cold, that he had lost his relish for divine things, and when he found himself turning with a kind of horror from the thought of attending another Odd-fellow's meeting and associating with men of such diversified moral and religious creeds as there assembled; when he remembered the two contrasting visions that had besieged his sleepless pillow, he saw the reason why. What a "beauty" and "venerableness" in the simple ceremonials of the Christian church! and beside them how horrible and ridiculous seemed the masquerades of lodge initiations!

To apply for a demit and leave the lodge forever was the one desire now in Stephen's mind. "Come out and be ye separate" seemed to sound like an audible command in his ears. "What concord hath Christ with Belial? or what part hath he that believeth with an infidel?"

His request, however, was received with strong demurrers, which in the case of a few of the members took a form nearly allied to threats.

"Now what should you want to leave us for?"

asked one. "Haven't you always been treated well
by the lodge?"

"I have no fault to find on that score," said
Stephen, briefly. "My reasons for withdrawing
have already been stated."

"Now I tell you, in your peculiar situation as a
temperance lawyer fighting the liquor party all the
time, you need the protection of the lodge, and if
you leave it you run more risk than you think."

This warning came from a man prominent in the
Van Gilder clique, and Stephen, considering the
source from which it proceeded, did not mind it
much till it was repeated in various terms by others
of much higher social respectability. His naturally
independent spirit cared very little for these undis-
guised attempts at intimidation, but it showed him
still another side of this many-sided order. It was
willing then to protect an honest man in his warfare
against evil, but he must buy that protection in the
same way a rogue buys his immunity from the grasp
of justice—by paying dues and learning signs and
grips! He wrote a long letter home—a letter which
caused much astonishment in the Howland homestead—in which he thus alluded to his experience
in the lodge the night he took his withdrawal card:

"I only did what I had a perfect right to do, yet
many in the lodge have taken great offense at the
step. To be sure they are the least respectable
members, but they are the very ones with the will to
do me harm. Honestly, such were the looks and
demeanor of some of those men towards me that I

should extremely dislike the idea of meeting them alone in the woods on a dark night."

"To think Stephen should have joined the Odd-fellows! Who'd have thought it! Would you, mother?"

This was Mr. Josiah Howland's first observation.

"Not that exactly," answered Mrs. Phœbe, as she folded the letter with hands that trembled, "but you know, father, we've both of us been a little troubled for fear Stephen might have backslidden, and lately I have been filled with such deep concern, and my whole soul has been so drawn out to agonize with the Lord for him that I have felt sure he was in some kind of a snare."

There is such a thing as spiritual second sight. Mrs. Phœbe was one thus gifted, and her husband reverenced it in her as something he did not himself possess, and did not quite understand. He had "lathered" his face preparatory to shaving, and now he stood before the little ten by twelve looking-glass thoughtfully "stropping" his razor.

"But I never dreamed *Stephen* would ever be trapped into any of these godless secret societies," he repeated, the idea every time he thought of it seeming to come with a fresh surprise.

"Why not Stephen as soon as any one?" queried Mrs. Phœbe Howland, as she put the letter away, and went quietly about some household task.

"Well, I don't know why," returned Mr. Josiah, as if this was a new view of the matter; "only I thought we had trained him better than that."

"Maybe the Lord is training him now, father."

Mr. Josiah pondered this over while he was shaving, as was his fashion of pondering his wife's sayings. These expressions of her finer spiritual nature that would never in the world have occurred to him, found a ready soil of appreciation in his heart where they blossomed in higher faith and profounder trust, for he had a timid and doubting side, and with all his New England patrimony of shrewd common sense it was beautiful to see how in every difficulty he turned to her clearer insight for counsel. "Somehow Phœbe could always see into things," he would say.

"Maybe that's so, mother. But I can't help feeling afraid for Stephen. Perhaps he stands in no danger from the Odd-fellows, but one can't tell in these secret societies, and I do wish he'd kept clear of them. They may do something to him yet. And there's the liquor men, they are dreadfully rampant out there. I was reading in the paper only yesterday how they set on a young temperance attorney in one place and beat him most to death."

Mrs. Phœbe Howland grew a trifle paler at these words, and drew her breath quick like one stabbed by sharp and sudden pain. Then she stood straight up before her husband with a deep, solemn light in her dark eyes.

"Father, you and I gave Stephen to the Lord as soon as he was born. *When did we ever take back the gift?*"

Mr. Josiah finished shaving in silence.

CHAPTER XXVII.

Jesse Dukes was sitting in his low cabin door. The river flowed past with a sweet, hardly definable murmur; the woods were a ring of emerald set against sapphire; a soft wind just stirred their leaves with a faint, spirit-like motion; the light wreaths of smoke which ascended from his pipe seemed only a part of all this tranquil beauty; and the figure of the trapper himself as he sat leaning back, his eyes half-closed, and every muscle relaxed in lazy enjoyment of the fine weather, presented no disturbing element in the scene. In fact Jesse Dukes came of a race who are gifted with far more of the Italian *dolce far niente* than of the Yankee restlessness and vim, and think nothing of taking their time to smoke and sleep out of any part of the day which suits them best. He knew that one his traps needed mending, and by and by he was going to attend to it. Meanwhile he felt in no hurry. The summer days were long in his little cabin, and there would be plenty of time to smoke his pipeful of tobacco before he set to work.

He was not ill-supplied with reading matter, such as it was. Copies of some ancient magazine lent him by the neighbors lay piled up on his rude table, and from the same source he often received the loan of an old newspaper. If a month or even a year had intervened since the date of publication, it made no difference. He read it with as much interest.

The mountaineer of the Southwest is by nature a fierce political partisan, and retains the freshness of first convictions to an extent apt to waken a smile in places where the mail comes daily, and the constant shifting of factions, reversing to-morrow the positions they hold to-day, and uniting to-day on questions at which they were at sword's points yesterday, so often makes the average voter doubtful of his real standing place. Nowhere else can be found the genuine Andrew Jackson Democrat, who, in his fealty which is, like that of an old French Legitimist, less to a person than an idea, cannot be made to realize that the party has chosen new gods to go before it. And it has its pathetic as well as its amusing side—this stubborn tenacity with which he will hold on to principles which that party has long cast out of its platform, and be ready to fight to the death for a political leader, years after that leader has stepped out of the ranks of the living. Jesse Dukes came of such a family. He was one himself and gloried in it. At the same time we must confess that he would have been a most inconvenient member to take active part in a Democratic convention of the present day.

Finally he rose up and stretched himself with a mighty yawn—he was over six feet and his head

reached nearly to the cabin roof—laid his pipe carefully away on the shelf, and was about to turn his
attention to the broken trap, when, in his search for
some paper to clean it with, he came across a part
of a Democratic political speech. To the majority
of newspaper readers it would have been like a piece
of very stale apple pie, but Mr. Dukes proceeded at
once to devour it with a keen appreciation of what
seemed to him the most telling points. He was a
prohibitionist, but like thousands of Southern Democrats who lean that way, he could not see how inextricably his beloved party had mortgaged itself to
the rum power; and if anybody wonders at such be-
nighted ignorance on the part of this simple Tennes-
seean, the blindness of the average Republican will
present him with as great a marvel. He was also,
as we have seen, an Anti-mason of the intensest
type, but he was entirely ignorant—an ignorance
shared however by the mass of historical students—
of that bit of American political history in which
the lodge played so important a part when it made
Andrew Jackson President, and thus prevented its
inveterate foe, John Quincy Adams, from filling the
Presidential chair for a second term.

He had finished it, and was about to appropriate
the paper to its intended use when his eye rested on
a local paragraph in which occurred a name that
had not crossed his mind for ten years save linked
with a curse. His face changed terribly when he
saw it. The lazy, shiftless, good-natured trapper
had the failings as well as the virtues of the moun-

tain race from which he sprung—grateful for the
smallest benefit, quick to avenge the smallest affront,
a trusty friend and an implacable foe.

It was the name of Dacey—James Dacey; a man
born of a good family, but with a decided bent for
the crooked and devious ways of the transgressor,
and with a faculty for keeping clear of the law that
much mystified many of his victims. He had been
married twice. The first time he had obtained an
unjust divorce through the help of an unprincipled
attorney who was like himself a high Mason. The
second time he had beguiled a simple-hearted, pretty
maiden into marrying him; then, after living with
her for a while, denied the legality of the marriage,
and left her, broken-hearted, in an equivocal position among strangers to support her two children as
best she could. Mr. Dacey's regular profession it
would have been hard to define. He never stayed
very long in one place, and with every change of
residence he turned his hand to something new in
the line of rascality. At the time Jesse Dukes so
unfortunately made his acquaintance he called himself a broker in real estate, though his methods of
conducting business were somewhat peculiar. He
was really the head of a bogus land company which
operated under fictitious names, issuing worthless
title deeds to confiding settlers in distant territories,
but he sometimes did a stroke of sharp business
nearer home, as in the case of Jesse Dukes. The
simple mountaineer, utterly unused to trickery and
fraud, bravely defended his title to his newly pur-

chased homestead, and when he realized that the suit had actually gone against him he could scarcely be restrained from springing on his adversary in open court. He swore vengeance as it was, and Dacey, whose forte was rather the smooth and graceful villain than the bully, thought it prudent to decamp, having about come to the end of his little game, rather than risk a charge of buckshot in his handsome person. He then became partner in a liquor saloon for a while. He operated a faro bank for a season. He dabbled in various lottery schemes, and indeed it would be difficult to name anything in the line of swindling and roguery to which he had not at one time or another given his attention. He was now agent for some worthless agricultural patents, and in consequence a very active grangeman. When the grange should discover, as it must before long, that it had been outrageously duped, he could rely on the close connection of that body with the Masonic lodge to clear him from the consequences.

Jesse Dukes sat for a long while with his eyes riveted on the paper. But this might be another James Dacey. Anyway he would find out, and if it *should* prove the one he sought, why—Mr. Dukes had no very clear idea of the form his vengeance was going to take, but he meant before he was through with Mr. Dacey to make him repent his action in that particular lawsuit which had broken up his happy home and reduced him to poverty.

At last with a fierce, determined look he rose to his feet, and not even stopping to put away his traps strewed over the floor, he left the cabin standing empty and desolate, and started forth on his quest for vengeance.

Before we proceed to tell how the quest came out, we have a word to say regarding the startling increase in our land of that form of lawless violence known as lynch law. In rude, semi-civilized communities it may be a deplorable necessity to dispense summary justice in this way, but when we find the papers filled with accounts of horrible lynching affairs, not perpetrated where the reign of law and order has not yet begun, but under the very shadow of our court houses, it is evident that there is something wrong in the working of our criminal laws. When a people know that swift and equal punishment will be meted out to all wrong doers, they are not generally disposed to take the execution thereof on themselves. But when the law has respect of persons, when it discriminates between the man who has robbed the State of a fortune and the poor boy who steals five dollars, because the one is a Mason and the other is not, is there room for wonder that they weary sometimes of the travesties of justice in our court rooms and become their own judges and executioners?

CHAPTER XXVIII.

"VENGEANCE IS MINE."

"I call this curious weather, Mr. Deming. Makes me feel kinder as though something was going to happen."

"Can't expect comfortable weather in dog days, Uncle Zeb," responded Mr. Deming, as he took a look around him at the horizon, which was curtained by a thin veil of clouds through which the sun shone with a strange, brassy radiance, while the very leaves on the trees seemed to fairly pant in the lifeless air.

"That's a fact," returned Uncle Zeb, as he seated himself in an easy attitude for conversation. "But human nater is dreadful onreasonable. When it's cold we want it hot, and when it's hot we want it cold. Makes me think a little of the weather we had that year Harrison was elected. I remember all about them 'Tippecanoe and Tyler too' times. Maybe you don't quite so well. You was a trifle younger."

"Parties have changed a good deal since then," sententiously remarked Mr. Deming, and Uncle Zeb went on.

"Well, politics is a good deal like a chessboard. It's a move here and a move there, and to them that

don't understand the ins and outs, why, it's all gam-
mon.   That's the way I look at all this nominating,
and canvassing, and stump-speaking.   But the Prohibitionists now—they seem to be going on a different tack.   I see there was a W. C. T. U. woman ad-
vertised to speak not a great ways from here, and I
thought I'd chirk up and go and hear her.   And if
she wan't a master head for facts and figgers!   Some
of the things she told fairly made me cry like a
baby.   I've been all kinder stirred up ever sence a
thinkin' on 'em over.   It didn't sound a bit as
though she was making a speech; she seemed to talk
right from her heart as the Lord give her the words.
I tell you, Mr. Deming, I've *about* made up my mind
if I live till next fall to vote the Prohibition ticket
and let both the old parties go—to grass."

Now Mr. Deming, it must be said, was a Republican, who had always prided himself on being sound
in regard to all the great moral questions of the day,
but he had never yet reached the point of leaving
his party; and now to hear such an energetic expression from Uncle Zeb, a Democrat of that easy-going
type who take up naturally with the party whose
platform presents the fewest troublesome issues,
touched his conscience as with a vague reminder of
the words of inspiration, "The first shall be last and
the last first."

"Well, I am waiting to see who the Democrats
will put up," he answered cautiously.   "A good deal
depends on that."

"I understand"—and Uncle Zeb chuckled, for he

could not help uttering a joke even when it bore
rather hard on himself—"you know we Democrats
are the publicans and sinners. We can turn about
and enter the kingdom while you Republican Phari-
sees are balancing on the fence. There's a kind of
Scriptural illustration for ye, as you may say."

It was one, however, which Mr. Deming did not
enjoy, for he felt that in this matter as in that of
the grange, Uncle Zeb had the advantage. The latter had prudently abstained from making his usual
facetious allusions to "the machine," since the unfortunate Masonic experiment recorded in a prior
chapter, and Mr. Deming was so relieved by the
truce that he could have thanked the O'Sullivan goat
for its unwitting share in bringing it about, many
times as he had voted the animal a nuisance and resolved to complain to the owner for not keeping it
more strictly confined.

It is one of the laws of the grange that no political questions shall be discussed in its meetings, yet
"the machine" is one eminently adapted to gain
office for the leaders; for who would suspect a society
of simple farmers of engaging in political schemes
and plottings? least of all those same innocent-
minded farmers themselves? Fairfield Grange,
though ostensibly devoted to advancing the peaceful
art of agriculture, was really a hot-bed of partisan-
ship, and Mr. Israel Deming had felt very percepti-
bly the pulling of certain wires; but whose hands
manipulated them or the secret of their workings
were hidden mysteries. Of the men for whom there

was this invisible but strong pressure brought upon him to vote at the coming election, he knew literally nothing except that they were grangemen, who, he was assured, would use their official position to advance the farming interests. He was never told, however, that every one of these same seekers for political power were high degree Masons, who were using the simple grangers as the proverbial monkey used the too confiding grimalkin.

Dora was sitting in the open window, dressed in her light afternoon muslin—a most agreeable and pleasing object. She heard the conversation, but not to take any particular interest therein. Her father and Uncle Zeb were always talking politics nowadays, and lugging in that wearisome subject of prohibition. Of course she wanted rum-selling done away with, but what was the use of making such a fuss about it? And as to these W. C. T. U. women she did not understand them in the least. She was sure *she* could never spend her life as they did, thinking and speaking and writing of nothing but temperance all the time. And then to go round gathering up all these terrible facts which made her feel sick even to read or hear about! It was perfectly incomprehensible. From this train of thought Dora's musings branched off in another direction. She began to think how hot it was, and recall to her mind some of the latest compliments Mr. Dacey had paid her, and wonder whether he really meant them. To the language of polite gallantry Dora was a stranger, and she never thought that a single glance of honest admiration from one of her young farmer suitors, even when it remained unsaid or was expressed in the most awkward and bungling fashion, had in it a thousand times more of real knightly chivalry.

Mr. Dacey on his part took every opportunity to foster her foolish fancy, for he was by no means oblivious of the fact that Mr. Deming was the richest farmer in Fairfield, and Dora an only child. But he had no idea of appearing as an open and honest wooer where he was sure of meeting opposition—especially from Mrs. Deming. There had existed a settled antagonism between them from the first. She was suspicious that all was not right in regard to the grange business, and feared that he was leading her easy-minded husband into trouble with those agricultural patents. The very suspicion that he had designs on Dora would have transformed her negative dislike to him into positive fury. But he was sure he could in time prevail on the latter to consent to a secret or runaway marriage, and in fact he had already laid his plans to this end by paying her many clandestine attentions which, if she had not been thoroughly bewitched by his flatteries, would have put her on her guard. For her's was a frank and open nature. The secrecy of the grange in itself had no charms for her. We do not bait a trap with poison, but with a harmless bit of cheese. Dora's girlish love of pleasure and admiration provided all the attraction needed.

It grew more strangely still and dark and oppressive. What little oxygen there was in the air seemed to die out of it. Even her father and Uncle Zeb grew silent as if it was too hot to talk. Mrs. Deming, however, had not succumbed to the weather. She did not believe in succumbing to anything, and now she said decidedly to Dora:

"Come, child, don't be so idle. If you are at work you won't mind the heat half so much."

Dora made a pretense of going on with her sewing, but the gate clicked just then and set her foolish little heart to beating with the thought that it might be Mr. Dacey, who had mentioned to her the day before, in one of those clandestine walks which he always contrived to plan in such a way that Dora never really suspected that he meant they should be clandestine, his intention of visiting her father the next day on business. It did not prove to be him, however, but the strangest, roughest looking figure Dora had ever seen. He must be a tramp of the most desperate description, she thought. How very fortunate that her father was at home! Of Uncle Zeb's valor in case of any sudden call upon it she had a pardonably low opinion.

We, however, have no trouble in recognizing our old friend, Jesse Dukes. Weariness and hunger and thirst he had hardly felt in the fierce heat of revengeful desire that consumed his soul. He asked for a drink and sat down on the doorstep, unloosing his knapsack as he did so and setting his rifle carefully up against the outside wall.

Dora brought him water in a tin dipper. Jesse

Dukes looked up at her with something of the pleasure that one looks at a bright-hued flower or bird.

"Thank ye, daughter," he said, as he gave the dipper back.   But the hard, fierce, vindictive face only
softened for an instant.

"I've got an account to settle with a man," he answered reticently, to Uncle 'Zeb's ready questionings, "and I've tramped a smart forty miles on purpose to settle it.   So I'm feelin' a bit beat out."

There came a low rumble of distant thunder.

"I reckon there's goin' to be a shower," said
Uncle Zeb in his slow way.

The gate clicked again.   Jesse Dukes started up.
He felt as by intuition the approach of his victim,
yet Dacey was within a yard of him and his foot
almost on the door-stone before he recognized the
grim face of the trapper.   Then he stopped, trembling.   He had reason to tremble, remembering the
look of wild-beast fury from which he had cowered
in such miserable terror, when, helpless in the net
of Masonic injustice, Jesse Dukes had turned upon
him in the court-room ten years before.   Now to be
so suddenly confronted with it was almost like an
apparition from the dead.

He attempted at first to ignore his enemy; then
with a poor feigning of sudden recollection he held
out his hand affably and tried to assume an air of
old acquaintanceship.

Jesse Dukes took no notice of the motion but
stood directly in his path, a grim and frowning bar-
rier to his further progress.

"You ain't fit to step your foot over a decent man's threshold," he said in a low, fierce voice; "and I'll stop your doing it if I kin. Didn't you cheat me out of every cent I had in the world, all because you was a Mason and could count on a Masonic judge and jury to help? And when my wife lay a dyin', and I had only a cabin to shelter her, and no medicine, nor food of the right kind for her, she'd want me to read to her out of the Bible, but when I did my eyes would always be a lightin' on sich ar texts as these: 'He turneth the way of the wicked upside down.' 'On the wicked he shall reign snares. Fire and brimstone and an horrible tempest shall be the portion of their cup.' When the Lord comes to reckon with ye, ye miserable varmint, passing yourself off for an unmarried man when you've got a wife and two children—off, nobody knows where—ye'll find there's a court up above where they don't make much account of Masonic signs and grips."

Dora gave a low, quick cry, that nobody heard in the excitement of the moment. It was as if wrapped in a somnambulist's dream she had been standing on the sheer edge of a dreadful precipice, and Jesse Duke's terrible accusations against the man she was foolish enough to think she loved was the voice in her ears that had wakened and saved her.

Dacey would have run away, but aside from the lack of dignity in such a proceeding it would have been about as safe to attempt flight with the fangs of a bull-dog already fastened in his coat. As a last resort he appealed to the group in the doorway.

"This fellow, you must see, is insane, Mr. Deming. How can you allow him to insult and abuse me with such a pack of lies. Uncle Zeb, as a brother Mason"—

Here Uncle Zeb rose up in mighty wrath.

"You needn't 'brother' me. I was green enough once to jine the lodge, and I've made a kind of a joke of it when it was a sin I'd oughter have repented of. And if a thousandth part of what I've he'erd jest now is true, I'd advise you to be repenting, and in a mighty hurry."

"This is prolonging a most unprofitable interview," said Dacey, taking refuge in the coolest effrontery he could muster to hide his inward scare. "Here is a man ready to take my life, and not one of you stirs a finger."

But Mr. Deming had enough of the Anglo-Saxon sense of justice not to interfere till really obliged to do so. He knew very well that but for these revelations now so strangely made by this unknown man he might in the next hour have been in Dacey's power—how deeply and inextricably he trembled to think. Such a villain ought to be in state's prison, and though a good fright would go but a small way towards paying him his deserts, it was better than nothing.

So pre-occupied were the group that no one saw the black curiously-shaped cloud with lurid greenish edges so swiftly approaching from the southwest, bearing desolation and death in its track. Yet the

very birds had felt the awful shadow of its coming
and flown away in terror.

"Ye sneakin' varmint!"—and with the old panther fury blazing in his eyes Jesse Dukes would
have sprung on his adversary, but a Hand parted
them.

Those in the house heard a dull, distant roar, but
there was no time for flight before, cutting for itself
a path even and clean as if done by a mower's
scythe, the tornado swept past, wrecking farm and
outbuildings, felling trees, and filling the air with
the flying dust and debris.

The storm demon did his work of destruction in
that one brief, dreadful instant. Dora had shut her
eyes in shuddering terror when the blow came on.
She opened them to find herself, rather to her own
surprise, still a denizen of this world. Uncle Zeb
was groaning and praying like an old-fashioned
Methodist. Not one of the group had been injured
by even a scratch.

But assailer and assailed!—where were they?

Jesse Dukes had really no intention of taking
Dacey's life. He meant to chastise him soundly
and show him up for the unprincipled villain that
he was. The justice Masonic courts refused to give
him he meant to administer for himself according to the rude ideas of justice prevailing among his
primitive mountain race. But Dacey's insulting
words had heated the furnace of the trapper's wrath
seven times hotter. There was murder in his soul,
murder in the fierce grip with which he held his

enemy till wrenched apart by that terrible Power.

*   *   *   *   *   *   *   *   *   *

He knew nothing more till one flash of vivid lightning rent the gloom, followed instantly by the reverberating crash of the swiftly descending thunderbolt. The rain descended in sheets, in cataracts. Jesse Dukes raised himself from the sodden earth and suddenly realized that he was alone—that the form stretched lifeless on the ground a dozen yards away was that of James Dacey. God had avenged him of his adversary, and saved him from blood-guiltiness.

He staggered to his feet, gave one dazed glance around and covered his face with his hands, moaning, "O Lord, I'm a poor sinner!"

CHAPTER XXIX.

GOING DOWN INTO EGYPT.

The political contest had assumed new features, and as usual the saloon and the lodge were both active. By this means some curious complications were preparing which would be a surprise to many who never thought while so confidently predicting results to make allowance for these two important factors—particularly the latter. "The way of a serpent upon a rock" is about as easy to trace as the way of the lodge in politics, but we will essay the task, first giving the reader a map of the political situation that he may better understand what follows.

The Republicans nominated as their choice for Governor Judge Dyer, a Christian man of strong temperance principles—in all respects an irreproachable candidate. The determined stand made by the Prohibitionists at the previous election had forced this concession from the unwilling party leaders. To nominate again a demagogue like Gen. Putney, even at the bidding of the Grand Army, would be too much of a risk. On the other hand the Democrats nominated as before an ex-confederate who stood high in favor with the saloonists. Had the Republican choice been less worthy the Prohibition ranks would have stood firm, but when to its nominee's unquestioned character for integrity and patriotism were added vague promises of submitting a prohibitory amendment to the people, even the staunchest third party men wavered. Stephen Howland himself, after a little inward struggle, left the prohibition Moses and joined the rest who flocked to Judge Dyer's standard in the sanguine belief that they already saw the dawn of a new day.

But Martin Treworthy was not so hopefully inclined, though if he could have conscientiously cast his vote once more with the party of his first affections, so inseparably associated with the memory of his old battles for human freedom and the name of his mourned and martyred chief, it would have rejoiced him from his heart.

"Mr. Treworthy, what do you think of voting for Judge Dyer," asked Nelson, who was now in his new position of foreman at the works.

He was tolerably sure of keeping it, and could speak lightly of his own losses to Stephen Howland as compared with others whose all had been swallowed up in the bank's failure. At the same time to have to begin over again the task so nearly accomplished of earning a home for himself and Martha was not a very inspiriting outlook. Besides this there were disagreeable things connected with his new position, for while the majority of the men liked him, he knew there existed an unfriendly element which made itself felt in various ways, and which would not only have gladly ousted him from

the situation, but would doubtless have succeeded
in doing so with an employer of less stubborn make
or less firmly his friend than Matthew Densler, who
turned a deaf ear to all complaints, grimly assuring
the fault finders that he was boss over his own concerns, and if they didn't like the new foreman they
might leave and welcome—the sooner the better.

Martin leaned forward in his leathern arm-chair,
and was silent a moment before replying.

"Judge Dyer is a fine sort of a man. He's clear
of the lodge; I've taken the pains to find out that.
And once, at least, he's wrote or said something
against it. And he's got a good clean temperance
record, but then I don't know —"

"Whether it is best to vote for him?" inquired
Nelson, as Martin seemed to go off in a deep reverie,
leaving the unfinished sentence suspended on his
lips. "I don't see as there is any other alternative.
I have said I would never go again with the Republican party, but I think I shall vote for Judge
Dyer."

" 'Woe unto them that go down to Egypt for help!' "
repeated Martin slowly and solemnly to this declaration; " 'to strengthen themselves in the strength of
Pharaoh and to trust in the shadow of Egypt.
Therefore, shall the strength of Pharaoh be your
shame and the trust in the shadow of Egypt your
confusion.' "

But Nelson could not see that this Old Testament
prophecy had the slightest bearing on the subject,
and answered wonderingly:

"What do you mean, Mr. Treworthy?'

"Didn't the Jews go for help to a nation eaten up by false worships? And ain't that just what the prohibition Israel is doing to-day?—seeking help from a party given over to the heathenism of the Masonic lodge?"

"Not more than the Democratic party, surely."

"That ain't the question. Masonry controls 'em both. Do you think I want the Democrats to win? Don't I remember their rule thirty years ago under Pierce and Buchanan, when I was whipped and put in prison and chased by bloodhounds? But that is all over and done with. I don't owe the Democratic party anything now, nor they me."

"Then why not vote for Judge Dyer? such an exceptionable candidate—I really can't see."

"No, you can't see," retorted Martin, with quiet sarcasm; "but may the Lord open your blind eyes. Here you be, you and other prohibitionists, and you can't see that a vote for either of the old parties is a vote for the lodge, and a vote for the lodge is a vote for the saloon."

Martin Treworthy shut his lips and said no more.

But it was a very cheerful going down into Egypt. The Republicans were confident of victory now they had captured the prohibition vote; the Prohibitionists equally so now that the Republicans had seemingly acceded to their demands. And though there were some like Martin Treworthy to feel suspicious of this era of peace and good will, they were in too small a minority for their votes to be missed.

CHAPTER XXX.

LODGE AND SALOON.

"The politicians of late years have been playing a game of chess intent wholly upon the board, but never giving a thought to the table under the board. But the table was alive, the back of a people which began to stir, and in the twinkling of an eye chessboard and men went to the devil."

This vigorous paragraph from St. Beuve on the French Provisional government of 1848 is quoted partly because it contains a warning which American politicians would do well to heed, and partly because the last clause describes very exactly the feelings of many good people when Judge Dyer was ignominiously defeated and his Democratic rival elected to the gubernatorial chair.

The old nursery rhyme of Cock Robin is founded on a deep-seated principle of human nature. If even a pan of milk is overturned it is always consoling to know exactly who or what did the mischief. In obedience to this philosophic instinct of humanity we will now resolve ourselves into a coroner's jury and inquire into the cause of Judge Dyer's untimely political death.

Masonry never forgets or forgives. On one single occasion, years before, he had written a letter condemning the lodge. Lodge leaders remembered it, and silently and secretly they combined together to prevent his election. How did they do it? The answer is easy. They united with the liquor men, and on some slight pretext "bolted" to the Democratic side in just sufficient numbers to turn the scale. But even Judge Dyer never suspected the hidden hand of Masonry. His defeat was ascribed to liquor bribery, to the defection in the German vote, to any and every cause but the true one.

The lodge leaders took care that the blame should be thrown on the shoulders of the prohibitionists, and their ideas were reflected in leading Republican papers by such paragraphs as the following: "The utter uselessness of making concessions to prohibition fanaticism has been proved once more. As usual it has been a disturbing and disintegrating factor which has not strengthened the party but only brought upon it defeat and loss. It is too costly a folly to be again repeated."

The liquor men were of course jubilant, and with astonishing unanimity the very saloonists who were such strong Republicans at the previous election, now that victory had perched on the Democratic banners, made haste to doff their new political livery and veer round to the winning side: while behind them stood the lodge Judas smiling complacently at the clever way in which it had tricked the simple temperance folks, betraying them wholesale to their ancient enemy.

But out of the dead lion came forth honey.   The
W. C. T. U. had no idea of giving up the battle for
a change of parties.   The prohibitionists, sadder
and wiser, fell into line and the work went on to the
mingled anger and consternation of the saloon men
who had reckoned securely on having things their
own way.   And now to have the cup of triumph
dashed from their lips, as seemed eminently probable if the bill for submitting a prohibitory amendment to the people could be made to pass the Senate
by a non-partisan vote the following winter, was certainly enough to warrant them in declaring, with
many unnecessary expletives, that "these W. C. T.
U. women never knew when they were beat."

Martin Treworthy heard the result of the election
in grim silence, and did not even say to Nelson, "I
told you so."

Stephen Howland, on his part, was astonished.
He had been very sanguine regarding Judge Dyer's
election, but he felt that the two old parties were
coming closer and closer together every year.   To
be sure, the Republicans retained something of their
former moral superiority—the momentum generated
by the sacrifices and sufferings of their early leaders.
Corrupt and self-seeking as was the average politician of that party, now and then they put up a pure
candidate, nor had the rank and file quite lost the
memory of their first baptism in blood and tears as
the party of liberty and moral progress.

Altogether it was a far more promising instrument for the lodge to make use of for the betrayal

of the temperance cause than its Democratic rival, of whose reform promises, though it should charm never so wisely, all true reformers would ever remain reasonably shy.

Stephen Howland, about a week before the election, was much surprised to hear the Good Templar acquaintance previously mentioned allude in a doubtful way to the result of the contest, and remark that "he was sorry the Republicans had not put up a stronger ticket."

"It is a thousand times stronger in all that constitutes real strength than the ticket put up last year," responded Stephen, warmly. "Judge Dyer has got no tricks of the demagogue about him. He is a plain, honest man, and as such he ought to command the people's vote."

"Well, Col. Morrison said to me only yesterday— you know he is Republican and enough in politics to get an inside view of the way things are going— that Judge Dyer would never be elected. And he went on to tell how it was perilling the German vote; 'and besides,' says he, 'Dyer isn't personally a popular man.'"

Col. Morrison was one of the "bolters," willing to betray his party for the sake of the lodge, and the above is a very good specimen of the way in which he and other Masonic politicians worked against Judge Dyer—less by downright falsehoods than by vague insinuations which carried all the sting of positive charges. But it must not be supposed that Masonry defeated him under her own name. She

hid behind the secret liquor leagues, but lent them
her halls, animated their counsels, and did for them
in brief precisely what she formerly did for the
Southern Ku-Klux who hid their disguises in Masonic lodge-rooms, and whose exploits in burning
school houses and killing defenseless negroes were
really nothing but Masonic masquerades.

It has been computed that every saloon in the
country must control on an average ten votes, which
gives us two million saloon voters.   Add to this the
dark, silent, invisible factor of the secret lodge, and
is it any wonder that pure men should be defeated
at the polls and demagogism thrive as in a hot-bed?
Yet many good people stand aghast at the idea of
joining religion and politics, as if it might be like
those chemical unions in which the composing elements are harmless enough when kept separate, but
as soon as they come together develop explosive
properties.

But is the union of the saloon and politics, or
Masonry and politics, any less dangerous?   Can the
pulpit afford to keep silent regarding questions on
which all the dramshops and gambling hells and
secret lodges have their freely-expressed opinion?

CHAPTER XXXI.

A LIQUOR MOB.

The Jacksonville Legion was not a military company, as the reader may innocently imagine, but the name under which the liquor sellers of that city had banded together to prevent the passing of temperance laws and the execution of those already on the statute book. It was really a branch of a secret saloon association that could bribe and cajole and threaten and flatter the candidates of both parties; that always had delegates at the primaries and caucuses, and plenty of funds with which to corrupt public officials and defeat and betray prohibition measures. In fact the Legion was a power with capacities for mischief that far transcended the Order of the Red Mark.

Stephen Howland still continued to worry the liquor men and be the recipient of curses that he did not hear, and which would not have much troubled him if he had. But little as he suspected it his most formidable enemies were among his former Odd-fellow brethren. His defection was an unpardonable offense, an insult to the order. And considered in this light it is not strange that a very active desire to punish him for it in some way was

developed in the breasts of many of the members?
And what easier way to do this than through a Masonic understanding with his saloon foes?

The Jacksonville Legion was freely sprinkled with
Masons and Odd-fellows of the Van Gilder type who
had never borne very friendly feelings to the young
lawyer, and now rather enjoyed the opportunity of
hitting him in the dark. Stephen did not even know
of the existence of the Jacksonville Legion, but he
was soon to learn by disagreeable experience that
liquor malevolence with the spur of lodge malice
behind it is capable of desperate things.

Stephen was announced to speak one night on the
pending Constitutional Amendment in the First
Presbyterian church in Jacksonville. This church
was very unpopular with the rum party for the advanced ground which its members took on prohibition, and also as being a gathering place for the
W. C. T. U. So the trustees, shortly after the announcement, received an anonymous note from the
Jacksonville Legion which read as follows:

SIRS:—*This is to inform you that if you let your
church be used by that lying blatherskite of a temperance lawyer, Stephen Howland, to spout his injurious
nonsense and defame better men than himself, we shall
find ways and means to destroy the building.*

BY-ORDER OF THE JACKSONVILLE LEGION.

The trustees quaked in their shoes, and with some
reason, for it was not long since an attempt had
been made to dynamite a temperance hotel. It
would be just as easy to dynamite a church, and it

was finally decided to hold the meeting in a public hall.

Stephen was not without a goodly share of phyical courage, but when he found on entering the place a crowd of irate whisky men filling up all the front seats next to the platform, he felt glad that the measure on which he was going to speak was such a one as to make it not incongruous, but on the contrary highly reasonable and proper that he should open his address with prayer.

The meeting was not entirely in the hands of the mob, and it was a positive inspiration to catch sight of Martin Treworthy in the audience—grim old hero of a hundred by-gone battles; and to meet Nelson Newhall's flashing eyes, that Stephen always said to himself had in them the look of a born leader; and see the calm, earnest faces of women that would any day dare a mob for the protection of their homes. But Stephen had put far from him the pride of fleshly confidence when he turned away from "the unfruitful works of darkness" at the call of the converted rumseller, Peter Snyder, and in an hour like this he felt that the eternal Jehovah himself must be his stronghold.

His prayer was audible to but few, the mob in front keeping up a perfect Babel of groans and hisses.

St. George had met the dragon!

If Stephen's heart had been a trifle lifted up with his popularity—and it was natural that it should be, for he was young, and flattering voices had not been wanting to prophesy for him a brilliant political future when the new party of prohibition should take the helm—it was strangely humble when he faced once more the riotous crowd. That reverent bowing of the head, that brief, simple petition had been altogether unpremeditated. It was a sudden impulse, the feeling of his own weakness coupled with such an inrushing sense of the divine power to uphold that he did it without a thought of anything singular in the action.

It was the first time he had ever fronted such an assemblage. But he had that crowning gift of the orator, a fine, sonorous voice, and was not easily put down.

At one point in his speech a few rotten eggs were hurled, bespattering a brand new suit. This was disagreeable as it was a nice one, and his funds would not at present warrant him in getting another.

"I am glad to meet some of our saloon friends in argument," he responded as coolly as if it had been a bouquet of roses, at which there was laughter and applause mingled with other demonstrations not so flattering. "I object to the style of the argument, but I will put up with it if it is the best they can muster. I am not here to-night in the interests of any man or any faction."

Jeering cries interrupted him, but he went on with perfect good nature.

"You distrust what I say—that I am not a demagogue swayed by selfish or at best class interests. A man has no right to pronounce an opinion in pub-

lic on any great question who has not first examined
it carefully on both sides, and considered it intelli-
gently and its relations to all classes in the community. If women should have the right to preserve the peace and virtue of their homes intact; if
business men and artisans have the right to pursue
their several callings unburdened by enormous and
unnecessary taxation, liquor sellers have also their
rights which I now propose to spend a few moments
in considering."

There was silence now. Even his foes were a little curious to see how Stephen would handle this
novel subject. He went on.

"The saloonist thinks that if he pays fifty or a
hundred or five hundred dollars to the State or the
city for a license to sell liquor, he has a right, clear
and incontestable, to sell it. Certainly so far as it
goes he has the best of the argument. The distiller,
if he pays ninety per cent tax to the government,
thinks he has a right to carry on his business without let or hindrance, and so far as human law can
give it to him has he not that right? This is not a
subject which we consider sufficiently. Of those
who denounce the liquor seller, nine out of ten have
never thought of putting themselves in his place, or
reflected that he has rights like other men—the
right that the government under which he lives
should deal fairly by him, and, if his be as legitimate
a business as shoeing horses or selling tea and sugar,
should impose no more restrictions on him than it
does on the blacksmith or the merchant. Now there

is no middle line between an honest and a dishonest business, between one that injures and one that benefits society; and the Government in taxing liquor-selling so utterly out of proportion to other trades is either guilty of the most high-handed oppression or the basest partnership in crime.

"Yet to-day our nation halts between two opinions. Shame on such cowardly vacillation! Either the business is a legitimate one and should not be taxed at all, or else it is the contrary and should be prohibited forever. Better that our law-givers openly proclaim the rule of the Drink Moloch than to worship him in secret. Better they should fling wide open the doors of the saloon and force the question to an issue. In the name of justice, of common sense, of patriotism; in the name of ruined homes, of delicate women suffering nameless atrocities, of children crying themselves to sleep with cold and hunger, of the thousands who fill our asylums and poor-houses—sacrificed between the two mill-stones of national and individual greed, give the liquor seller his rights!"

Stephen stood erect and defiant. He felt as if he would not have minded a pistol at his head. He had reached that height of spiritual exaltation where walk the souls of martyrs palm-crowned. He would have gladly thrown his own life a sacrifice into the chasm of this awful wrong.

In the beginning of the disturbance some of the most determined among the temperance men fearing personal violence to the young speaker, had forced their way through the mob to the platform and made a kind of body guard around him, while one or two of the more timid had quietly slipped out and applied to the Mayor for police to quell the disturbance. The mob were composed mainly of barroom loafers, convenient tools for the saloon and the lodge; but they quailed before these evidences of a determination to preserve order, and Stephen finished his address in comparative quiet.

As may be imagined, he did not find the evening's exciting scenes a good preparation for sleep. He still occupied the same office, though it did not now look so bare and cell-like as when we first showed it to the reader. He had indulged himself in a student's lamp of neat and chaste design, a set of new law books, and an easy chair which happened to take his fancy at an auction sale because it was so like one which at home always occupied a certain corner of the family sitting-room, and had been his favorite refuge in many a childish trouble. Instead of directly seeking his couch he threw himself into its capacious arms, thinking that he would sit there a few moments and enjoy the darkness, and silence, and solitude. A soothed, comforted, restful feeling began to creep over him. The scowling, derisive faces ceased to float before his eyes, the tremor of his nerves grew still, and Stephen at last fell into a sound slumber, from which he was suddenly roused with a feeling that he had been repeating an old adventure of his boyhood, when one night in driving home the cows he was caught in a thunder storm.

But as he recovered from his bewilderment he grew conscious that it was a real sound which had awakened him—the firing of a volley of shot into his office window.

He hastily turned up his light. The pane was shattered, and in the ceiling directly over his sleeping place were lodged two bullets. Stephen felt a shivering sense of awe. Never before had he come so near to touching the hand of a protecting Providence, for plainly the object of the miscreants who had fired the bullets was assassination.

The outrage caused, as was natural, intense excitement, but as it had been planned in secret conclave by members of the Jacksonville Legion, bound by oath in true Masonic style to keep each other's counsels, the perpetrators were never discovered.

CHAPTER XXXII.

The bill for submitting a prohibitory amendment to the people stuck hopelessly in its passage through the Lower House. Legislators trembling under the threats of the autocratic rum power are surpassingly fertile in ways and means by which to evade the demands of temperance constituents.

But the W. C. T. U. again set up their banners in the name of the Lord for "no license" in Jacksonville. Again they marched to the polls in a body to beseige the hearts and consciences of the voters, and this time they conquered. Jacksonville stood committed for prohibition by a large majority vote, and a band of rejoicing women gathered in the churches to sing Te Deums, and offer up glad thanksgivings from a full heart, only one thing marring the joy of the victory—the resignation of their beloved leader, Mrs. Haviland.

Physicians had at last told her that she must quit her life-work—that she was sinking under a mortal disease; and the sweet motherly face, with its silver curls, was missed forever from their counsels.

It was all clear now to Martha—that strangely excited manner, that wail as from a strong heart breaking. She was seeing what Martha could not see—a shadowy hand beckoning her silently, steadily, out of the conflict into the peace everlasting.

"Yes, they are going," said Martha to Nelson, with a trembling lip, "one by one. But the question in my mind is not whether we who take their places will be more devoted. That we cannot be. But shall we be wiser? Will the time come when the W. C. T. U. will see that the lodge has been all the while fighting them behind masked batteries?"

"I don't know," answered Nelson. "Rum and secrecy are two pretty formidable enemies to give battle to at once."

"Yes, but there's no help for it. 'One war at a time' is a maxim that sounds very well, but unfortunately you and I have been born in an exceptional age. We have got not only rum and the lodge, but infidelity, Sabbath-breaking, Mormonism, and ever so many other tremendous evils to battle with, not a single one of which can be safely let alone."

"Well," answered Nelson, "we are going to have a contest with the liquor men here in Jacksonville. This has been their stronghold so long that they are perfectly furious and determined to fight the law at every step. That outrage on Stephen Howland was only a specimen of what they would gladly do to others."

"Yourself included, I am afraid."

"Myself included, I *hope*," said Nelson with a laugh. "You surely would not wish me to have their goodwill."

Martha's answering smile was rather grave, for she never could get rid of a haunting fear for Nelson. And in fact at that very moment three burly foreigners, who could neither read nor write, were being treated to divers glasses of raw whisky in a saloon kept by a member of the Legion, as a fit preparation for the commission of a dastardly deed quite worthy of the two dark sources with which it originated.

The votes which had turned the scale against the liquor party in the last election were cast largely by young workmen whom Nelson had influenced to come out on the prohibition side. Why should not the saloonists hate and fear him? That they certainly did almost as much as they hated and feared Stephen Howland. And how easy to make a few ignorant foreigners their tools of vengeance by cramming them with stories that he was unfriendly to his own class; that in the recent strike he had taken sides against the laborer, and that his sympathies were all with the rich aristocrats and monopolists.

But utterly ignorant of any trap laid for his feet Nelson left his place of employment as usual to find Martin Treworthy waiting for him outside the works. He had got into a way lately of doing so, alleging sometimes that he wanted the walk, and sometimes that he wanted a conversation, but the real reason covered by the excuse was in a certain feeling of uneasiness in Martin's mind; though he took good care not to let Nelson see that he was the object of this peculiar surveillance.

"I looked over the prohibition returns this noon as I was eating my dinner," remarked Nelson, after starting several subjects of talk and not getting much reply, for Martin seemed unusually abstracted and silent. "Take the country at large and the gain over last year is wonderful. At this rate it won't be long before the third party will sweep all before it."

"You're young, lad, you're young," dryly answered Martin.

Nelson laughed. He was not averse to being called young, even if in his old friend's mind the expression stood for something akin to verdancy. He liked to feel that he had the larger half of his life before him. It always gave him a thrill to think that he was standing on the threshold of the world's mightiest conflicts, with forty, or even perhaps fifty, years in which to watch the unfolding of the grand panorama.

"I tell you," said Martin, his eyes kindling, "this ain't going to be no 'ninety days' struggle. Why, you just look at it a minute. See how Satan is setting the battle in array, and do you think he'll run like a whipped spaniel at the first fire?"

"Mr. Treworthy," said Nelson, half humorously, "you are, what do they call it, a pessimist? You are always looking at the dark side of human affairs."

"I don't daub with untempered mortar," said Martin, bluntly. "There's enough of that done nowadays by the ministers and the politicians."

Nelson relapsed into silence, and when Martin spoke again it was in a slow dreamy fashion almost as if talking to himself.

"That's a grand chapter in Revelations now about the Leader on the white horse. I remember reading it first in camp—in a pouring rain, chilled to the bone. That was in Kansas before the war begun, under Capt. John Brown. Them were hard times —to see the ministers and churches all going agin us, and the government joining to hunt us down. It was that chapter I was reading when the Lord revealed to me that there was a great war coming. And it did come, and the churches and ministers and government drank the cup of trembling and astonishment. And now they are doing the same thing right over, upholding and petting the secret lodge for every other foul thing to hide behind. And if they don't take warning they'll have the same cup to drink again."

Nelson had heard Martin Treworthy talk in this way before, but now there was something strangely solemn in his manner. He was about to reply when he heard his name suddenly called, and looked around.

"Hold on a minute!" he shouted, thinking it was one of the men at the works who had some matter about which he wished to speak to him.

A suspicion crossed his mind on a nearer approach that he might be mistaken in the identity of the individual addressing him, and to clear up his doubts he said, inquiringly:

"It is you, Mike?"

In the darkness he failed to notice the other fig-ures lurking behind. An oath answered him, and three clubs, wielded by the three stout arms that had been hired by the saloon and urged on by lodge vengeance, descended on Nelson's head and shoul-ders.

He had separated from Martin Treworthy, though the latter had not gone on but was quietly waiting at a short distance, and when he heard the execra-tion and the dull thud of the falling blows, he sprang forward and bursting into the ring which surrounded Nelson received himself the brutal rain of blows and kicks. Martin had once possessed a strong right arm of his own, and did not fully real-ize how his rough experience on Kansas plains and Southern battle fields had robbed it of its early vigor, but the diversion gave Nelson a chance to grapple with his assailants and hold his own till help arrived from an unexpected source.

The assault took place in the outskirts of the city, where there were few passers-by who dared to inter-fere. Only one tall, broad-shouldered, muscular stranger seemed to have no notion of waiting the tardy movements of the police, but pitched at once into the melee all unarmed as he was, and with a few skillful blows that showed pugilistic training knocked two of Nelson's antagonists *hors du combat*, and held the other with firm grip till the officers of the law came up and relieved him of his prisoner.

It was Peter Snyder, who was now in Jackson-

ville engaged in the double errand of looking out
for some stray sheep that within sound of a dozen
church bells still persisted in straying, while nobody
except a few such self-appointed evangelists as he
seemed to regard it as particularly their business;
and negotiating for the lease of his old saloon which
it had occurred to him was in a convenient locality
for a mission that he proposed starting. He had
left the Salvation Army. Even there he found the
same difficulty in speaking against lodgery that be-
sets the regularly-ordained minister of the Gospel
who can preach against rum and tobacco, or lying
or cheating, and everything be as calm as a summer
sea, while the least adverse allusion to secretism
stirs up a perfect seething whirlpool of angry com-
motion; and he had finally made up his mind, as he
expressed it, "to serve the Lord on his own hook."

Nelson, who was not seriously hurt, though somewhat bruised and battered, felt too great an anxiety
for Martin, who lay insensible, to show the surprise
he might have otherwise felt when we recognized
the Gideon who had so providentially appeared for
his rescue.

"I guess he'll come to in a minute," said Peter, as
he made rough efforts for his restoration. "But
them were hard knocks for a man of his age to
take."

Nelson groaned as he hung over the prostrate
form. But before long Martin Treworthy opened
his eyes and managed to stagger to his feet, and together, as tenderly as two sons might a beloved

father, they assisted him to his own domicile, but he fainted away when they reached the threshold.

* * * * * * * * * *

"I am all right, Martha. It's Mr. Treworthy that's got the worst of it. We must see to him now. He has fairly given his life for mine."

And Martha, to whom the tidings had come that Nelson had been struck down by saloon ruffians and nearly killed—and to whom for an instant that took in a whole lifetime of buried hopes and sweet womanly joys which might never come to the blossoming, everything had seemed to spin around in one dizzy vortex of anguish—knelt down by Martin's bedside and kissed his rough hand with sobs.

"Oh, Mr. Treworthy, you must get well for our sakes."

Martin smiled.

"Supposing Nelson had been killed, had you ruther—now think well—would you ruther he'd been indifferent to the rum business, as so many folks are, and so saved his life?"

"No," said Martha, with white lips. "If the martyr's crown was waiting for him I wouldn't be the woman to keep him from it."

"Then look here a bit. I reckon the woman I should have married, if she'd lived, and that I have been married to in my soul these twenty-five years, would have said the same thing."

"I think she would," responded Martha. She bent her head and kissed his hand again, and this time there came over her a strange feeling as if for

the moment. there had been a sense of spiritual kin-
ship and communion between her and Martin Treworthy's early love—the fair-haired girl who had
slept so quietly for a quarter of a century under her
low prairie mound.

But there was another to whom the tidings came
in an exaggerated form, and that was Dora Deming.

She had not quite forgotten her brother Nelson—
how tender and careful he used to be of his little
sister in the years of his over-grave boyhood. A
great change had passed over Dora since that summer day of awful experience. Dacey's death, the
way in which he had swindled the grange, and its
utter and hopeless collapse in consequence, together
with many unsavory details of his former career
now brought to the light, had been the talk for days in
circles wider than their immediate neighborhood;
but no one dreamed of the brink of ruin on which
Dora had so carelessly sported. It was all a secret
between herself and God. Perhaps in the years to
come, with her grandchildren about her knees, when
the wonder and terror had faded out of her life and
left her only the memory of the deliverance, she
might tell them the story for a warning. But now
the very thought of it made her shudder with a kind
of nightmare horror as one might shudder remembering an incautious footfall on the sheer edge of
some bottomless abyss.

"Mother," she said, after sitting a moment in silence with white cheeks and a great yearning at her
heart, "I wish I could see him—just once."

"Well, child; I don't know why you shouldn't," returned Mrs. Deming. "He is your own brother."

And so the very thing came about in the most natural way in the world for which Martha had longed and sometimes even prayed—that she might see Nelson's sister—she had none of her own—and get acquainted with her.

Martha, like most plain women, loved beauty, and her heart went out at once to the sweet girlish face that looked up at her with such beseeching entreaty.

"Tell me!" gasped Dora. "Is he dead, my brother Nelson?"

"No; he is alive and well. You were told wrong. It was Mr. Treworthy, an old friend of his, that was badly hurt in trying to defend him. I have often heard Nelson speak of his sister Dora. He will be glad to see you."

"I heard of it only this morning," said Dora, with quivering lip. "It seems so dreadful."

"It *is* dreadful," answered Martha, taking Dora's little, soft, clinging hand in her's. Martha's hands were not very small, but there was power and character in every fibre. They were the kind that Joan of Arc might have had, or any of those heroic women of our early history who could rock a cradle or shoulder a musket. "It is the same dreadful thing that has been going on so long. Only now it has come a little nearer. We grow callous. We read of rum's doings in every paper we take up till it gets to be an old story. We women who lead such peaceful happy lives need to have it brought home to us once in a while so that we may feel as we ought for other women. Don't you think so?"

Dora knew vaguely that her father had been a drinking man, and they had all been very poor and wretched in consequence, but she was too young at the time to retain any bitter personal recollections. She had not meant to be hard and unfeeling when in her bright, careless way she had protested that "such things didn't concern her anyway;" she had only been a butterfly happy in her painted wings and caring nothing for the worm crushed under foot. Something in Martha's face impelled her to be frank.

"I have not been interested in temperance—much. I have been selfish, I am afraid, but I wish I could help put down this dreadful drinking."

Impulsively Martha took off the bow of white ribbon that she wore and pinned it to Dora's dress.

"Then we are doubly sisters, for now you belong to the white ribbon ranks as well as I," she said. "We will work and pray together, can we not? And oh, Dora! can't you love me just a little? I have always wanted a sister so."

Dora's cheeks flushed, and then with a little cry she put her arms around Martha's neck, and clasped together in that close embrace Nelson found them.

*   *   *   *   *   *   *   *   *   *

Though there were a few days in which it seemed as if Martin Treworthy's natural vigor of constitution might re-assert itself, he had no such thought.

One night when Nelson was watching by his side,

Martin seemed to rouse suddenly from a stupor and spoke his name with sudden, eager earnestness.

"Nelson, in my tin box on the shelf you'll find a paper that'll tell you what I want done with what I leave behind. And there's one thing—two things you must promise me."

"Anything within the bounds of possibility, my dear old friend," said Nelson, with a choking voice.

Martin raised himself up and his eyes gleamed with the fire of other days.

"You said a year ago you could see no hurt in the lodge. Do you see any now?"

"I see a world of Satanic mischief," responded Nelson, emphatically. "Fighting slavery taught you to hate it. Fighting rum has taught me."

"Then take my place when I step out of the ranks. My life has been a rough one, but I can't say I hain't enjoyed it. I come of fighting stock. There was a Treworthy fell with Wolfe on the plains of Abraham; but my battle for the slave was a grander one than his. God grant that your's may be a grander one than mine. For I'm going, my boy, and you mustn't mourn for me nor feel bad— you nor Martha. There's only one thing more. When I am gone lay me by the side of *her*."

He said no more for a long time. Suddenly he raised his head and exclaimed joyfully, "I see Him —the Leader on the white horse." And with his eyes riveted on that wondrous vision, the man whose greatest earthly pride was that he had once fought under John Brown went to join his captain.

CHAPTER XXXIII.

THE CONCLUSION OF THE MATTER.

A story, like a human life, must draw to its conclusion some time, and as very little remains to be said regarding the fortunes of the characters with whom we have traveled thus far, we will proceed to the inevitable winding up.

Martha and Nelson stand in the front of the greatest moral conflict the world has ever seen. It rages hot and heavy, a battle all along the line. They, no less than the old anti-slavery reformers, live in a time that tries men's souls.

The paper in Martin Treworthy's tin box made Nelson sole heir to his bit of city property, and paved his way for the purchase of what is now one of the best farms in the State. And in the hermitage, moved to more congenial surroundings, they spent the first years of their married life, which were gladdened by the advent of a little Martin Treworthy Newhall; and even when fortune prospered them and they built a new and commodious residence, they still sacredly preserved it, converting it into a kind of summer-house half hid with creeping vines. And if the reader visits it once more, as we now invite him to, he will find the settee and the

leathern armchair in their old places; even the pot
of ivy and the vases of dried grass which Martha is
at the present moment engaged in arranging. Nelson is watching one of the most glorious of summer
sunsets, and as the radiant level beams convert the
broad acres of wheat into a living lake of emerald,
he hums softly,

"Green fields beyond the swelling flood."

Martha came and stood behind her husband.

"It is almost like a bit of the New Jerusalem let
down to earth," she said.

"It makes me think of Tom," he answered.

Martha's only reply was to lean her cheek on his
shoulder, and they stood thus together for several
moments in silence.

Nelson had not forgotten Tom, but though he had
lost a brother he had found a sister. On the principle of the attraction of opposites, Dora had con-
ceived for Martha that passionate attachment which
a weaker nature often shows for a stronger one.
She is happily married to one of the worthiest of
her farmer suitors, consults Martha in all household
difficulties with even more freedom than her energetic mother, and bids fair to develop into a model
of a young American matron.

"Judge Howland! this is an unexpected pleasure,"
exclaimed Nelson and Martha both in delighted uni-
son, as a visitor suddenly makes his appearance—a
tall, fine-looking man, whose decidedly familiar
features convince us that it is indeed Stephen Howland, now privileged to write Judge before his name,

and one of the foremost political leaders in the great party of national reform.

That Puritan couple have to-day no occasion to be ashamed of the Daniel they have given their country—and here pardon us one moment's digression. There is much bemoaning nowadays over the loss of the old spirit of integrity that characterized our forefathers, but if we would have sons of the Puritans filling again our legislative halls and judicial benches there is one way, and only one way, by which it can be accomplished—restore again the Puritan home.

"Business took me in this direction," responded Judge Howland, as he shook hands with his old client; "and I could not resist the temptation to turn aside and congratulate you on what I presume is no news. I hear your name prominently mentioned as candidate for a seat in the next legislature."

Martha's cheeks flushed with fond pride as she looked at her husband, who answered quietly:

"My highest desire is to be worthy of the honor. Then I can bear success or defeat with equal composure. But I want to know, Judge Howland, if you have any idea of the cause of your failure to be re-elected last fall."

"Yes, I have," slowly responded the Judge, "though I may not be acquainted with all the facts. I know my enemies got up a malicious story of bribery on my part, and one man even swore to my giving him a large sum of money to buy up votes with—a sum larger than my whole personal estate. The story was purposely started nigh on the eve of the election so as to give me no time to deny it till it had done its work in defeating me. Masons and Odd-fellows were the originators and propagators of the whole ridiculous charge. A public man, as soon as he displeases Masonry, is politically doomed."

"Well, now," said Nelson, "what is to become of the country when the reputation of no candidate for public office is safe; when he must fall down and worship before the brazen image of the lodge, or be cast into a fiery furnace of cowardly defamation and slander?"

"I don't know unless the moral sense of the nation awakes to what is now the real Question of the Hour. That question is not so much whether we shall put down this or that great evil—not even intemperance, blasting, gigantic iniquity though it be, but whether Christ shall rule our nation through Christian rulers, or Satan through the godless secret lodges. I do not mean to belittle the other great issues which are pressing upon us, but I do assert that this is the one grand issue which contains all others as in a nutshell. I do not wonder that men seeing the tremendous amount of misery and woe wrought by the saloon, and *not* seeing how this secret, irresponsible lodge power backs up that and every other evil, should think the temperance question the most important. But how long is it since a Masonic clerk, by neglecting to record the minutes of the Constitutional Amendment passed in this State, killed all the hopes of the temperance men and women who had labored so untiringly for its passage? How often the County Commissioners and Excise boards are Masons standing in fraternal relations to the rum power? How often liquor cases are tried and juries fail to convict because there is a secret understanding with a Masonic judge or attorney? How many cases are put off on a friv-olous·pretext and never tried at all for the same rea-son? Temperance men and women must wake up to these things; they are waking. This grand party of Christian reform which has risen up to combat their secret enemy bears the destiny of the Ameri-can race in its bosom over our stormy political waters as the Mayflower bore the seed for the na-tion's planting; and its platform embodies lessons experience has been teaching them through years of disappointment and frustrated hopes, and which once learned can never be unlearned."

Nelson was thinking of Martin Treworthy, who would have so rejoiced in this new party but died without the sight.

Judge Howland paused a moment, and then he said with slow and solemn emphasis:

"'How long halt ye between two opinions?' —that is the question God is asking the American nation to-day."

THE END.

APPENDIX.

CHAPTER II. Page 13.—The qualifications required are that the candidate must be a free, white man, twenty-one years of age, of good moral character and sound health, and a believer in the Supreme Being, the Maker and Ruler of the Universe.—*Donaldson's Oddfellow's Pocket Companion, p.* 19.

Chinese, Polynesians, Indians, half-breeds or mixed bloods are not eligible to membership.—*Ibid, p.* 320.

CHAPTER V. Page 57.—Another movement which lost us the active co-operation of thousands of excellent and able men was the substitution of close for open organizations. Prior to the formation of the order of the Sons of Temperance *all* our public meetings were opened to the world. * * * Seven-eighths of our weekly temperance meetings now are held in private rooms. Few of the aged are there to give the proceedings the dignity and gravity which their presence generally confers, and the children are left at home; and worst of all, the drinking portion of the community, the very portion which we wish to influence by our arguments and appeals are excluded. *They* have not the password. * * * Those petty rivalries which are now frequently occurring between the different orders where they exist in the same community, and often between subordinate and neighboring organizations of the same order; and those unbrotherly strifes for office and honors which too often occur now, were unknown in the open organizations, absolutely unknown. * * * In less than fifteen years the style of operations I have described [open temperance work] so far revolutionized the public opinion of Massachusetts that the license system was abolished in more than three-fourths of the counties of the State. The old style of operating gave place in the years 1840, '41 and '42 to the Washingtonian system, and that very soon to the Sons of Temperance and other forms of close organization, and they have had the field almost exclusively for over twenty-five years; and what is the present status of temperance in that State as compared with what it was in 1843? It may be doubted whether we are stronger at the polls now [1872] than we were twenty-five years ago. For myself I believe that had the work of reform been prosecuted for the last twenty-five years in New England in open organizations with such added provision as experience might have suggested, the liquor traffic could have been crushed before the public attention could have been diverted from that issue by the great struggle for the preservation of the Union.—*Dr. Chas. Jewett's Forty Years' Fight with the Drink Demon.*

CHAPTER VIII. Page 123.—What regeneration by the word of truth is in religion, initiation is in Odd-fellowship.—*Grosh's Manual, p.* 90.

It was a leading characteristic of all the ancient rites that they began in sorrow and gloom, but ended in light and joy.—*Ibid.*

This internal, truly living spirit of Love and universal fraternity, pervading all our rites and ceremonies; * * this soul of all its teachings and workings is Odd-fellowship, the hidden name in the white stone which he knoweth best who most truly possesses it.—*Ibid, p.* 78.

CHAPTER XXII. Page 273.—Flora, the goddess of flowers and gardens among the Romans, the same as the Chloris of the Greeks. Some suppose that she was originally a common courtesan who had left to the Romans the immense riches which she had acquired by prostitution and lasciviousness, in remembrance of which a yearly festival was instituted in her honor.— *Lempriere's Classical Dictionary.*

CHAPTER XXIII. Page 286.—The case of Jacob Strycker is given for an instance related by Rev. Mr. Brockman, and recorded in the minutes of the State Grand Lodge of Pennsylvania for the year 1871, p. 486.

John Randolph professed to have found that the philosopher's stone consisted simply in these four words: "*Pay as you go.*" But an Odd-fellow will more surely find it in the *three* words: "*Pay in advance.*"—*Grosh's Manual, p.* 192.

In a perfect financial system of dues and benefits there is no place for charity; and every dollar taken from the sick fund for mere charity is robbery of that fund.—*Jour. Proceedings Supreme Grand Lodge, Session of* 1880, *p.* 8213.

P. G. M. Joseph Gardiner gives officially the total receipts for the thirty-nine years of existence of the Grand Encampment of N. H. Odd-fellows, $121,896.90; "total relief of Patriachs," widows, etc., $31,124.31. Thus it would seem that this charitable society gets to its beneficiaries a trifle over one-quarter of its receipts. —*Christian Witness.*

According to a report of the work of the Odd-fellows for 1883, they paid out during that year $2,015,-832.52, while they collected $5,350,181.24.

CHAPTER XXVI. Page 318.—Lodges cannot abridge the liberty of the citizen, nor dictate to him what he shall eat or what he shall drink. All good Odd-fellows despise as such the *abuse* of intoxicating drinks, and in "their war against vice" they look upon drunkenness as incompatible with every principle of the Order. But neither will the laws nor the principles of Odd-fellowship descend to the restriction or the regulation of the beverage of its members.— *White's Digest,* *Art.* 975.

While *temperance* is a cardinal principle of the order and must be observed, they will not attempt to enforce *total abstinence,* a principle never intended by the framers to be engrafted on our order.—1849, *Journal.*

THE
Christian Cynosure!

A LARGE SIXTEEN-PAGE
WEEKLY REFORM JOURNAL,
OPPOSED TO SECRET SOCIETIES.

EVERY Christian and every patriot *needs* the CHRISTIAN CYNOSURE. In these days of journalistic competition this is a broad assertion; but we believe it is true, for the following among other reasons ·

1. Because it is the *only* paper adapted to general circulation having the special object of opposition to organized secrecy. Besides the ablest editorial, contributed and selected articles weekly upon this topic, which is of more than national importance, it also has interesting sketches of progress and incidents from the reform lecturers in all parts of the country, reform news and notes, letters from the Old World, etc., etc. It is the especial organ of this movement in America—a movement which is sustained by the utterances of some of the ablest statesmen and divines whom the country has produced. Every person interested in either the family, government, or religion—the most sacred interests of humanity—is *directly affected* by secret societies, and *needs to keep posted in this movement.*

2. Because it is *uncompromisingly right on* ALL questions of the day. On temperance, tobacco, Sabbath desecration, Mormonism, the Southern and Indian questions, civil-service reform, monopolies, the rights of labor, and every other question, its only aim is to be RIGHT and advocate the TRUTH. It is hence FEARLESS and OUTSPOKEN.

3. Because politically it emphasizes the fact that an enlightened *conscience* should reign in political as in all other affairs. It supports the American party as the best embodiment of correct political principles. It exposes the lodge-bound chicanery and corruption of the old parties.

4. Because in addition to these features, it contains a choice selection of wholesome reading for the family, from oldest to youngest, with religious and secular news, market reports, etc., etc. It is thoroughly Christian, but entirely undenominational. It is owned by and is the organ of the National Christian Association.

$2. per Year, Post-Paid; Clubs of Ten, $15, and a copy free to sender.

Every friend of reform is appealed to, to aid in spreading needed truth by sending in his own subscription and those of friends. Sample copies, subscription blanks or any desired information regarding publications, free on application.

W. I. PHILLIPS, Publisher,
221 West Madison Street, CHICAGO, ILL.

www.ingramcontent.com/pod-product-compliance
Lightning Source LLC
Chambersburg PA
CBHW051518100726
47898CB00005B/1503